BRAINJACKING

BRAINJACKING

The Science of Influence and Manipulation

Brian Clegg

ICON

Published in the UK and USA in 2026 by
Icon Books Ltd, Omnibus Business Centre,
39–41 North Road, London N7 9DP
email: info@iconbooks.com
www.iconbooks.com

ISBN: 978-183773-151-0
ebook: 978-183773-152-7

Typesetting by SJmagic DESIGN SERVICES, India

Printed and bound in the UK

Appointed GPSR EU Representative: Easy Access System Europe Oü, 16879218
Address: Mustamäe tee 50, 10621, Tallinn, Estonia
Contact Details: gpsr.requests@easproject.com, +358 40 500 3575

For Gillian, Rebecca and Chelsea

CONTENTS

ACKNOWLEDGEMENTS

My thanks as always to the team at Icon Books, notably Connor Stait, Steve Burdett, Rhiannon Morris and Elle-Jay Christodoulou. This is particularly true in this case in encouraging me to look into a distinctly different topic.

Thanks to the people I interviewed or asked questions of – you will discover them as you make your way through the book – and for those writing the books, papers, articles and podcasts you will see referenced. One recurring theme here is the replication crisis in psychology and how many studies in the field are now considered questionable: this is in no way attempting to reduce the importance of this work, or to suggest that researchers have deliberately set out to mislead.

Most of all, thanks to my late parents and those involved in my education who have encouraged me to look beyond the constraints of a single science to take a wider interest in how science influences and reflects the world around us and how we fit into it.

WE'LL TELL YOU WHAT TO THINK

1

Will you take the red pill?

In case that opening sentence means nothing to you, it references the storyline of the 1999 film *The Matrix*. In the movie, the hero Thomas Anderson, a.k.a. Neo, discovers that his apparent reality – everyday, late-twentieth-century life – is an illusion. Nothing that he experiences is real. For obscure (and totally impossible) reasons, Neo and most of the rest of humanity are comatose in pods, plugged into an immersive virtual-reality environment.*

The concept of experiencing life-like virtual reality was not original to the imaginations of the Wachowskis, the siblings behind the movie. For example, there was a similar concept that was remarkably also called the Matrix in the *Doctor Who* TV show, first appearing in the story 'The Deadly Assassin', broadcast in 1986, while the 1992 novel *Snow Crash* by Neal Stephenson featured a realistic (though consciously occupied) virtual-reality world that gave us the term 'metaverse'.

* In *The Matrix*, the justification for humanity being stored in pods is that they are being used by the controlling artificial intelligence to generate power for a hellish future Earth. Unfortunately, this makes no sense, as it takes significantly more energy to keep human beings alive than they generate – people do not produce energy from nowhere. The movie's key concept breaks a fundamental law of nature, the conservation of energy.

Introducing brainjacking

The Matrix film portrayed a visceral, fictional kind of brainjacking, which is the term I'm using to indicate mechanisms that enable our brains to be changed by others, often without conscious awareness that this is happening. This is entirely different from brainwashing, where the experience is all too obvious to and traumatic for the victim. Brainjacking is a more subtle, far more widespread, and more interesting activity. I won't be covering brainwashing here, but see the Further Discovery section at the back of the book for a recommended title on the subject.

The vivid reality of the Matrix experience, indistinguishable from the real world except when there was a 'glitch in the Matrix' certainly won't become practical any time soon. Early attempts at virtual reality have aptly demonstrated that we have a long way to go. Whether you have experienced *Second Life*, which has offered a crude virtual world environment since 2003, or have seen the entertainingly basic metaverse implementation that caused Facebook's parent company to rename itself as Meta in 2021, you won't confuse what you see with reality. However, if we put aside the aspect of fooling our senses into believing a virtual world is real, there's another type of brainjacking that goes on in the movie.

At one point Neo, along with Trinity, one of the other main protagonists, is stuck on the roof of a building in the Matrix. Like Neo, the real Trinity is lying on a couch, literally jacked into the system,* but the virtual Neo and Trinity need to escape the building, which handily has a helicopter parked on the rooftop. Neo asks Trinity, 'Can you fly that thing?' and she enigmatically replies, 'Not yet.' Trinity then calls the real-world 'operator' – her minder outside of the Matrix – and says that she needs a pilot program for a B-212 helicopter. The operator taps some keys, the

---

* The jack plugs used in the movie are so enormous that they would almost certainly destroy the spinal cord.

ability to fly the aircraft is pumped into her brain, and seconds later, they are ready to take off.

It might be tempting to think that this kind of thing – inserting information directly into the brain by electronic means – is all that could be described as brainjacking. But in reality, and in far more subtle ways, human beings have been influencing each others' thoughts for as long as the species has existed. We'll start to explore this by looking at the apparently simple but core human activity of storytelling.

Tell me a story

Though storytelling was first limited to direct person-to-person communication, it has been expanded by technology ever since the introduction of cave paintings, and even more so by writing, film and video. Everything we read or see influences our thought processes to some degree, potentially in a profound manner. But this is not the limit of real-world brainjacking. When we consciously attempt to get into another person's brain and influence its workings – when we go from simple argument to something more sophisticated – it can become far more of a dark art.

From the basic brainjacking that has developed from storytelling, we will see the rise of advertising and propaganda. As information technology has improved, particularly with the rise of the internet and AI, we will see the rapid growth of mental influence and manipulation. The more we find out about the brain and psychology, the more we can see opportunities arising to influence human behaviour and beliefs. We will also take time to explore the places that psychology has attempted to expand the potential of simple storytelling, from nudges to subliminal influences and priming.

I started this introduction in the world of science fiction. This is rarely a good predictor of the future. It's not what it's for. But in the field of dark brainjacking, fiction can sometimes offer real and valid warnings. The movie *Minority Report,* for example, showed advertising specifically targeted at an individual as his retinas were scanned and identified. In the classic novel *The Space Merchants,* even more science-based marketing techniques were featured, ranging from subtle influencing to deliberate addiction to a product. We will visit these possibilities later in the book.

Brainjacking also takes us on a journey through advertising and marketing's attempts to understand and influence our thoughts and desires, reaching more subtle and even subliminal influences. In discovering how science intersects with our desires and decisions, we will see both how these techniques can have a genuine impact on our lives, and also how they can be, and often have been, overhyped.

This is going to be a different kind of science book to many that deal with the mind and the brain. I read a lot of popular science and must confess that my eyes rapidly glaze over when I'm faced with a whole list of different parts of the brain being identified as having a responsibility (or not) for various aspects of our cognition. The reality is almost always 'but it's really more complicated than this'. To some, I'm sure, this labelling of brain bits is fascinating and fun, but I'm more inclined to the Richard Feynman viewpoint.

Feynman, one of the twentieth century's greatest physicists, found his postgraduate physics course a little limiting: to broaden his experience he attended biology lectures at the same time. A story he tells of his experience in his classic collection of anecdotes, *Surely You're Joking, Mr Feynman!,* describes how in one of the biology class exercises he had to comment on a paper in which the electrical impulses in the nerves of a cat had been measured. Feynman wanted to put the interior parts of the cat mentioned into context, so went to the library and asked for a map of a cat, much to the librarian's amusement.

When Feynman later reported on the paper to the class, he began by explaining just what went on inside the cat. His fellow students pointed out they had already memorised the names of the cat's muscles and so on, so knew what went where. 'Oh,' said Feynman, 'you do? Then no wonder I can catch up with you so fast after you've had four years of biology.'

In a similar way, I don't think there's much to be gained by giving you a map of the brain and pointing out the various parts that get activated by mental influences, unless there is a very specific reason for doing so. To paraphrase something else that Feynman said, a lesson he learned at an early age from his father was that science isn't about knowing the labels for things, it's about understanding what's going on.

Informing, influencing, manipulating

Instead of taking a clinical, solely objective approach, *Brainjacking* will be a more personal take on the subject than I would ever use in a book on, say, quantum physics. We all have minds – and we have all had those minds influenced throughout our lives. It would seem silly and wasteful to ignore personal experience, and so I will crop up as an individual in the story of brainjacking significantly more than I would usually expect to. After all, influencing minds is what my job is all about.

In the previous sentence I used 'influence' in a vague fashion. We will discover that brainjacking can be used at three levels: to inform, to influence and to manipulate. Information is typically about facts that have no consequential impact on our behaviour. A hydrogen atom has one proton in its nucleus. If you didn't already know this, you are now so informed. If it sticks in your mind, then I have changed your brain in a small way, but it's unlikely to make any difference to what you do in future.

Influencing and manipulation, by contrast, both have the potential to change beliefs and future actions. Although we tend to think of manipulation as being worse than influence, either of these processes can be undertaken for good or evil (depending on your definition). Manipulation is a more difficult concept, because the word now has negative connotations. The initial meaning was changing something by hand (*manus* is Latin for hand), but it came to mean more general handling and dexterity. It wasn't until the nineteenth century that a suggestion of deviousness crept in.

If we take influence and manipulation to mean a conscious attempt to make a change, then there is no doubt that plenty of this does occur in storytelling – and some of it does delight in deceit. In the way I'll be using the terms in this book, the difference between the two isn't about whether or not the content is factual. It's possible to influence with a lie and manipulate someone to do something good. But manipulation encourages a decision from the heart rather than the head. Influence is more about winning someone over using intellectual argument.

All informing, influencing and manipulating sit on a continuous spectrum – the types of brainjacking subtly shade into each other. But we can often see attributes of each in different ways of talking or writing about the same thing. Take these three statements:

> The famine in Romanda is now severe. Each week at least 100 children are dying of starvation. Without aid things will get worse.
>
> You can help the children of Romanda with a few clicks. A £10 donation will keep a family of four from hunger for a week.
>
> Little Syra in Romanda doesn't understand why her mummy can't help her. She wakes up every morning hungry. You can change her life.

Each statement has a different type of influence on your brain – but the way it does so and the impact it has is different dependent on the position on that spectrum. With all that in mind, let's take the first steps we all need to understand, benefit from and survive the sometimes insidious but always present work of the brainjackers. And it begins with the concept of story.

Are you sitting comfortably? Then I'll begin.*

---

* If you aren't British or were born after the 1970s, 'Are you sitting comfortably? Then I'll begin' may seem an odd phrase. It was used as the regular introduction to stories on the BBC radio programme *Listen with Mother,* which ran between 1950 and 1982.

ONCE UPON A TIME 2

Biologists don't like admitting to human exceptionalism – the idea that we have a special place in nature, quite distinct from other animals. But I would argue that this attitude is because they are too close to their subject. Admittedly, in one sense they are perfectly right. We are, after all, not unique in being either a mammal or a great ape. Yet looking at our ability to produce technology, to develop sophisticated cultures and to transform the environment (for good and bad alike), it is surely perverse to suggest that *Homo sapiens* is not in some sense special.

What makes us unique?

There has been plenty of argument about what makes us seemingly unique among the animals. In his book *Consciousness*, English biologist John Parrington, based at Oxford University, suggests that there are three factors that enable us to stand out. These are our use of language, the way that our deployment of tools and technology has enabled us to radically transform our environment, and the fact that we have a uniquely complex brain structure. For me, these all come together in one clear and distinctive aspect of human behaviour – and it provides the foundations for brainjacking. We are storytellers.

In *How Life Works,* science writer Philip Ball notes: 'One of our attributes that most distinguishes us from other animals is our construction of complex cultures, which rely critically on systems and technologies for passing on information and learning – and thus *causal influence* – between generations through means other than genes.' Arguably, the most important system here is storytelling.

American lecturer in English Jonathan Gottschall refers to us not as *Homo sapiens,* but *Homo fictus* – 'the great ape with the storytelling mind'. He points out that children don't have to be trained in what stories are – they are inherently part of being human. He notes: 'Children don't need to be tutored in story. We don't need to bribe them to make stories like we bribe them to eat broccoli. For children, make-believe is as automatic and insuppressible as dreams.'

Strictly speaking, not all use of story is brainjacking. One of the ways we stand out from other animals is as a result of our internal storytelling. Rather than live our lives primarily in the moment, we are constantly telling ourselves the small stories that are responses to questions such as 'What if?' and to the deployment of 'How?' or 'Why?' or 'What?'. Questions like:

> How should I get my next meal?
> What do I need to do to make this happen?
> What if there's a predator behind that bush?
> What happens when I die?

This internal ability to ask ourselves questions that each in turn can generate small stories of what might be and how things might be achieved gives us the ability to plan, to consider future risks and opportunities, and to act accordingly. However, the additional leverage that arises from storytelling that has propelled the human race to a new level is when the stories are passed from person to person, changing human brains in the process. It's in this process that brainjacking began.

You may by now be thinking that I've gone totally over the top. Perhaps storytelling brings to mind sitting on the floor as a child while an adult reads a book. Or, dare I say it, those arty storytellers who bang on about keeping the oral tradition alive that you find at folk festivals and *eisteddfods*. And that is one version of storytelling – the oldest version that involves simply standing in front of people and talking at them, which developed into oratory and political discourse. But combined with technology, storytelling has become far more. It gives us art and music. It gives us education and books, film and TV, and all the wonders of the internet.

In a sense it's obvious that story in the broad sense has an impact on our minds. I read something and remember it. I see an advertisement and buy a product. I attend a political rally and the speeches encourage me to vote a certain way. But Jonathan Gottschall points out that from the second half of the twentieth century there has been a significant amount of research to back up the common-sense premise that story moulds our minds. As he puts it: 'Research shows that story is constantly nibbling and kneading us, shaping our minds without our knowledge or consent. The more deeply we are cast under story's spell, the more potent its influence.'

Gottschall notes that it is not just non-fiction that we learn from; we are shaped by fiction, whether or not it reflects reality. As an example, in my spare time I write murder mysteries: police procedurals. These contain a fair amount of detail of what police officers do in their line of work. But I had to admit to a book group asking how I'd researched my books that I've only twice been in a police station and have rarely done any research. Almost all my understanding of police procedure is taken from fiction, with a small amount from popular science, where the work overlaps with, say, pathology – and usually I can get away with it.

Gottschall tells us that Tolstoy thought that his job, the job of an artist, was to 'infect his audience with his own ideas and emotions' far more than to inform: Tolstoy clearly saw it as influencing and manipulating. Gottschall goes on to relate how a study has shown that 'scary stories leave scars' – and fiction is more likely to do so than real-world horrors. Like me, you may sympathise with this view. I remember being terrified when young by a book featuring a comic-strip monstrosity called a caltrop. I was convinced that one lived on the dark corner of my grandmother's staircase, and I would rush past the corner with my eyes closed.

From the storytelling coal face

Let's get some assistance in pulling apart the concept of storytelling to see how it can have such an effect. Roger Ashton-Griffiths has a doctorate in creative writing from the University of East Anglia. He has also been an opera singer and an actor. If you are a *Game of Thrones* fan, you would recognise him as Mace Tyrell, though he has appeared in everything from Hollywood blockbusters to *Doctor Who* and *Coronation Street*.

I met Roger ten years ago when we were both on the Lancaster University team for the TV show *Christmas University Challenge* – we will be meeting the other team members later in the book. All four of us are professional storytellers, but each in a very different way. Before finding out more about the nature of story from Roger, though, let's take a step back for a moment and notice the gentle brainjacking that took place over the last few paragraphs.

The mere fact that you are reading this book gives me a small amount of ability to impact the workings of your brain. Even if you never consciously revisit the topics covered here, apparently forgetting everything you read, some remnants of the ideas from the book will remain, insidiously lurking in your brain. When something relevant comes up, those fragments will be there, even if you don't directly recall them, contributing to the way that your brain deals with the issue. That is just the standard, base level of brainjacking associated with any book, whether it be fiction or non-fiction.

But a couple of paragraphs back, I also indulged in some more targeted work on your brain. By noting that Roger has a relevant doctorate, I potentially gave his opinion a little more weight. Even though we live in an age when experts are not awarded as much importance and respect as they once were, it may have had a small influence. And, as film and TV are very much part of the storytelling family, Roger's experience of those gives an additional degree of weight. If you happen to be a *Game of Thrones* fan, we've got some extra interest from a familiar character. And this is potentially important because personal interest and emotion are key tools in amplifying the effectiveness of brainjacking.

Even if you have never watched *Game of Thrones*, there is still the potential to gain a little extra traction from that association, because almost everyone has at least heard of the show. In essence, my brief introduction to who Roger is provides both simple storytelling in its own right, and also an intentional piece of brainjacking to prepare you for his responses.

Storytelling as preparation for life

I started by asking Roger what 'story' is. He told me: 'My unsubstantiated opinion about what the arts in general and storytelling in particular *is*, is about ways of preparing for life. In the sense that you're imagining situations that you either have not or are unlikely to encounter, and that you do so by putting yourself in imaginative space to rehearse this.'

He went on: 'You're aware, I'm sure, of Booker's book about story structure:* he defines seven basic plots. It all arises because you have a bit of a problem, and you work out how to solve it, then you solve it, and you get the princess in the castle, and you live happily ever after. I can see stories as a means of rehearsing life's situations. It's like when you come into the house and you've got to remember the code for your alarm, and you think about it before you go in – you go, "Whoa, the code is that," and when you go in, you can press it. Storytelling has that kind of function: it prepares us for life's eventualities. And beyond that, it's something we like doing, so we carry on doing it.'

At first sight, this may seem to be overburdening a story. Obviously, the whole panoply of brainjacking, taking in education as much as fiction, does in some sense prepare us for life, but if we take the picture literally, as American psychologist Steven Pinker does in his book *How the Mind Works*, that fiction in particular provides us with tools to cope with life's eventualities, it's worrying how much of what we absorb in fiction is about how to get it wrong. Jonathan Gottschall describes it instead as a form of low-tech simulation where 'our minds are firing and wiring, honing the neural pathways that regulate our responses to real-life experiences', rather than providing direct guidance.

We tend to think of a story as being primarily about words, or words and visuals if the story comes in the form of a comic strip, TV show, film or play. But I wondered if it was reasonable to consider all of art and music to be a form of storytelling. Roger responded: 'Yes, absolutely. Are they also preparing us?

* In fact, I wasn't aware of Booker's book at the time. Roger was referring to Christopher Booker's *The Seven Basic Plots: Why we tell stories.* (More details in the Further Discovery section.)

In a different way. I think it's preparing an emotional response: stretching, exercising, working out your emotional responses. In evolutionary terms, emotional responses are things that people save, enabling us to behave in appropriate ways.'

As primarily a non-fiction author, I wondered about the position of non-fiction in the storytelling universe. For me, narrative is just as important in non-fiction as it is in fiction – and a purely factual book (like this one) will attempt to make changes in someone else's brain, though the toolkit is certainly notably different.

Do stories manipulate?

I probed Roger on how non-fiction fitted in, unintentionally using wording that opened up a divide in our thinking. I asked: 'Non-fiction might do some emotional manipulation, but obviously a lot of that is informational?'

Roger's response was telling: 'Let's take out this idea of emotional manipulation, which is what – I don't know – sales personnel might do to you. They might make you feel guilty because you don't shower every day, so buy my shower gel. I don't think that's the same thing. In storytelling you are not manipulating emotion so much as facilitating.'

This feels defensive (something we will return to at the end of the book). I don't think there is any doubt that storytelling involves manipulation, underpinned by emotion – and I don't see why that is a bad thing. It's markedly true of that insidious combination of music and visual storytelling that happens when you get a good movie soundtrack. The moments when I take a sharp intake of breath and attempt to hold back the tears when watching a film almost always coincide with an emotionally manipulative piece of music. Even when there aren't images on the screen, such music can have an effect.

A classic example of cinematic manipulation that gets me every time is the ending of the 1970 Lionel Jeffries film of the E. Nesbit children's book *The Railway Children*. As a father of two daughters, the moment when Jenny Agutter's character Bobbie sees her father on the station platform and says, 'Daddy, my daddy!' inevitably starts the waterworks. Genuinely, my eyes are tearing up as I type this. This was underlined some years ago, when listening to a radio programme on how film music amplifies feelings. They played the music that goes with that scene without the dialogue – and because of my existing association, the tears still came. Of course, music doesn't require images to stimulate emotion – its purpose is always in part an emotional response – but there was something different in the way that this particular scene had become embedded in my brain, tied to the musical cue.

I don't doubt that Roger is right that storytelling facilitates emotion, but I think it would be naïve to suggest that master storytellers do not write or direct in a way that is, consciously or not, attempting to manipulate the recipient as well. Calling it manipulation does not make it bad (though, of course, it can be – think, for example, of Leni Riefenstahl's documentary film *Olympia* and the way it portrayed the political setting of the 1936 Olympics in Nazi Germany); it's just what people do when they tell stories.

Roger went on to consider the universal nature of storytelling: 'Everyone through all walks of society seems to engage with stories one way and another. It might be people who watch soaps on ITV right up to those who watch Danish dramas on BBC4,* but everyone in every strata of society appears to be

---

* For those not familiar with the social hierarchy of UK TV channels, ITV is a popular middle-of-the-road commercially funded channel, while BBC4 is the BBC's 'highbrow' channel. Arguably, and perhaps ironically, BBC4's biggest success has been in bringing foreign language crime series with a wide appeal such as *The Killing* (Danish), *The Bridge* (Danish/Swedish) and *Spiral* (French) to a UK audience.

engaged in it one way or another. I think it has this universal quality. Take, for example, sci-fi, which is not really about an imagined future, it's about the people of the imagined future, and without that, it's rubbish: it's not something you can engage with. It has to be "once upon a time in the future", and if it's not that, it's no good.'

Finally, I wondered if stage acting, with an audience for the actor to interact with directly, is a different type of storytelling to acting to a camera for film or TV? 'The experience of telling a story is different, but I don't think the impact of the story varies. It's a dissimilar sort of process, but then writing novels rather than non-fiction involves different processes, even though aimed broadly at the same thing. Take the case of poetry: in Kipling's poem "If", there's not really any story, but it engages the imagination. It's about putting the listener into the mindset of this person who can do this, or who could do that. The emotional engagement is exactly the same, even though there isn't the same sense of linear storytelling.'

I concluded: 'It seems to me you're saying that storytelling is a way of seeing into someone else's brain?'

Roger answered: 'It's precisely that. And this is the reason why there are so many different stories, even though Booker says that there are only seven basic plots. We keep reiterating them because there are uncountable ways of addressing the problems, rehearsing in different ways.'

Why we tell stories

It's worth taking an excursion into the world of Christopher Booker's *The Seven Basic Plots*. This is an extremely chunky book (certainly not an easily digestible story in itself), running to over 700 pages. The first section looks at those seven plots and their variants,* the second explores the nature of a happy ending, the third looks at where the model doesn't really work, before finally dealing with the aspect that particularly interests us: why we tell stories (this part also explains why many stories *don't* have a happy ending).

Booker says that the universality of plots implies that 'stories emerge from some place in the human mind which functions autonomously, independent of any storyteller's conscious control ... the real key to understanding stories lies in seeing how they are ultimately rooted in a level of the unconscious which is collective to all humanity; and how the "secret" which "sits in the middle", giving them their underlying shape and purpose, is always trying to put over the same fundamental point.'

This isn't a particularly logical deduction. It's almost like saying 'as there are only three directions at right angles we can move in, the three dimensions emerge from the collective unconscious'. If there are only a handful of permutations of plot, it doesn't have to have anything to do with the collective unconsciousness (assuming there is such a thing: it's not a scientific concept); it can simply be due to a structural limit. There are only so many ways we can re-arrange things.

From this generalisation, Booker moves on to creation stories. Interestingly, he includes some scientific theories in this set of stories, as well as religious creation myths. Perhaps not surprisingly, given that Booker was a journalist with a history degree, the scientific aspect evades his understanding. We are told that in this story initially there was an agglomeration of hydrogen atoms a few millimetres across and of almost infinite mass. This exploded with such force that all the elements we now have, including those that make us up, were formed.

* It's not essential to know these for our purposes, but they are overcoming the monster, rags to riches, the quest, voyage and return, comedy, tragedy, and rebirth.

Impressively, every single statement in those two sentences is incorrect.

Should we expect Booker to get the basics of a scientific theory right? I think, if you are to assess a theory as a story, then yes, we should. This is especially true for Booker's subsequent framing of evolution, which totally misses the point, giving the process a teleological aspect. But evolution does not have a goal: that's the whole point of it. This is the problem if we, as Booker does, only see story from the limited viewpoint of fiction with a 'hero' and a plot. He never explains how, despite putting the big bang theory on a par with creation myths, this can be the case. He does not seem to understand the difference between a creation myth – a story that explains *why* something happened, but that can't usefully explore *how* something happened – and a scientific theory – a story that explains *how* something happened with no interest in or even concept of the *why*.

In this sense, then, Booker gets things entirely wrong. But he points out one interesting thought. In some religious traditions, as well as having a creation there is also a fall, where humanity is expelled from paradise. He draws a parallel with the difference between humans and other animals in being detached from the instinctive, unquestioning relationship with nature that is the state of all other life. This genuinely does give us a suggestion as to why we tell stories (as opposed to what stories are). It could indeed be an attempt to deal with our conscious ability to make decisions – where both we and others suffer the consequences, good or bad, of those decisions.

Narrative-emotional technology

In another book on the nature of story, *Wonderworks*, American professor of story science Angus Fletcher gives us a better take on what it's all about that nonetheless echoes Booker's point. According to Fletcher, literature was invented as 'a narrative-emotional technology that helped our ancestors cope with the psychological challenges posed by human biology. It was an invention for overcoming the doubt and pain of just being us.' Fletcher tells us that our ancestors developed a toolbox of techniques that enabled literature to 'improve daily health and happiness' – inventions that have since passed out of use and haven't been taught for many centuries.

Fletcher attributes the mechanism for discovering these techniques to Aristotle, the fourth-century BCE Greek philosopher, as a two-stage process of first identifying what literature is doing and then uncovering how it succeeds in doing it (perfectly logical, if easier said than done). Aristotle then goes on to uncover such a technique which is described as 'lifting the soul' – admittedly a fuzzy concept, but one that seems to point towards a sense of wonder arising from the experience of consuming the story. The 'how', Aristotle puts down to the reader or audience being presented with a sequence of events that have a predictable progression, followed by a sudden and unexpected change of direction. What we'd call a plot twist.

Fletcher extends this mechanism into what he calls 'the stretch': making everything more intense than the everyday, which has been associated by some neuroscientists with an enhancement in the sense of wellbeing – Aristotle's lifting the soul. This might seem a little odd when Aristotle's reference point was largely Greek tragedies. If you've ever sat through one of these, you will realise that they are not what anyone would think of as cheerful. But Aristotle's idea, much as Roger Ashton-Griffiths came to in his assessment of the nature of story, was that we can achieve catharsis from our own past traumas by the impact on our brains of watching or reading a drama unfolding.

Fletcher tells us that there are studies backing this idea up, as well as research finding that it works even better if we move our eyes from side to side while revisiting the trauma (conveniently matching the action of watching a play or reading a book). I'm not sure about this. The eye-movement effect is backed up by a 1980s psychology study – prime time for bad psychology papers (we will discover more about these as we progress). Fletcher also references 'recent studies on mice' – always a worrying thought because, well, mice aren't people.

I personally find tragedies (Greek or otherwise) depressing and avoid them as much as I can. When I have watched one, I certainly haven't found any impact on my dealing with the biggest traumas I've had in my life. Nothing. Nada. For me, the goals set by John Reith, the formative director-general of the BBC, for the broadcaster's role as a public service are far closer to what story seems to deliver, and certainly what I want from it: to educate, inform and entertain (not necessarily in that order) – with an added dollop of influence and persuasion. Perhaps this is because I'm not a great fan of literary fiction, which is more likely to have wider pretentions.

Fletcher goes on to deliver a whole smorgasbord of literary devices that can influence our brains, 25 in all. I won't list all of them, but they include concepts like courage (in a protagonist), romance, exciting curiosity and freeing creativity, freeing your mind, warding off heartbreak, deciding wiser (sic), believing in yourself and lessening your lonely (sic). If these seem like extracts from a New Age self-help manual, I ought to say that many of these concepts are linked to studies that claim to support the abilities of this aspect of story.

The second look

To give one example of story influencing the brain that is particularly apt in the context of brainjacking, Fletcher dives into the 'neuroscience of our gullibility'. He starts with a story of a Japanese emperor in 1913 and the circumstances of a meeting the emperor undertakes. He then asks the reader if they believed the words that he had written, and suggests that 'the way your brain evolved, you believe every new thing that you read. You're having a hard time accepting this biological fact about the brain, I know. That's because I have just made you suspicious.'

Our brains are far more complex than those of our earliest ancestors. Where originally the brain largely dealt with immediate response to stimuli, we are now able to analyse and assess what we take in. This reflects the two-systems approach that Daniel Kahneman made famous in his book *Thinking, Fast and Slow*. (More on this later.) Typically, we take the fast response first and then sift through what has happened when we have the luxury of time. As Fletcher puts it: 'Rather than deciding what to believe, [the brain] decides what *not* to believe.' He suggests that we accept everything as true in the instant, then begin to question it.

This is, arguably, an over-simplistic interpretation. We don't really accept everything we read as true initially, but rather accept everything that fits with our worldview as true before we can analyse it in more depth. So, for example, if I read a book eloquently putting the case for a flat Earth (is there such a book?), I would not believe it for an instant. But, for example, Fletcher's Japanese emperor story is a null event in my worldview. I have no existing opinions or knowledge and so, yes, I did initially believe it.

Fletcher points out a distinct danger for brainjacking (he describes it as brainwashing, which as we've already discovered is not the best description of what is happening here). Because it takes additional effort to disbelieve, he suggests, then if we are stressed, tired or distracted it makes it easier to go along with an assertion that on proper reflection would not make sense. However, according to Fletcher, literature has a mechanism to slow down the brain, overcoming instant assessment.

He describes this as 'the second look' – literary techniques that make us reassess what we have read so far, potentially seeing the information in a different light. It might be a subtle implementation, such as Shakespeare's Mark Antony repeatedly telling us that Brutus is an 'honourable man', where the repetition pushes us into a meta-reading, asking, 'Why is he saying that so much?' Or a more full-frontal approach where the author deliberately takes the reader back to something they've already read, forcing them to revisit it.

This isn't, of course, a technique limited to the written word. In film, Fletcher points to the Japanese film *Rashomon* (which is linked to the Japanese emperor story). For me, M. Night Shyamalan's *The Sixth Sense* is the ultimate example. Here, a whole string of events are portrayed in a way that misleads the viewer for much of the movie, but are then unpicked to reveal the reality of the situation. (Watching the film for the first time, oddly, the thing that suggested to me that something strange was happening before the reveal was the idea that a well-off American adult and child would use a bus to go anywhere.)

Fletcher suggests that the answer to being overwhelmed by brainjacking is to 'try clearing your mind with an alienating book' such as James Joyce's *A Portrait of the Artist as a Young Man*, or Kurt Vonnegut's *Slaughterhouse-Five*. I'm not convinced this is a useful everyday tool. A far more effective approach would surely be to develop a sceptical viewpoint and to apply a more scientific assessment when presented with new information of significance. It's easy to overdo scepticism and end up with cynicism. But something you will find happens again and again in this book is that we do need to take a second, sceptical look at what we are told, making sure that we aren't relying too much on the fast-thinking part of the brain.

Stories and religion

When I spoke to Oxford University's Helen Carasso about advertising and marketing (we'll find out more about her in Chapter 3), she brought up one area where storytelling has a huge impact: religion. Although I mentioned this briefly above in the context of Booker's thoughts, it's important to explore this a little more in Helen's company. I ought to be clear that this is not an attack on religion. All too often religion and science are portrayed as being in opposition – but that is an optional viewpoint. And saying that storytelling is central to religion does not equate religious teaching with fiction. As we have seen, non-fiction is just as much about story.

All religions have story at their core. The stories may be different, or they may be overlapping (as they are between Judaism, Christianity and Islam). The stories may be found in central texts, or in a verbal tradition. But religions enable us to explore deep truths indirectly through myths. 'Myth' is a word that has become loaded with negativity, often now used to label something untrue. But religious myths attempt to give insights into, for example, the creation of the universe through stories that some take literally, but many accept as metaphorical teaching.

We can also see that religion is responsible for a huge amount of brainjacking. Religious stories still shape the way that the majority of humanity sees the world and reacts to events. This doesn't require a theocracy – in a primarily secular country like the UK, despite humanists' moans, everything from our legal structures to our approach to charity has been strongly influenced by religious storytelling.

Helen said: 'Religion gives us a moral framework, it gives us a story of how we're here, and why we're here, and what we're here for. I think most people, however much faith they do or don't have, accept there is a narrative that's built up around whatever you believe is the core truth of what that literature of faith is, and that seems to me to be an extreme example of where, by having a story, you find a way of coming to terms with the big questions, without getting into what actually happened in the big bang, and what is evolution and so on. It seems to me it's often something that helps you to put order into chaos.'

Famously, the Spanish founder of the Roman Catholic Jesuit order, St Ignatius Loyola, said: 'Give me a child till he is seven and I will show you the man.' Leaving aside the inherent sexism in that remark (to be fair to Ignatius, he was writing in the sixteenth century), the implication that getting your brainjacking in early will result in a shaping of our mental attitude to the world is not without foundation. Having said that, many children rebel in their teen years – and there is good evidence that we don't have a truly adult outlook on life until our twenties.

Education as brainjacking

It is far less likely that the influence on children and young adults referred to in the quote would come from the Catholic Church now than was once the case. But a huge amount of brainjacking of young minds goes on in the process of education. This is a particular form of storytelling – but unfortunately the implementation of education often destroys the point of story. Our insights into the nature of story all stress the way that story helps the recipient to develop a better relationship with the world around them. This requires the recipient to be in charge of the process of what they get from the story. But in education through to tertiary level, just as much as the Jesuits did, we spend far too much time telling students what to think: how they should react to our educational stories.

Before I began writing books, I spent some time giving training in creativity to businesses. My co-presenter, Paul Birch, told a story about his days in primary school. The class teacher had played a piece of music (it was Tchaikovsky's *1812 Overture*). The teacher then asked: 'What does that make you think of? What picture does it bring to mind?' Paul lived in a rural area, where fox hunting was still common. He excitedly told the teacher: 'It makes me think of a fox hunt, with galloping horses and baying hounds and horns.' The teacher shook her head. 'No, it's not that. Anyone else?'

Far too often, schools expect 'the right answer' from their students. This is fine if you are doing STEM subjects such as maths or physics. There *is* a 'right answer' to solving an equation* or working out the current that flows when a particular voltage is put across a resistor. But many of the questions that are important to us as humans have a multitude of right answers. All too often, education can shut down creativity. There is a lurking form of brainjacking that says 'it's not safe to be creative – follow the path that is set'.

Of course, there are good reasons for avoiding some aspects of childhood creativity. If a small child thinks that glowing coals in a fire look pretty and wants to play with them, although this is a form of creative impulse, it is right to say 'No, you mustn't' and explain why. But there is plenty of childhood creativity that we suppress unnecessarily.

This isn't always as crudely enacted as Paul's teacher's intervention. Our educational establishments from kindergarten right through to universities tend to instil a particular set of values and approaches. There is not an issue if the topic is scientific, or involves discussing moral and political topics where there is a chance to explore the alternatives, but there are two circumstances – when the approach taken is based on bad science, or when moral and political topics are presented as if there is only one right answer – where the negative side of brainjacking does come into play.

Bad science brainjacking seems to come through particularly strongly in fads that are employed in primary schools (the four to eleven age group in the UK). One example that was common when my children were in primary school was Brain Gym. This was a commercial system intended to enhance the children's thinking abilities. Some basic aspects of the Brain Gym methodology were simple, well-established factors – like it being good to take regular breaks when learning, the benefits of exercise or the

---

* Even in solving an equation, though, there can be more than one right answer.

value of basic breathing exercises. However, much of the rest of the process has been shown by Dr Ben Goldacre to have no basis in science, despite using pseudo-scientific terms in its literature.*

Specifically, Brain Gym had a strange attitude to water and incorporated odd rituals. The claim was made that it's important to drink a glass of water before activities, and to hold the water in the mouth to transport oxygen to the brain. Drinking fluids is certainly a good thing – but the Brain Gym approach to this doesn't make any sense. To begin with, it specifies that only pure water satisfies the body's needs for hydration, when in fact we take in water from almost all food and drinks we consume. And holding water in the mouth won't transport oxygen to the brain. According to Goldacre: 'They're keen on drinking water, because "processed foods" – I'm quoting from the Brain Gym manual here – "do not contain water." This is just not true, and it would be irrelevant even if it were.'

There were also special massage-like movements in the Brain Gym routine, which were said, for instance, to stimulate the blood flow in arteries to carry more oxygen to the brain. Again, these made no physiological sense. Most of the influence from the exposure to Brain Gym brainjacking seems to have faded, but I do wonder if it is why a whole generation seems obsessed with carrying water around with them at all times to avoid becoming dehydrated.

Our bodies are, on average, around 60 per cent water, and everything from our digestion to the operation of individual cells would not function without it. It's not surprising that we can only go around three days without drinking water, as we are constantly losing it and need to keep levels topped up to avoid dehydration. But the good news is that keeping hydrated is nowhere near as difficult as you might have heard. (Just as well,

---

* Ben Goldacre's analysis of Brain Gym is from his book *I Think You'll Find it's a Bit More Complicated than That* – see Further Discovery for details.

when you consider how many millennia humans have managed without being able to buy sports drinks.)

It is often said that you need to drink eight glasses of water a day – around two litres or three-and-a-half pints – but there is no scientific basis for this. A fair amount of research has been done to track down where this tenacious bit of misinformation came from. It may have been a 1945 US National Research Council recommendation that adults should have a millilitre of water for each calorie of food. Two litres is, indeed, a typical required amount of water if you aren't exercising so hard that you sweat profusely, but we don't need to *drink* this amount. We get about half of it from our food.

As for the rest, Heinz Valtin, a kidney specialist from the Dartmouth Medical School in New Hampshire, reviewed* the available evidence and showed that there is no need for this to be pure water. Tea and coffee, for instance, are fine (provided you aren't drinking so much that there are problems with caffeine). You may have heard you should avoid these (and colas) because they are diuretics, which make the body lose more fluid than it gains – but a study† showed there was no difference in the effect on hydration levels between water and caffeinated drinks.

Mindset manipulation

A more recent example of bad science in school brainjacking is the deployment of 'growth mindset'. This is the apparently common-sense idea that if you believe it's impossible to change

* The 2002 review of what can make up the recommended two litres of water is '"Drink at least eight glasses of water a day." Really? Is there scientific evidence for "8 x 8"?' by Heinz Valtin.

† The 2000 study showing the difference in hydration levels between water and caffeinated drinks is 'The effect of caffeinated, non-caffeinated, caloric and non-caloric beverages on hydration' by A.C. Grandjean et al.

because talent is what people are born with (a so-called fixed mindset), you won't put in the necessary effort and thus you won't achieve your full capability. But if you believe in the ability to change (growth mindset), then you will study or train harder and will get better outcomes as a result.

The underlying idea that you will do better if you study or train is hardly a surprise – but the practice in schools is different. Some individuals have monetised the growth mindset concept, and what's of scientific interest is whether or not their programmes and specific methodologies recommended to encourage a growth mindset make any difference to learning in schools. There have been a large number of studies on the impact of growth mindset – and this is where it becomes noteworthy.

These studies have been pulled together in a number of meta-analyses,* which originally collectively showed a very small but real effect. However, once these results were subject to some scrutiny, and studies with small sample sizes or that didn't set out their approach in advance (opening them up to the potential of falling into the various statistical traps common in soft science research – see page 228 for more on this) were discounted, there was no significant impact. This has resulted in a vitriolic exchange between supporters and doubters of the growth mindset approach.

Dubious brainjacking in education can also result from both over-simplification and political bias among the educators. Over-simplification is a common problem when, for example, teaching science to children. Sometimes keeping things simple is acceptable, because it is a starting point in a staged build-up of knowledge. For example, telling children that light is a wave, or

* A meta-analysis is not an original study but accumulates findings on a topic from other studies. Not all meta-analyses are equally good: to work well they need to take into account the quality of the studies that they are collating.

that all a plant needs to thrive is water and sunlight is a starting point which will (hopefully) be built on later, when the students are capable of understanding more sophisticated details.

Unfortunately, all too often the simplified version is not expanded on, leaving the wrong impression embedded. This may not be so significant where the topic is abstract. Only a would-be physicist (or at least someone with an interest in the subject) needs to know that it isn't sufficient to describe light as a wave. But, for example, we teach children environmental issues from primary school onwards, and often these are presented in a grossly over-simplified fashion. It's even the case that some of the simplified science we teach young children that doesn't get corrected later is downright wrong. We have more than five senses, for example, and Newton's seven rainbow colours were selected entirely arbitrarily.

Teaching differently

Given the unquestionable brainjacking power of learning – for good or evil – it is arguably time for a radical overhaul of the way that education is undertaken. We will see in the section on misinformation some specifics on whether or not we can help children to be better able to cope with filtering the vast amount of information they now receive from diverse qualities of source. But it's about more than that. While universities are at least starting to get there in terms of understanding the importance of skills in handling online information, our schools still mostly take a pre-digital approach.

Don't get me wrong – I am not advocating that we abandon books. (As an author, this would be an extremely unwise move.) If anything, because of a shortage of funds, schools don't make as much use of books as they should. However, what we haven't seen is the introduction of an education process that is focused on giving students the tools they need to deal with the vast amount of information now available from many different sources and media, information that is issued in the hope of influencing their brains.

We currently teach to exams, using curricula that spend far too much time on giving students the basics they might need for various careers. This means for many of us most of the material taught in school will never be used again. In science, for instance, I'd suggest we would be much better giving students a broad, popular-science style background to history of science, key developments and how they have led to applications, rather than plodding through the basics of mechanics or optics.

If students develop an interest in sciences and head towards a specialisation, then they can pick up these basics extremely quickly – but for most they are useless and put many off an interest in science in the first place. I have often given talks on science to both primary and secondary school children. In the primary schools almost everyone is excited by science. It only takes a couple of years of secondary school teaching to wipe out this enthusiasm in most students.

Taking the suggested approach, we could make science far more interesting. For example, the basics of the special theory of relativity, including time travel, can easily be handled with no more maths than basic algebra. This would be far more interesting than anything in the current physics curriculum. Combine this with education in how to research information – for example, how to find and check out an academic paper if you are suspicious of a claim you see in the media – and we will have set up a much more effective mindset than the kind of lessons that are only designed to generate passes in the current exams.

Our examinations typify the worst aspects of bad brainjacking in formal education. Existing exams are often little more than a test of memory. There's nothing wrong with knowing some basics by heart. But going further by being required to regurgitate large amounts of information is a total waste of the brain. All exams should have read-only access to the internet (unless the intention is for students to collaborate), testing both the students' ability to find information and to assess its quality and use it appropriately.

When I did my master's in operational research at the University of Lancaster, one of the best-known aspects of the final exams was the Jumbo. This was an eight-hour examination with a single question. (That question was several pages long.) It was pre-web, but the exam was open – we could go to the library, researching anything required. For me, wider use of this approach, though with modern information sources, would set the pattern for a much better style of exam than current structures.

Education is the most structured brainjacking that will ever happen in a person's life. At the moment, much of that opportunity is wasted. I know many teachers and lecturers, and they are usually fed up with the latest educational fads being foisted on them. I am totally aligned, for example, with the primary school teachers who bemoan the waste of time in teaching ten-year-olds what a fronted adverbial is. I mentioned Feynman and his map of a cat in the previous chapter. We don't give students any benefit by making them regurgitate pointless labels. But there is little doubt that the education provided by schools would benefit hugely by starting from scratch, designing a system that gets a better set of information and skills into students' minds.

The stories we tell in education may lead to students growing up instilled with a particular set of views and lacking some key mental tools. But on the whole educators are at least trying to do what they believe to be right. Most storytelling in schools and universities is done with good intentions. In the next chapter, we will see how another form of brainjacking, which is intended to pass on accurate facts, can be distorted, as news edges into propaganda.

PROPAGANDA OR NEWS? 3

Just as is the case with education, news reporting is intended to impart facts that will influence the brains of recipients, in this case providing information about what is happening in the world. But news reporting is even more burdened with the potential for shifting from fact to political viewpoint, so much so that extremely slanted news has its own name: propaganda. News both informs and influences, but propaganda deliberately sets out to manipulate.

Spreading the word

The word propaganda, first used in English in the 1670s with reference to the missionary work of the Roman Catholic Church, comes from the Latin *propagare* (to propogate). Since the late-nineteenth century it has been used to mean spreading information that will support a particular viewpoint (often political), often in a biased or misleading fashion. Of course, though the word took on this meaning in the 1880s, propaganda has existed as long as there have been means of mass communication.

Some propaganda has had the clear intention to mislead. In 1926, the English politician Arthur Ponsonby wrote that propaganda involved the 'defilement of the human soul'. He also famously wrote: 'When war is declared, truth is the first casualty' (though he thought he was quoting an unknown source). Propaganda goes hand in hand with warfare, when states, rightly or wrongly, decide that it is important to control the flow of information to the people, sometimes providing wholly untrue information to bias the population in a particular way, or to help bolster morale in the face of bad news.

According to English professor of international communications Philip Taylor, the modern approach to wartime propaganda originated with the British in the First World War. He notes:

> It was no more the policy of the official British wartime propaganda machine to lie deliberately than it was to tell the whole truth. Facts were displayed selectively yet rationally, while falsehoods were eschewed in the belief that they would be ultimately exposed and thereby jeopardise the credibility of those facts that had been released ... The majority of wartime falsehoods – and there were many – were in fact circulated by a free and highly jingoistic press, not by the official propagandists, but the damage had been done.

It's hard to be precise about the origins of propaganda, but it has been argued that epic poems and, for that matter, grandiose architecture that date back over 3,000 years were a form of triumphalist propaganda in their glorification of power. Taylor suggests that some classical mythologies, particularly those of the Romans, were constructed for what we could now see as propagandist purposes. If we move forward to medieval times, in Europe the two prime vehicles for propaganda were public speech – notably from the pulpit – and the transformative invention of the printing press, releasing a deluge of propaganda, both religious and secular, onto those of the public who were literate.

It was, though, in the twentieth century, particularly with the introduction of moving pictures and then television, that propaganda was able to truly achieve its potential. If we equate propaganda to some degree with the manipulative level of brainjacking, bear in mind that a crucial element of this is emotional content. And emotion is best put across by a combination of visual and auditory means.

We can see this in a trivial but informative way in TV talent shows, which indulge in all three levels of brainjacking. The basic informational content is, say, the quality of the singing. The influencing comes from the verdicts of the judges and in later stages, where we see more of the competitors as people in their apparent personalities, though this has a consciously manipulative element, as what is shown is shaped by the show's director. But propaganda comes into play with explicit attempts at emotional manipulation, where we often hear of some sad event in the competitor's life and how, for example, a particular song choice is inspired by their dead grannie. This is so commonplace that it has regularly been mocked on satirical shows.

In a more sinister fashion, we can see propaganda in action in the way that lies are put across, particularly in populist politics, with emotional fervour. At the time of writing, probably the strongest example of propaganda in mainstream politics is the continued assertion from Donald Trump and his supporters that he won the 2020 US election – an emotion-led approach that enables every legal challenge that Trump faces to be treated as a witch hunt. In the next chapter we will see how misinformation and disinformation have become commonplace contributors to brainjacking.

Propaganda for good

Arguably, propaganda that does not contain lies does not have to be bad if used properly in a good cause – neither need it be a vehicle of the state or even of political movements and parties. A fascinating illustration of the way that propaganda can be positive and politically neutral comes in a TV drama based on real life, *Mr Bates vs The Post Office*, first shown on the British TV channel ITV in January 2024. This tells the story of a terrible miscarriage of justice in the UK that took place in the first two decades of the twenty-first century.

From 1999, the Post Office began installing a computer system called Horizon, provided by multinational computer giant Fujitsu, to handle the financial accounts of thousands of sub-postmasters (male and female) who were in charge of small, local post offices across the country. Over time, around 3,500 of these users found that the system began to say that they had sold stock they never had, leaving many of them owing the Post Office tens of thousands of pounds. When those running the post offices complained, they were accused of false accounting and fraud. Around 700 received criminal records, 236 were sent to jail and four of them committed suicide.

The whole business was handled scandalously by the Post Office, which repeatedly lied, telling each person involved they were the only one with a problem and (with the help of Fujitsu) claiming incorrectly that the data for individual post offices could not be changed remotely. The massive company threw its legal might against those small business people, ruining them. At the time of writing, only a relatively small percentage have received compensation or had their convictions overturned, and nearly 80 per cent of the compensation paid in the first successful legal challenge went to costs.

The reason this case is so interesting from the brainjacking viewpoint is that this four-part docudrama has had a huge impact on the action taken on the scandal. Reporting on this miscarriage of justice itself is nothing new. It was first reported in *Computer Weekly* magazine in 2013, has been covered by national newspapers and magazines, and was subject to two BBC *Panorama* documentaries in 2015 and 2020, along with a BBC Radio 4 series in 2020. There was plenty of media coverage. But none of it had anywhere near the impact of *Mr Bates vs The Post Office*. Why? Because the docudrama was propaganda. Good propaganda, certainly, but it went beyond the influencing remit of the documentaries and articles.

As Jonathan Gottschall notes, 'fiction seems more effective at changing beliefs than non-fiction, which is *designed* to persuade through argument and evidence'. He recounts the words of English writer Somerset Maugham who said that 'fiction writers mix the powder [medication] of message with the sugary jam of storytelling. People bolt down the sweet jam of storytelling and don't even notice the undertaste of the powder.'

Because the drama could take us directly into the experiences of those who were suffering (presented through acting), it is far more visceral than the documentaries, even though these featured real people talking about their pain. Being told about something will always have less emotional weight than witnessing it. Emotion was leveraged to the full in the TV show.

Manipulation as dramatic tool

What was particularly fascinating was that the series was followed by a documentary – *Mr Bates vs The Post Office: The Real Story*. This programme featured the real people who had appeared as characters in the drama – and, for me at least, it was much easier to identify with the real sub-postmasters because I already 'knew them' through their dramatic avatars. I had been in 'their' homes. The drama had without doubt manipulated me into considering these to be people I knew, and hence would be more likely to care about.

One good example of conscious manipulation from the drama makers was the role of the central 'villain', Paula Vennells, chief executive of the Post Office between 2012 and 2019. Focusing almost entirely on a small number of individuals is a common approach in such circumstances. Vennells was not the only Post Office senior executive to be complicit, nor, for that matter, were the handful of cases explored necessarily typical of all those whose lives were damaged by the scandal – but to get proper emotional engagement (and hence effective propaganda), it is important to focus on a small enough set of people to maximise connection.

Before this drama, Vennells was a name practically no one knew. But when I started typing it into Google to check the spelling of her surname, by the time I had typed Pa she was the first response. When I got as far as Pau she remained first, putting her ahead of Paul McCartney. In the programme, Vennells, played excellently by Lia Williams, typifies corporate indifference to human suffering. But the true hand of the propagandist shone through in one short scene. Vennells is shown dressed as a Church of England vicar, giving a sermon which touches on the very Christian values she was so clearly failing to show.

This wasn't a fantasy scene – Vennells genuinely was a 'non-stipendiary' minister – a vicar who isn't paid but performs the role through a sense of duty. (She stepped down in 2020.) This was a brilliantly manipulative scene. It had nothing to do with the Post Office story per se. But it underlined the hypocrisy of Vennells's stance at work. Was this a bad thing to do? No – it made a valid point impressively well. But that didn't stop it having the hallmarks of propaganda. And that was why this TV drama was able to put the Post Office scandal at the top of the UK news agenda for days on end, with interventions all the way up to the prime minister. Nothing like this happened after the documentaries or newspaper articles.

The journalist's viewpoint

I brought up the topic of *Mr Bates vs The Post Office,* and how it had more impact than factual material, with the second of my *University Challenge* teammates. Ranvir Singh is a newsreader, presenter and documentary maker who has worked for both BBC and ITV. She said: 'I think it's a really interesting phenomenon, and lots of people are scratching their heads including journalists, because you think the power is in research and doing it properly and telling the story first – actually it makes you think, "What was missing?" All the writing that was done, the *Panoramas* and all of that was obviously thorough, factual, truthful, balanced, impartial, and all that good journalism is – uncovering a scandal.

'But, it was a technical scandal. It was about what the non-human computer system did. What the drama added was all about the emotion. When you watched it, the Horizon system was just this little sinister red flashing light under the desk. What we were witnessing was the unravelling of human lives, and the pain that the computer caused. It makes you realise that humans respond to humans and not necessarily to technicalities. Fundamentally, as journalists, we've always known to ask, "Where's the human interest angle in this?"'

Ranvir also noted that drama has a lower threshold for engagement for the audience than a documentary does: 'They can tell truths in an unexpected place at nine o'clock at night in a drama with an actor you'd really liked in another show. You might think, "I've had a hard day: do I want to sit down and watch a documentary on the Post Office scandal?" It's just a matter of how we react to things: we go, "No, thanks, there's enough shit in the world, I don't want to watch something else."'

That 'actor you like' part, she believes, is also important: 'I heard a good thing the other day: if you are currently in a corporate scenario somewhere in the world and you are in litigation or there's something going on, ask yourself: "In the ITV drama of the future would Toby Jones play me?" If the answer is no then you know you're in the wrong!' Ranvir was not alone in commenting to me that she watched the drama because of the presence of this actor, who seems particular adept at playing the little man versus the machine.

Few would argue that there is any problem with the use of drama as propaganda in *Mr Bates*, where the topic of persuasion is central to the drama itself. What can cause more irritation to viewers is when propaganda is shoehorned into drama without an obvious reason. There have been periods, for instance, in the existence of the long-running BBC science fiction/fantasy drama *Doctor Who* when there have been such heavy-handed messages that the storyline took second place – never a good look. The same can be said for soap operas such as ITV's *Coronation Street*, which has regularly picked up on the social and cultural debating points of the day, but at least that can be said to be reflecting the real world, which is hardly the point of *Doctor Who*.

Mr Bates vs the Post Office demonstrates that propaganda, while often dubious, isn't inherently bad, even if it can be selective with the truth. But where do we draw the line between propaganda and 'real' news? Remember Taylor's comment about the majority of falsehoods in First World War British propaganda coming from the free press? Just because many news organisations are not under control of the government does not mean that they will not indulge in propaganda.

This is easy to see in newspapers and in the work of TV channels such as Fox News in the US, or GB News in the UK, where the political alignment of the news channel is no secret. But this is not the only source where the dividing line between news and propaganda is fuzzy. The BBC in the UK, for example, prides itself on its impartiality – yet many critics suggest that it has a bias towards the views of a left-leaning, liberal, metropolitan elite. This is not company policy, which is to be strictly impartial, but rather appears to reflect the political and cultural makeup of most BBC staff.

The nature of news

I asked Ranvir about what news was *for*: 'Doing the job which you can't do in your daily life, telling you what's happening around you and the state of the world ... It takes you outside of your own home. It also lets you know that perhaps you're not alone if you are feeling a certain way about your street, or crime in your area, or whatever it might be ... There's the old adage that people in journalism use – and it's a very crude one – if it bleeds, it leads. And that's why there's a huge responsibility on the news. When I worked in regional newsrooms, we used to say that you could fill an entire half-hour show every night with just crime, because there's enough of it around. But that isn't a true reflection of society, so you have to be mindful of what news you are giving and how often: it can give a distorted view of the way things are. And, of course, everything is subjective. Editorialising is a subjective art.'

But can news ever be pure information or does it always involve influence? Ranvir said: 'I would say that there is a striving for it to be as pure as possible and what it means in practice is, "Is it balanced?" Have you taken the perspective of all parties in this situation? Have you given enough time to all sides to set their story out? But is it ever really pure? It's a really good question and I feel put on the spot that I can't say, "Yes!" immediately.

'For example, how pure is [the reporting of] any war? There is disinformation and propaganda and the pushing of agendas: as a journalist you're fighting all of these different things and making split-second judgements about where you're heading with your storytelling each night. You might adjust it each night slightly, so that over the course of a week you get to a sense of purity. Because you can't always tell ten different stories in a six-minute piece every night. So, you might only tell two sides of the story one night, but then the next night you might tell another two sides of that story. I think there is always a striving for purity, but I don't think you can always achieve it in the time you've got.'

I asked if part of the problem was that even the words you choose can influence how people see the situation. 'Absolutely, journalism is all about the words … It's a bit of a tug of war sometimes when you're writing copy and the editor's writing headlines. Headlines can be a nightmare because there are so many different things in play: space on the page or time when you've got one minute to write the bongs [TV headlines between strikes of Big Ben on the ITV News]. You are trying to get information into a small space with the greatest impact. Because you're trying to get people to watch … and that's what clickbait is. Clickbait is literally using words that don't even reflect the story just so you click on it, so that the site can sell advertising. Ask how many people when they click on a story are really disappointed with what came next, probably the majority of the time. Clickbait uses language to influence and manipulate.'

Should news and documentaries go beyond information?

There is no doubt that a news source that attempts to be impartial, such as the BBC or ITV, engages in at least the influencing level of brainjacking. It may report some information, but on issues ranging from climate change to politics there is a clear intent to influence too. And though high-quality news organisations would like to think that they don't engage in manipulation, the reality is that news reporting often deploys emotion – for example, asking interviewees how they *feel* – rather than putting across emotionally neutral facts.

This becomes even more obvious in documentaries. Ranvir commented: 'In the documentaries that I've been involved in where there's been an element of uncovering scandal or trying to get underneath the skin of something, you try to force the light of day into dark corners that people don't want you to go into … So you're trying to figure out "What is my angle going to be?" And then you've got to be careful of confirmation bias. That's probably as close as it gets to opinion. Opinion is something you try to leave to the viewer or the reader. But what was really a massive lesson that journalists had to learn during Brexit was "Is being fair and balanced the same as telling the truth?" Because if you use time as a crude weighing scale – five minutes for each side, say – what if one side are saying things that can't be proven to be true until after the event? … Gaza and Israel is another example: as a journalist you are attacked relentlessly for being one side or the other. But those stories still have to be told – it's not an exact science; it's not maths, it's human behaviour. It's people and it's pain and it's policy, and all of these things are always, knowingly or unknowingly, being manipulated by the people telling the story, because you have a point of view.'

Some documentaries, of course, are made with the explicit intention of making a change. 'You can have campaigning journalism, where you are trying to get a policy change, or, say, to get the NHS to change their guidelines on something because it's outdated and it doesn't reflect the current science. I did a documentary on foetal alcohol syndrome* and we challenged the NHS and the BMA on their guidelines in the UK about how much alcohol is safe in pregnancy. We presented lots of evidence

* *Exposure: When Pregnant Women Drink*, 2015.

from America and elsewhere – we were talking to those doing the latest research – and [the NHS] did then change their guidance, recommending that it's better to not drink at all: not even have *one* during pregnancy. Social pressures and social norms can sometimes outweigh science: in campaigning journalism you have an idea in the back of your mind that you hope the right people will listen to and take action and update their policies or change the law.'

Polling problems

One feature that frequently crops up in the news is the opinion poll. At first sight, this is one of the few sources of pure information on the brainjacking spectrum. After all, it appears as pure fact: a snapshot of the public's views on whatever you might wish to ask them about. However, polls present two possibilities for brainjacking to go further.

The first is that the information is not, to use Ranvir's term, 'pure'. Just like any scientific experiment, poll results are highly dependent on the quality of the study. After all, a poll typically attempts to tell us something about the population at large by interacting with a much smaller subset. To be effective, the people who are polled should be representative of the population that is being modelled, but that can be very difficult to do (and is why major polls on, for example, the Brexit result in the UK have failed to reflect the outcome).

Just like any other study, an effective poll has to have a large enough sample size – if you are looking for a country-wide outcome, even for a relatively small country like the UK, this needs participant numbers in the thousands. And (this is the really difficult bit) the distribution of those polled has to match the whole population in all ways that would reflect on how they will answer their questions. A simple example: if you want to predict the result of an election, you won't get far by just polling the members of one political party.

Even after a poll has been taken, modern pollsters modify the results. When you see numbers who intend to vote for party A or party B, these will not be the actual numbers who said they would vote that way. The polling organisation weights the numbers to correct for any difference between the sample used and the real distribution of the population. As an example, in a YouGov poll of voting intentions in the UK some years ago, out of 1,667 polled, 492 said they would vote Conservative – but the published poll showed the number as 457.

Getting the right match to the population is one of the main reasons that polls can go wrong – and in such circumstances if the poll misleads it is not usually intentional. But it's also the case that more unscrupulous pollsters can use the phrasing of questions, or even the order in which questions are asked, to bias the outcome of a poll. Asking which party you will vote for in the next election is a neutral question. But how you word, say, a question about whether or not a politician is deceiving the nation can make a significant difference to the way it is answered.

So far, we have considered polls as information – but in reality they can be far more. Poll results cannot be detached from reality. Unless it's a private poll that is never published, the target audience of the poll – for example when the results are shown in a news programme or newspaper – *is* the voting public. And it is impossible to believe that members of the public would not be influenced in any way when such polls are published.

There has been a significant amount of research on this over the years, though most of it does date from the period when there is considerable doubt over the accuracy of social science research. Nonetheless, there seems to be sufficient consensus to suggest that one of two suspected factors does have an effect on outcomes, while the other is relatively negligible.

One suspected impact is the 'bandwagon effect', where people see a candidate or party doing well and take this as a positive indicator, increasing their chance of voting the same way. The other, opposing, impact is the 'underdog effect', where voters see a party or individual trailing in the polls and decide to vote for them to help them. A number of studies suggest that the bandwagon effect does have an impact but, perhaps surprisingly, the underdog effect does not.

These aren't the only possibilities, though. Political parties are always wary of complacency that might lead to voters not bothering to turn out because their party of choice seems to be doing so well that it's not worth the effort – a negative bandwagon effect. There also appears to be a greater tendency for tactical voting from supporters of certain parties, particularly when the driving issue is to avoid another party or candidate getting in at all costs. Again, polling can have an influence in shifting voting intentions by suggesting the best way to avoid an undesired result.

News and manipulation

I spoke to Helen Carasso, who we will return to on the subject of advertising in Chapter 7, about both news reporting and manipulation. Helen has held a range of marketing and PR roles in public sector organisations such as the UK government's information service and Oxford University's public relations office. She now researches and teaches higher education policy. Like I did with Ranvir, I asked Helen if it is possible to be purely informative or is there always influencing or manipulation?

'Absolutely there's manipulation. When I worked at [BBC] World Service, my senior colleagues in the newsroom always held they were absolutely impartial, funded by the

Foreign Office, but absolutely impartial, and I said, "I know you're trying to be, but you're not. You come with a perspective, with a background – of course if you're doing a bulletin for the Arabs you lead with a different story than if you're doing a bulletin for the Thais. You still have a perspective, and you're not covering everything." You cannot listen to everything, see everything, write everything, tell everything. So, however much you try to be neutral, you're still saying it's more important that somebody understands not to use the hairdryer in the bath, because they might kill themselves, than it is that they understand that it will cut out if it overheats. You're still making a judgement.'

Thinking of the three levels of brainjacking, I asked if Helen thought there was a judgement to be made between neutrally passing on information and actively trying to change people's opinion.

'I think there is a spectrum, but the road to hell is paved with good intentions, and there clearly is a difference between certain American-style "news" channels and a BBC news channel, a *Channel 4 News*, whatever. In some senses you could say Fox News is clear what it is, it's honest. It wears its colours on its sleeve. It's not a view I would like to adhere to, but at least you know what you're getting if you listen to that. But then, that assumes a sophisticated audience, and of course that's the other thing. You are assuming a level of critical insight into the messages that come to you. I know people laugh at media studies but it's like the way that studying literature, rather than just reading the book, enables you to understand the context, the metaphors, the positioning, all those sorts of things as opposed to just "here's a poem" or "here's a book".'

The comment about Fox News was interesting, given that some public service news broadcasters in the UK are, perhaps, less likely to put an emphasis on impartiality than the BBC. A good example might be *Channel 4 News*. Channel 4 is an oddity in the UK – it is publicly owned, but funded by advertising, unlike the BBC, which at the time of writing is funded by a licence fee. *Channel 4 News*, produced by Independent Television News, has always prided itself on giving more depth of coverage and debate than its competitors. But in recent years it has shown a noticeable shift to the left. Michael Crick, a distinguished UK news broadcaster, said in 2023 on a podcast* that by the end of his time at *Channel 4 News*, the approach had become too political. It started off relatively neutral, but it ended up with a strong left-wing liberal bias, with which he felt quite uncomfortable. Arguably, any bias is more insidious with a source like *Channel 4 News*, which is a public service broadcaster, so viewers may well assume it would be impartial.

Something that many news organisations now attempt to do explicitly is to point out to their audience the distinction between the factual reporting they espouse and the twin distortions of misinformation and disinformation. In the next chapter we will see how these can result in unwanted brainjacking.

* Michael Crick, the former *Channel 4 News* political correspondent, was talking to Roger Bolton on his podcast on British broadcasting and the BBC, *Beeb Watch*.

MISINFORMATION AND DISINFORMATION

4

The two words 'misinformation' and 'disinformation' are often used interchangeably, but the technical distinction is that misinformation is about getting the facts wrong without the intent to, erm, misinform, while disinformation requires the deliberate intention of misleading the recipient. Despite this, the two are usually lumped together in the attempts we see to prevent the public from confusing fact with fiction.

Checking the facts

The need to highlight misinformation and disinformation seems manifest in the widespread development of fact-checking organisations, some dedicated to sifting the data, others being adjuncts to news providers, such as the UK's national broadcaster's BBC Verify (the service formerly known as Reality Check). At the time of writing, this service's lead stories include the British prime minister missing key 2023 targets, the number of people reported killed in Gaza in 2023 and whether the UK Labour Party intended to institute a meat tax if they got into government.

A US example of the same kind of service is FactCheck.org – at the time of writing this included showing that a picture of the US vice president with accused sex-trafficker Jeffrey Epstein was a fake, revealing that studies apparently showing that Covid vaccines caused illness or millions of deaths in New Zealand were not real, and explaining that US Army cadets did not chant 'Fuck Joe Biden' at an American football game.

There is no doubt that facilitation of communication across the world by the internet has been a boon. Science, for example, has benefited hugely from the ability to get quick access to papers from every university at the click of a button (admittedly, often accompanied by their institution paying a hefty fee). But the internet has also made everyone capable of being an information provider. And this has a huge potential for the introduction of misinformation and disinformation.

Unfortunately, using fact-checking services has itself become subject to a kind of misinformation or disinformation response. When the fact-check does not agree with personal beliefs, it can be easy to assume that the service itself is biased, because it does not support the beliefs an individual holds to be true. Often this response is incorrect, though it would be fair to say that most fact-checking services do reflect the lack of political balance that is prevalent in academia,* and can seem to be attacking right-of-centre opinions more than they do those on the left.

Low calorie drinks and autism

I recently experienced misinformation live. One of my daughters gets a lot of her information about the world from the

* There is considerable variation in numbers between studies, but there is no doubt that academics significantly lean politically to the left more than they do to the right.

social media platforms TikTok and Instagram. As a result of one Instagram video, she informed me that one third of all US births resulted in Asperger's syndrome because of the mother consuming diet drinks containing aspartame during pregnancy. Looking at the video, which was from a Joe Rogan interview, the claim made was actually that 'one in three women who drank Diet Coke during pregnancy had an autistic kid'.

Looking into the claim a little deeper, it was inspired by a press release from the University of Texas Health Science Center at San Antonio, put out on 20 September 2023. This said that a study had found 'an association between autism diagnosis in boys and daily consumption of either diet soda or a comparable amount of aspartame by their mothers during pregnancy or breastfeeding'. The release went on: 'In this case-control study,* boys who had been diagnosed with autism were more than three times as likely as neurotypically developing boys to have been born to mothers who reported consuming one or more servings per day of diet soda, or comparable amounts of the leading artificial sweetener aspartame, during pregnancy or breastfeeding.'

We already have a couple of elements of misinformation or disinformation creeping in. The report saying the diagnosis was three times more likely in boys was transformed into the totally different statistic of a third of all children by the time I heard it.

As is often the case, newspaper headlines, echoing the Instagram video, grabbed the scariest part of the information in the press release and generalised it with, for example, the *New York Post* reporting 'Drinking diet soda during pregnancy

* A case-control study is an observational study where two groups with different outcomes on a particular input are compared with the intention of identifying a cause for the difference. They are significantly less reliable than randomised controlled trials.

linked to autism'. However, the UK's *Daily Mail** struck back, quoting scientists who called the research 'irresponsible', and pointing out a range of flaws in the study itself.

Firstly, the study was based on a relatively small sample size, comparing mothers of 235 children on the autism spectrum (the 'case group') with those of 121 children who weren't on the spectrum (the 'control group'). Secondly, the data relied on the mother's recall of what they had consumed long after the event – in some cases the children were already adults, so the mothers were recalling what they drank on a daily basis eighteen or more years earlier. I can't remember details of what I drank last week. Thirdly, we know that autism has a strong genetic component, yet no effort was made to eliminate this from the study. In fact, this was a key flaw, because around half of the control group of non-autistic children had the same mother as one of the autistic children, meaning there wasn't a proper distinction between control and case groups. Underlying the negative response to the study from professionals was the scientific mantra that correlation is not causation.

Correlation vs causality

It is perfectly possible for two things to be correlated – apparently associated numerically – without one causing the other. One example I was taught on my university course many years ago was that there was a period of time after the Second World War when the amount of bananas imported into the UK was correlated with pregnancies. More bananas, more pregnancies – but

* It is ironic that the *Daily Mail* countered the suggestion, given that this newspaper has a long-standing reputation for reporting on studies which they claim show that practically anything either causes or prevents cancer – sometimes both.

no one seriously suggested the bananas caused those extra births. It is often the case with a spurious correlation like this that there is a third factor that caused both observations – in the banana example it may have been, for instance, that increasing personal wealth led to more enthusiasm for having children and more eating of the then-expensive fruit. Or it could have been that people were assuming that A caused B, where it was actually the case that B caused A. In the banana example it could have been that pregnant women ate more bananas.* And then there are many purely random correlations.

With sufficient volumes of data, you can almost always find meaningless correlations. There are websites that highlight such correlations in data† where we can discover, for instance, that US crude oil imports from Norway correlate with drivers killed in collisions with railway trains, that the per capita consumption of mozzarella cheese is correlated with the number of civil engineering doctorates awarded, and that the people who would want to know the date on which they will die are far more likely than the average to feel that pizzas without a crust are just fine. We now have access to much more data than ever before – meaning spurious correlations are far more likely.

Can we protect our children?

Back with the diet drinks and autism study. The methods employed by the scientists were incapable of providing useful evidence that consuming the aspartame caused the autism. Arguably the study's authors, or the university's press office, verged on disinformation here, as they should have known that

* This may well not be true, but it's more likely than the bananas causing the pregnancies.

† For excellent examples of spurious correlations see www.tylervigen.com.

this was the case. There is no harm in doing such a study, which demonstrates that more in-depth research is required to get to the facts – but there is the potential for a lot of harm in presenting such a study to the public as if it were reporting facts.

Getting to the conclusion I present above is fine if you have the time to do what I have just done – spend an hour or so looking into the study itself, the press release and the responses from other scientists. But, quite reasonably, my daughter did not have the time to do this. She is arguably unwise using Instagram or TikTok as an information source – but this is hardly uncommon among her peers in their twenties and younger people. We are now bombarded with misinformation and disinformation that attempts to change our mindsets.

I asked Ranvir Singh, who has an eleven-year-old son, what can be done in such circumstances. 'It's very difficult – some influencers out there with massive followings espouse something that touches a raw nerve with the audience that they're talking to, and then they veer off into misinformation or disinformation in the next minute. But the audience is already hooked into the cult of personality on these platforms, and so that is very difficult to counter. [With my son] I'm like, "If you come to me and tell me all this stuff you've seen on YouTube, you've got to go onto these other sources and read articles about it, then talk to me."

'But it takes a lot of effort – when I was younger all we did was at 6 or 6.30 at night, sit down and watch the news. My dad was obsessed with it, as most immigrants are. They're desperate for information about the land they've left: the politics over there and here – they are a product of the politics, really. They've changed their life, making a big decision to abandon everything they know for a new place. People who have that life are intrinsically interested in the news in the way that if you have a safe, quiet life you can afford to ignore the news. Boredom is the privilege of an unworried mind: if you can be bored, great, it means you're not worried about anything.

'As I was growing up, the BBC was the holy grail – and the BBC in India was hugely trusted. I grew up with that in my household. But my son doesn't sit down and watch the news at a particular hour. He will come to me at various times of the day and say, "Mum, did you see that?" ... They're in their bedrooms with a million different voices, and there's just one of you saying, "Come downstairs, have your dinner" – you're fighting all the time, and you have to be so active – you can't take your eye off the ball for even a couple of weeks. Before you realise it, they start spouting things and you think, "Where did you get that from?" They can't even remember where they heard it, but they're now telling it as a fact ... I think all children are now accessing so much information and misinformation that as a parent or caregiver or teacher you are constantly having to put those conversations under pressure of truth, of source ... that's a lot for an eleven-year-old.'

I pointed out that it's not just a lot for an eleven-year-old – it's a lot for parents who aren't in the news business. Ranvir replied: 'Absolutely. I don't know what you do if you're not already naturally invested in the business of news and truth: I don't know how you cope.'

Inoculating against misinformation

Inevitably, there have been attempts to do something about the pervasive nature of misinformation and disinformation. Sander van der Linden is a Dutch social psychologist based at the University of Cambridge who specialises in social influence and is described on Wikipedia as 'an authority on understanding and dealing with misinformation'. In his book *Foolproof*, van der Linden describes misinformation as a contagious virus, and stretches the analogy to suggest it's possible to inoculate the public against this infection, just as we would prevent the spread of a real virus.

If this is true, we have a potential defence against this form of brainjacking. Van der Linden breaks down the 'DNA' of the misinformation virus into a number of components: he suggests that by enabling the public to understand and recognise these components, it is possible then for them to spot misinformation when it comes along and hence to prevent the 'virus' from spreading. The components he suggests we need to look out for are Discrediting, Emotion, Polarisation, Impersonation, Conspiracy and Trolling (the initials of each word spelling out DEPICT).

In principle, we could just learn what these components are and how to spot them, but van der Linden suggests that playing specially designed games provides a better way to build our recognition skills, stretching the analogy possibly to breaking point to suggest that playing such games constructs mental 'antibodies' so that we can then fight off misinformation reflexively, without consciously deciding the quality of the information. There are, however, significant problems with this approach.

The first is that, realistically, most of the general public will neither read van der Linden's book nor play his games. If the approach were effective *and* it could be incorporated into a nation's education system so everyone played the games at school, it could have some influence. But there has been considerable doubt expressed about the content as well as the method used to provide 'inoculation'.

University of Sussex philosopher Dan Williams* notes that four of the six components (discrediting, emotion, polarisation and conspiracy theories) are not inherently misinformative. For example, discrediting is something that science does all the time – it is how scientific theories move on. While in some contexts, emotion can be suspicious, it is not a marker of misinformation

* Williams makes this point in his blog post 'Misinformation is not a virus, and you cannot be vaccinated against it'.

in most cases – we have already seen how central emotional content is to getting a message embedded. In the Post Office Horizon system scandal, for example (see page 36), it is hardly surprising that there is a lot of emotion in the reporting, bearing in mind that many people lost their jobs and homes, several hundred faced criminal trials and some were jailed. But that emotion does not make information about this scandal misinformation.

Polarisation is a particularly odd component, as there are plenty of causes where there are polarised viewpoints, especially in the modern world. What is often the case in such causes is that there is no clear right and wrong answer – each side of the polarisation has positive and negative points. But it certainly isn't an inherent flag for misinformation. And although some conspiracy theories are ludicrous, perfectly reasonable theories can be labelled as conspiracy theories by those who have an interest in countering them. Take, for example, the reasonable idea that the Covid virus was the result of a lab leak. The pandemic did, after all, start in a city where a major lab that works on coronaviruses is located. Yet what was at the very least a coincidence worthy of thorough investigation was treated by authorities as a conspiracy theory for several years before it began to be taken seriously.

As such, it's hard to see any of these components as reliable markers on which to base 'inoculation'. Williams also suggests that highlighting these as features of disinformation tends to make people consider all content, whether or not it is true, as suspicious. Arguably this is better than naïve acceptance of misinformation, but it is not ideal. A final concern that Williams raises is that the examples of misinformation used in experiments to test this approach are constructs, designed to show the required characteristics, rather than true examples of misinformation.

Part of the problem with the inoculation approach is the amount of focus put on the feel of the piece of information. There is nothing wrong with taking this into account. If, for instance, the information is all in capitals (or yelled in a video), badly spelled, presented in an amateurish way or full of ad-hominem attacks, we have some initial red flags. But in the end, it is more fruitful to put significant weight on the claims themselves. As science communicator Carl Sagan made clear, extraordinary claims require extraordinary evidence. What evidence is being provided? Are there links to legitimate sources? What do you find with a quick Google search on the topic?

While the inoculation analogy breaks down rather easily, one thing that does ring true from van der Linden's work is the need for better education in dealing with information. As we saw in Chapter 2, schools still have a very twentieth-century approach to teaching. A number of years ago, the Royal Society of Arts proposed a new type of school curriculum where what was taught was primarily the tools for finding information, assessing it and making use of it, rather than traditional subjects. These tools would then be deployed in a wide range of projects that covered the requirements of more traditional curricula.

Getting the basic tools

An education approach that centred on information-handling tools would certainly be hugely helpful in dealing with misinformation and disinformation – and I would suggest it is only by making such a fundamental change that we could achieve something close to a universal ability to deal with such issues. It is also something that is even more necessary now that generative AI, such as ChatGPT, can be used to produce essays and other schoolwork – knowing how to check the correctness of such material becomes crucial. (More on generative AI in Chapter 10.) I would also suggest that it would be useful to look at the way that the BBC radio programme *More or Less* deals with numerical issues in the data we are presented with by the media.

Without getting heavy mathematically, the Radio 4 show and podcast presented by Tim Harford helps listeners to develop antennae for spotting numbers that seem unlikely to be true. Unexpectedly large or small numbers don't immediately make the claims they are used to support invalid, but are indicators that further digging is required before believing them. This approach is also very effectively covered in Michael Blastland and Andrew Dilnot's book *The Tiger that Isn't* (see the Further Discovery section) – Blastland was central to the development of the *More or Less* show.

It was using this kind of thinking that made it easy for me to take the first steps in looking at the aspartame and autism misinformation mentioned above. When I was told that one in three US children were now born with autism as a result of diet drinks, that seemed a phenomenally large number. I don't know off the top of my head the birth rate in the USA, but I know the population is over 300 million, so it seems reasonable there would be several million babies born a year; the implication that at least a million babies are born with autism as a result of their mothers' diets per year doesn't feel right. Equally, it would mean a school class might have as many as ten such children – again, it feels wrong from experience.

Of course, it made it easy to start in a state of suspicion because the source was Instagram. It is perfectly possible that a TikTok or Instagram video will contain correct information – I'm sure many do. But that surface-level indicator of a potentially dubious source played a part in the need to dig deeper.

Press office problems

The issues with the original press release that started the aspartame and autism story show the amount of care that needs to be taken in the way that science stories are presented to the public by scientists and by university press offices. This is by no means the only example of a press office misleading journalists or enabling what started out as information to end up as misinformation or disinformation.

My favourite example of this happening is harmless, though it does demonstrate the extent to which an attempt to grab headlines can result in an extreme distortion of the facts. This story, dating back to 2013, involves the *Star Wars* weapon the lightsaber.* Now, I loved the early *Star Wars* movies, but one of the more bizarre aspects of them was the introduction of this device. Can you imagine the reaction of the military if they were told that scientists had perfected a lightsaber and it was going to be issued as a sidearm? It would be difficult to be sure if they would laugh or cry. As a practical weapon, the lightsaber is a nightmare.

There's a good reason why soldiers stopped using swords. They're absolutely no use against an enemy carrying a firearm that works from a distance. Though *Star Wars* creator George Lucas fudged the issue by showing Jedi masterfully stopping incoming blasts with flicks of their lightsabers, we all know that it wouldn't work in the real world. Even if it were possible for human muscles to respond fast enough to hit an incoming projectile (not to mention the beam of a blaster heading towards a Jedi at light speed), while the fighter wielding a lightsaber was busy stopping a blast to the head, another shot would have taken them out from a different direction.

Why, then, are lightsabers so wonderful if we wouldn't use them as weapons? Because they are very attractive to play with. They make highly entertaining toys. Take away the unpleasant effects of slicing through flesh and who wouldn't want to take part in a lightsaber battle, clashing insubstantial glowing blade against blade to a soundtrack of that glorious ripping

---

* I know that the correct UK spelling is 'sabre', but 'lightsaber' seems to require the US alternative.

buzz? There's a reason that there's a toy lightsaber on my desk, rather than a *Star Trek* phaser. It's much more fun. But even so, perhaps newspapers, magazines and TV channels should have been a little more careful when in 2013 they carried headlines that included 'Star Wars lightsabers finally invented', 'Scientists Finally Invent Real, Working Lightsabers' and 'MIT, Harvard scientists accidentally create real-life lightsaber'.*

One problem here is that *Star Wars* is not science fiction: it is fantasy, a fairy tale with magic swords dressed up in scientific clothing. There is no physical way that a laser-like light beam can emerge from a weapon, then suddenly stop after travelling a metre or so. Light doesn't work like that. So why were media outlets carrying those headlines? (I do, incidentally, love the word 'finally', carrying the suggestion that it was surely about time that physicists stopped messing about and managed to do this.) Those headlines were written because the press release from the universities carried a quote from Professor Mikhail Lukin of Harvard saying: 'It's not an inapt analogy to compare this [discovery] to light sabers.'

In reality, the remark was both inapt and inept. What the scientists had done was use a special form of matter, called a Bose–Einstein condensate, only viable at extreme low temperatures, to make two photons of light briefly interact with each other in what were described as 'light molecules'.† That is interesting, without doubt, and worthy of reporting. Generally, photons totally ignore each other. This is just as well, as otherwise all the light and radio signals passing by as you read this would collide with each other. But the phenomenon has nothing

* Quotes on the invention of lightsabers are from *Fox News*, the *Guardian* newspaper and *Time* magazine.

† The paper referred to by the press release is 'Attractive photons in a quantum nonlinear medium' by Ofer Firstenberg et al., published in *Nature*.

whatsoever to do with lightsabers – and it is certain that no one had 'finally invented a real working' one.

This delightful and harmless example shows the way that misinformation (and disinformation) can spread due to three different constituencies coming together that all have good intentions, but are each trying to do something different. The scientists want their work to be better understood by the public. The university press officers want to make sure the organisation's achievements are widely publicised, in part to ensure that funding continues to come in. And the media outlets want eye-catching headlines, ideally linked to something the public can relate to – like a lightsaber.

By default, most scientists are trained to be highly cautious about their discoveries and would like to surround everything that they say about them with caveats and limitations. A few, especially those who have already had media exposure or lucrative TV contracts, may be inclined to wild exaggeration, but most attempt to be careful and precise. But such care and precision does not satisfy either the press officers or the journalists – so in reporting a study or experiment, those caveats tend either to be ignored altogether or pushed down to the bottom of the article where they get far less attention. The combination of the headline and first paragraph is what counts here – and the temptation when writing these will be to go for the most eye-catching distortion of reality. Some readers or viewers will absorb the whole piece – but many consumers of the media will take the brainjacking impact of the opening as the key message.

Do intermediaries help?

One attempt to get around this problem in the UK, now followed in a number of other countries, is the establishment of the Science Media Centre. This is a body that is not affiliated to a particular university, but rather can act as a filter between scientists, science press releases and the media, providing what is intended to be an informed, appropriate response to a news story, rather than one that strays into misinformation to garner attention.

Fiona Fox, the head of the Science Media Centre in the UK, points out a difference in response to two vaccine scares. In 1998, the MMR (measles, mumps and rubella) vaccine was linked to autism as a result of an irresponsibly flawed study by the now discredited former medical doctor Andrew Wakefield. Newspapers carried the story without significant warnings that it could be spurious, and the result was a huge drop in MMR vaccination uptake across many countries, resulting in severe illness and deaths of children. By contrast, reporting of another potential vaccine scare in 2009, when a schoolgirl died after having the new HPV (human papilloma virus) vaccine, was much better handled by the press, who were guided by the Science Media Centre, established in 2002.

Fox does not claim sole responsibility for the difference in approach by journalists, but giving scientists a professional way to present information has certainly helped. In the particular example above, though, it is worth noting that Wakefield's commercially driven PR machine was actively promoting the imagined dangers of the MMR vaccine, while, by contrast, there was no equivalent concerted attempt to discredit the HPV vaccine. Having something like the Science Media Centre does nonetheless help both overcome the potential for exaggerated claims from press offices and the inability of many media outlets to understand scientific studies. The latter problem results both from a tendency for the vast majority of those employed in the media to have a humanities background and the reduction in the use, particularly by newspapers, of dedicated, appropriately trained science reporters.

Dangerous third parties

Even with a better feed of information from scientists to the media, interested third parties can also distort the public's understanding through misinformation and disinformation. We will see in the next chapter how tobacco companies engaged in deliberate deceit. However, in the complex chain of information reaching the public and influencing our minds, those third parties don't have to be so clearly intent on benefitting themselves. One of the biggest problems here is when a third party with apparently good intentions gets it wrong, and as a result spreads misinformation.

Often, this is done where the third party makes decisions and sets policy based on emotion rather than logic. Perhaps the clearest examples come from the green movement. In principle, organisations such as Greenpeace and Friends of the Earth have the best of intentions. Who doesn't want a better environment, benefiting everything from wildlife to the future of humanity? But time and again such organisations have misunderstood or ignored the science, and as a result have spread misinformation.

Two clear examples of this are over genetically modified foods and nuclear power. Genetic modification of plants has held the promise of better nutrition and saving millions from starvation for decades now. But many countries, including those in the European Union, have effectively banned GM products, in part as a result of strong opposition from green organisations. That opposition was based not on good science, but on the reality that some GM producers were out to make money by means that weren't particularly pleasant. This meant that, for example, because manufacturers of a weedkiller were promoting GM plants that were resistant to that weedkiller, the green organisations prevented the deployment of nutrition-enriched golden rice that could have had major benefits in the fight against malnutrition.

Of course, the public discrediting of GM, pushed by the green organisations and parroted by the press, was not presented as preventing profiteering – instead efforts were made to ensure that the technology was seen as unsafe, with opposition from the likes of the UK's King Charles (then the Prince of Wales), based on GM being unnatural and hence dangerous, frequently being quoted by the popular press. This misses the reality that nature is often extremely bad for us. Many of the deadliest substances, such as ricin and botulinus toxin, are natural – our success as a species has, in part, been as a result of being able to defend ourselves from nature, whether it's the impact of viruses and bacteria, or earthquakes and water shortages. The clear scientific consensus that GM was safe and effective was submerged in a tsunami of scares and tabloid headlines about 'Frankenfoods'.

Nuclear power, similarly, has produced a knee-jerk reaction from green organisations and green-minded political parties, resulting in the madness of some countries such as Germany moving part of their energy production from nuclear to the far more environmentally damaging coal. This action ignores the overriding importance of tackling climate change – for which nuclear is an important green source of energy that isn't subject to the variable nature of wind and sunlight. The emotional response to nuclear has watered down the importance of dealing with the biggest environmental danger that the world faces.

There is good science to show that nuclear power is a safe way to generate electricity – but the myth is still wheeled out that it is dangerous, and many people still have this incorporated into their mindset, a direct result of alarmist brainjacking. To give a feel for the reality, we can look at the main ways to generate electricity and assess how many deaths occur per terawatt hour* generated. Coal results in about 24 deaths, oil about 18.4 deaths, natural gas about 2.8 deaths, hydro power about

---

* A terawatt hour is roughly the amount of energy used by 150,000 UK households in a year.

1.3, wind 0.04, nuclear 0.03 and solar 0.02.* Bearing in mind how much brainjacking is influenced by emotion, it doesn't help, of course, that many people have a mental link between nuclear power and nuclear weapons because of the word 'nuclear'.†

Organisations such as Greenpeace and Friends of the Earth demonstrate that even those with access to good data and the tools required to interpret it can fall foul of misinformation – and can enthusiastically spread it. We are never going to be able to entirely prevent misinformation and disinformation from taking hold. Plenty of people don't have the time or the inclination to dig into a story even for a few minutes – but there is no doubt that we can do more to equip ourselves to have at least partial resistance to dubious information.

My examples here have primarily been about misinformation and disinformation in the scientific sphere, but they have also become commonplace in the political output of some individuals. We already saw in the propaganda chapter the assertion that Donald Trump won the 2020 US election. We don't know for certain whether the Trump camp really believes this assertion, making it misinformation, or if it is a disinformational ploy. Either way, it has the same effect of convincing millions of supporters that the former president has been shamefully mistreated.

Outright lies in politics used to be relatively rare – politicians would rely more on ignoring difficult questions – but there is no doubt that in a world where 'personal truths' are accepted as reality by some, untruths are deployed far more. More insidious

---

* Figures on deaths from energy generation from ourworldindata.org. Note that levels for both hydro power and nuclear are exaggerated by a very small number of accidents and would be considerably lower without these outliers.

† The brainjacking impact of the word 'nuclear' is so strong that medical devices based on a phenomenon called nuclear magnetic resonance (NMR) were renamed magnetic resonance imaging (MRI) scanners.

still is the possibility of disinformation in the form of fake audio and video, misrepresenting what an individual has said or done: we will come back to this in the chapter on artificial intelligence.

Disinformation is a form of deception that plays out particularly within the news and social commentary sphere – but before we leave the dark side, we need to dig deeper into deceit and the ways in which individuals can attempt to deliberately mislead and set up incorrect understandings in the minds of others.

DECEPTION 5

Storytelling may feel like a harmless, pleasurable activity, but we have already seen that it can have a dark side. There is always brainjacking involved – so it's important to take stories seriously – but there is more danger when the story is an untruth. This isn't the same as fiction. Storytelling has always had a powerful fictional side, so much so that many people mistakenly think that narrative and creativity are limited to fiction. But the difference between fictional stories and untrue stories is that fiction comes clean. We know it's not true, except when we see the weasel words 'based on a true story', which is often another way of saying 'we made most of this up, but we want you to think it's true'.*

The most dangerous brainjacking involves deception of some sort. Lying, misleading or otherwise fooling our brains in their interpretation of what they hear or see in a more direct and substantial way than is involved with most disinformation. Of course, such deception doesn't have to be bad – it can be

* I am thinking here of fictional films and the like that use this phrase (such as some horror films), rather than docudramas.

undertaken for the purposes of entertainment, for example. But often it is done for entirely the wrong reason.

Deception to entertain

To ease us into the world of truly deceptive brainjacking, I am going to refer to the work of Derren Brown. Brown will crop up several times in this book, so it's worth a brief introduction for readers who aren't familiar with his work. A TV and stage illusionist, Brown very successfully combines a number of the brainjacking-enabled entertainment vehicles: magic, hypnotism and mentalism. There is no doubt that he is a master of the art – his shows are brilliant, though the man himself splits opinion.

All stage magicians practise deception by fooling our senses, but Brown is unusual in taking the deception content of his act to a different level. As he admits in his excellent, if oddly written book *Tricks of the Mind*, while he never claims to do 'real' magic, or to have psychic powers, he does regularly use apparently scientific mechanisms to provide a misleading explanation for his tricks, which are in reality based on a totally different principle.

It seems fair to say that Brown has had a lifetime obsession with deception. He describes spending some time while at university with a fake injury on his face, simply to obtain a reaction from those around him. As he says himself, this was attention seeking – a frequent mark of the performer – but he also relished the way that he knew something that his audience of fellow students didn't. Whether or not deception takes place with an end in mind that is far less acceptable than entertainment, it often carries with it that sense of superiority gained by having knowledge that others don't.

I ought to say in mentioning Brown's undergraduate antics that I can hardly be too critical, as I also resorted to a degree of deception while at university. I regularly gave palm and Tarot card readings. This doesn't mean that I believe in fortune telling – it wouldn't have been deception if I had (apart from deceiving myself). But I had always been interested in the occult – and was fascinated by people's reaction to it. I did go to the effort of reading up on the basic lines identified by traditional palm readers – not as trivial an effort as it would now be with the internet available – but I confess that I simply said whatever came to mind when the Tarot cards were laid out. And had great fun doing it.

Stage magic is perhaps the purest form of deceptive brainjacking, in the sense that we all know that the tricks we watch in amazement are faked in some way – part of the pleasure comes from trying to work out how the tricks function. In that sense, they bridge the gap between fiction and the more manipulative form of deception. It's rare that stage magicians explain how their tricks work, but in his book, Brown not only describes the mechanics of a simple coin trick, but shows how applying layer upon layer of deception can be used to make the performance more intriguing and entertaining.

The basic trick involves making a coin disappear. (If you want to know how to do it, read Brown's book, referenced in the Further Discovery section.) But, Brown suggests, the mere act of making a coin vanish is not enough to evoke wonder. We've seen it far too often before. So, he extends the trick, and here's where the brainjacking really takes off, by briefly 'showing' the coin is still in his hand before making it disappear. In reality, the coin has already gone, but it seems that by doing this quickly enough, most of the audience will take on board the suggestion that they have actually seen it.

To take things to the next level, Brown adds an introductory act to the trick. The coin is first picked up from the table in a normal fashion (as opposed to the slightly artificial way necessary to make the trick work). After attempting to make it disappear, the would-be magician admits that the trick has gone wrong and puts it down. This partly makes the success more surprising, but more importantly, it weakens the attention to the real trick. Even this isn't the end. Brown finally appears to pass the coin from one hand to the other, even though it has already been disposed of. He gives the impression of manipulating it, struggling to make it disappear, before finally revealing that it's not in either hand.

Magic tricks often rely on the power of misdirection – getting the audience to look at the wrong thing when a manipulation is taking place. Brown describes an extreme version of this which took even him by surprise. In a different trick, he produced three cards, previously selected by three close-up audience members, from a shuffled pack. Once he had done this and the trick was apparently over, he placed each of the audience members' cards under their drinks on the table in front of them all. Because they thought the trick was finished, the audience were off their guard. Even though he positioned the cards perfectly openly, the participants were still shocked to discover that their cards had turned up under their drinks.

Our deceptive senses

What makes this apparently unlikely outcome possible is a fundamental mistake we make about the way our brains interact with our senses, notably vision. We see the world around us as if we are witnessing a clear, continuous stream of visual imagery. It seems to be like a video. But the reality of the human visual sense is totally different, and this explains why Brown's subjects could see a coin that wasn't there, or did not notice the cards being placed under their glasses.

Let's start by unpacking what happens when you see a simple still-life image: a red apple, sitting on a table. The initial requirement is to have light available. This travels from a light source – the sun, a lamp or whatever – and hits the apple. The atoms on the surface of the apple absorb photons of light that have travelled from the source. This means that the light's energy is used to increase the energy levels of electrons in the apple's atoms. A very short time later, some of the photons are re-emitted from the apple.

Assuming you are looking at the apple in white light, such as sunlight, the incoming photons will have a range of energies corresponding to all the colours of visible light, plus some invisible infrared and ultraviolet photons as well. The photons that are re-emitted, though, will have a different energy distribution. In the case of the apple, the re-emitted photons will mostly be of the appropriate energy to be seen as red light, so you will see the apple as being red. But that part of the process hasn't happened yet.

Those emitted photons head away from the apple and some of them pass through your pupil. They are absorbed by the retina at the back of the eye. This has a number of types of sensor known as cones, responding to different colour ranges. The red photons will be detected primarily by red cones, photoreceptors that produce a tiny electrical charge in response to photons in the appropriate energy range. These electrical signals are passed through the optical nerve into the brain. To do this, there is a significant amount of pre-processing, because there isn't a fibre for every sensor, so the signal going up the optic nerve has already been simplified.

Most of the signals go to the opposite side of the brain from the eye in question, though some end up on the same side to enable 3D vision. In the brain, the information received will be processed to deal with things like motion (not a lot of this is involved when looking at the apple), pattern and shape recognition, colour handling and more. Your brain gets a pile of data from which it makes up the picture that you 'see'. This is totally different from a camera, where the equivalent of the retina simply measures numbers of different coloured photons hitting it and recreates the image. Your brain's mechanism is far more complex.

This process of rebuilding the image enables the brain to overcome some shortcomings that would require significant AI to be ironed out by a modern digital camera. For example, if you were to take a picture of the apple, you would hold the camera (mostly likely your phone) steady, pointing it at the apple, and press the button. It is best not to wave the camera around while taking the picture. But when you look at the apple, your eyes are not fixed on it. They are constantly jerking around in high-speed movements called saccades.* Because of the way the brain assembles the image, it can edit these out, so your view appears to be static.

Similarly, the point at which the optic nerve meets the retina has no sensors. It's a blind spot where you can't see. If we built smartphone cameras like this, there would be a black gap near the middle of the image. But the brain rebuilds what's there by using data from both eyes. It fakes the appearance to make things look right.

This is all wonderful, but it does make it easy for the brain to be fooled about what it's seeing. This often helps enormously with stage magic, but it's easy enough to see it happening in optical illusions. On the next page is my favourite optical illusion of all time, the checker shadow illusion, produced by Professor Edward Adelson of MIT.

This optical illusion depends on the way the brain processes patterns and shadows. We know what a chessboard (used for playing the game called draughts in the UK and checkers in the US) looks like, and how a shadow influences colouring. This fools the brain into being unable to detect that the squares

---

* Saccades are the fastest movements of any body part – the eyeball can sweep through about 10 degrees in a hundredth of a second.

© Edward H. Adelson.

labelled A and B are exactly the same shade of grey. And even though I know that this is the case, I still can't see it. B still appears to be a much lighter shade.

Our eyes also make all kinds of correction for different intensities and colours of ambient lighting, so we can still see to the best of our ability in extreme conditions. As we will discover in the penultimate chapter, one optical illusion all of us have experienced when looking at the moon is that it appears a lot bigger than it really is. But moonlight also seems far more intense than is the case. We can see quite clearly by the light of the full moon, but it is around 300,000 times dimmer than sunlight.

Another example of vision correction in action is one I've spotted during a candlelit carol service. Our local church has a popular and atmospheric service at Christmas where the building is lit only by candles. Or it would be, if it weren't for the infra-red heaters, which add a strong red glow to the surroundings. After spending a few minutes in the red ambiance, the candle flames start to look green. My brain has detected that the overall lighting is unusually red, and compensates by reducing red sensitivity. This takes red out of the white light from the candles, giving them a ghostly green hue.

Deception by misdirection

Sometimes it can be difficult to focus on our surroundings as much as we want to, which gives ample opportunity for deception. If you have the opportunity, before reading further take a trip to this page: bit.ly/brainjacking6 – it's from the website of my earlier book *The Universe Inside You*. Watch the video, which requires considerable personal focus to complete a task successfully: watch it all the way to the end before returning to the book.

Whatever the outcome of undertaking the experiment in this video, it reflects the same opportunity for brainjacking that Derren Brown made use of in his card trick. The way that the brain creates images, and hence our conscious awareness of what we see, leaves open a gateway for deception and manipulation of our experience.

Professor Dan Simons of the University of Illinois at Urbana-Champaign and his colleague Daniel Levin of Vanderbilt University have undertaken several experiments to demonstrate this ability to manipulate the brain's perception of what is being seen. In a simple example, six cards are displayed on a PowerPoint slide. Someone from the audience is asked to point to one while the presenter's back is turned. She chooses the ace of spades. The presenter then moves onto the next slide – and now there are only five cards. The ace of spades is no longer there. Everyone is impressed – until it's pointed out that none of the cards now on show were on the previous screen. The focus on the ace of spades made the other cards effectively invisible.

In Simons and Levin's most famous study – apart from the 'count the passes' video I suggested above that you watch – they undertook another deceptive experiment where a passer-by was asked for directions in the street. Partway through the answer, two men carry a door up the street, passing between the questioner and the direction-giver. The conversation then continues as the directions are completed. What the direction-giver does not notice is that the person they are talking to has changed while the door went past.

One clear lesson from this is how risky witness evidence is in legal cases – someone didn't even notice a change in the person they were talking to in real time. The dubious nature of witness evidence has been known for a long time. In 1901, a murder took place in a lecture given by Professor Franz von Liszt at the University of Berlin. The professor's students were asked to write down what they had witnessed.

In the witness statements from the lecture, eight different names were given for the murderer. Some said that the killer had run away after shooting his victim (he didn't). The order in which events took place varied from witness to witness. The murder was faked: von Liszt, a criminology professor, wanted to demonstrate just how unreliable witness evidence can be in court – and did so beyond his own expectations. Yet, worryingly, although the police try to make use of less corruptible evidence such as CCTV these days, witness evidence is still widely relied on in court. It shouldn't be, unless the evidence is not open to this kind of confusion.

Powers of the mind?

We'll come back to Derren Brown's work when we look at subliminal brainjacking and hypnosis. But the entertaining side of deceptive brainjacking is a relatively small part of the activity. More often than not, the aim of deception is more sinister. What

Brown does involves a little deception for entertainment purposes, but he never claims any special abilities. However, some assert that their abilities are due to special powers – what is sometimes called 'psi' – encompassing telepathy, telekinesis, psychic abilities and more.

Although these individuals are still often entertainers, the degree to which they are manipulating their audience and their beliefs is significantly greater because they claim genuine abilities. What is particularly worrying is when such performers manage to fool scientists. Being human, scientists are just as susceptible as anyone else to the abilities of stage magicians, but there is a danger that by trying to test the abilities of those claiming special powers without a suitable knowledge of the techniques used by the performers, scientists can give them undeserved respectability.

Perhaps the best-known example is the case of Uri Geller, the Israeli-British TV personality who claims true psychic abilities. Geller has done numerous TV broadcasts: a good example of Geller's trademark ability to bend spoons, forks and other cutlery came on his first live TV appearance back in 1973, on the show of current affairs broadcaster David Dimbleby. At one point, a tray of cutlery was brought on. While Dimbleby held one end of a fork, Geller rubbed it near the tines. He then took the fork and soon after, the head dropped off it. Geller pointed out that while stage magicians can duplicate this kind of thing, they aren't able to do so under such controlled conditions as he was experiencing.

All very impressive, but for two issues. One is that it is easy enough to get cutlery to break with very little pressure if it is pre-treated, for example by repeatedly bending it. Secondly, in many demonstrations, the cutlery is not constantly in view, as Geller tends to move around a lot during his act. This wasn't the case when he bent Dimbleby's fork – but those controlled conditions that Geller claimed simply didn't apply in this case.

What did not come out on air was that Geller had asked for the tray to be placed in his dressing room before the show. He was left alone with the cutlery with plenty of time to prepare it.

What sets Geller apart, though, is that he has also been tested by Russell Targ and Harold Puthoff, scientists at the respected Stanford Research Institute (SRI). Surely there was much more control employed in these experiments? That was certainly the scientists' intention – but it is worth noting that these were laser physicists, whose experience was dealing with light, rather than the less trustworthy experimental subjects that are people. A paper describing the experiments was published in *Nature*, though the editors of the journal said that details of the experiments were 'disconcertingly vague', and they were publishing the report despite this because it was better to have a debate than simply allow unsceptical media coverage to continue with no scientific input.

The reliability of the study depended on the controls involved to ensure no cheating. In one set of experiments, Geller attempted to reproduce a set of images, despite being closed away in a sealed room with no way to contact the outside. In another set, he predicted the result of shaking a six-sided die inside a closed metal box. Clearly, these experiments would only have value if, in the case of the image reproduction, Geller could not communicate and did not have a collaborator, and if he was unable to interfere with the box in the experiment featuring the die.

For some of the image experiments, Geller was in what was described in the report as a double-walled, steel room with an audio monitor that allowed sound out but not in. Targ and Puthoff made the claim that there was 'no sensory leakage' between the room and the outside. Unfortunately, the room was not soundproof, which was not surprising, as there was an 8.9-centimetre- (3.5-inch-) wide hole between the room and the adjacent one where the images and the experimenters were located. The hole had been stuffed with some gauze – which would not stop sound carrying – and was found to have fallen out on the one occasion that Geller made a near-perfect reproduction of the image.

What also isn't mentioned in the paper is that Geller's stage assistant, Shipi Shtrang, was in the room from where the images were being 'transmitted', on the other side of that gauze-filled hole. Shtrang had every opportunity to see the images and to communicate with Geller through the hole. Of course, there were others present, but this would not stop a sound code being used – or even a piece of paper being passed through the hole by someone with plenty of stage magic experience.

As far as the dice experiment goes, it's worth seeing exactly how the experimenters described it taking place:

> A double-blind experiment was performed in which a single ¾-inch die was placed in a 3 x 4 x 5-inch steel box. The box was then vigorously shaken by one of the experimenters and placed on the table, a technique found in control runs to produce a distribution of die faces that does not differ significantly from chance distribution. The orientation of the die within the box was unknown to the experimenters at that time. Geller would then write down which die face was uppermost.

It sounds impressive and much better controlled. But, again, the paper fails to provide sufficient detail of the situation. The secret to a good trick is to ensure that some aspects are clearly observed, leaving others ignored. Firstly, the box was not sealed in any way. Secondly, as far as the description of the experiment in the paper goes, it appears that Geller was sensing the value on the die remotely as it sat in the box on a table. But in reality, Geller was in the room and was allowed to handle the box before his announcement of the value. For a significant amount of time, a stage magician was holding an unsealed box. All he needed was a brief distraction and he could peek inside. In eight out of ten trials he got the value right – but is that surprising?

What also wasn't apparent from the write-up in *Nature* was the lack of control the scientists had over Geller's behaviour. The Apollo astronaut Edgar Mitchell was present as an observer to the trial – not as a sceptic, but as a believer in Geller's abilities. Yet Mitchell remarked afterwards: 'They were so eager to keep [Geller] around that they worked themselves into a box by meeting his every whim and if he threatened to walk off they would relent and do what he wanted. Of course, they lost control of the situation and it just got worse and worse and worse ...'

The naïve researcher

Geller's work inspired the British mathematician John Taylor to undertake his own experiments, which he wrote up in a book called *Superminds*. There is no suggestion that Taylor was attempting to fake outcomes, but his work with the apparent mental abilities of a number of young people demonstrated how easy it can be for those who want to deceive to harness the naïvety of those who want to believe. Taylor devised what appeared to be a much tighter control on mental metal-bending abilities than was ever applied to Geller. Rather than use cutlery, Taylor provided his subjects with small strips of copper and aluminium. In some cases, these were contained in sealed glass tubes, yet the young 'superminds' were able to bend the metal with apparent ease.

To try to find out how this was possible, Taylor checked for a whole range of physical (but unlikely) influences, from heat and magnetism to radiation – but none seemed to be involved. However, there was a huge problem with the controls that Taylor applied. Here's his own comment on one set of experiments: 'two of the best metal-benders, after a week at home with all three types of tube, returned them with the aluminium strips fantastically distorted and none of the seals had been broken'.

In another experiment where the tubes weren't used, Taylor tells us: 'Another subject who had been left with a strip of copper proceeded to break it into pieces by producing softening, even going so far as to be able to pull off a small piece.' Note that the subject had been left alone with the copper strip, while those with samples in tubes were allowed to take them home for a week. Taylor allowed this as he believed there was a 'shyness effect' that meant the mental abilities would not manifest when the children were too closely observed.

You are welcome to believe Taylor, but two more observations are useful in assessing his findings. A team from Bath University, who had more experience of working with people, tested some of Taylor's protégés: when they left their subjects alone, they filmed them through a one-way mirror. As a result, they were able to observe the children enthusiastically bending the strips by hand. On another occasion, the American stage magician and professional sceptic James Randi turned up at Taylor's office posing as a journalist. Taylor proudly showed Randi one of the tamper-proof tubes in which metal had been bent after a week at the subject's home.

The tubes were transparent plastic, with a red rubber stopper inserted into each end. Each stopper was held in place by a screw through the plastic; the head of each screw had a black wax seal with secret markings to show if it had been replaced. Randi took the tube and, while apparently examining the metal within, fiddled with the stoppers. He discovered that it was relatively easy to remove one of the flexible stoppers without shifting the screw. The seal was nothing more than a distraction. All this goes to show that deceptive and manipulative brainjacking is well within the scope of children – and can fool lofty academics who don't have the right training.

Photos that fool

Having already admitted to my deceptive use of palm and Tarot reading, I have also to confess to another experience of deception in my youth – I enjoyed taking UFO photos. Let's be clear, I have never had any real experience involving unidentified flying objects,* though I would love to have done so. But I had fun faking them. This wasn't with the explicit attempt to deceive, but simply for the enjoyment of making the images. Sometimes I used plastic models I'd constructed, held up by fishing line. At other times I threw a hubcap in the air, spinning it like a Frisbee for stability, and took photographs.

Some time ago I was sent for review a book called *UFOs Caught on Film* by B.J. Booth. What I found fascinating was that several of these allegedly real UFO photographs had exactly the same problem that I'd had with my hubcap photos. When you spin a hubcap in the air it doesn't typically fly level, but at an angle, producing an odd-looking image. And this was the case with the UFO photos in the book too. Others looked like nothing more than streetlights or birds.

The most delightful image Booth included was a relatively well-known one, showing a fleet of UFOs flying over the Capitol building in Washington DC. This isn't a faked photo per se, but it is entirely misleading, despite being presented here as a striking photo of UFOs appearing over the hub of American democracy. The reason we know things aren't what they appear is that a complete version of the photograph shows significantly more of the scene than was reproduced here. In the full image you can see that there is a formation of lights along the front of the building that exactly matches the layout of the apparent

---

* The preferred term now is UAP, or unidentified aerial phenomenon, as quite a lot of 'UFO' sightings are not flying objects at all, but optical effects.

UFOs – they are nothing more than reflections in the camera lens.

I would defend my own efforts, because I never claimed they were real; I was just trying to make the images as realistic-looking as possible for fun. But the use of such photos in books like this one reinforces the idea among the susceptible that the UFO phenomenon involves real alien vehicles. Just as was the case with the psi testing, this demonstrates how easily we can be deceived when the deception supports our beliefs – and this susceptibility can be used not only by UFO enthusiasts, but by those who aim to indulge in brainjacking for nefarious purposes.

Deception online

One of the joys of the internet and email is that it has opened up many to an opportunity that in the old days was only available to the select few – to be the potential mark (or victim) of a con. Most of us receive phishing emails which claim to be from a respectable source – our bank, our internet provider … anyone who might have a vague reason for getting money out of us. Many such attempts are very crude, littered with spelling mistakes or badly copied logos. There is even a theory (though I haven't found quality research to back it up) that these obvious errors are sometimes intentional – because potential victims who take the bad fakes seriously are more likely to be gullible.

Some phishing, though, is significantly more subtle. I had a phone call in May 2023, claiming to be from my broadband provider, BT, to tell me my account had been hacked. They said that to prove it was really them, they would send me an email with a PIN. An email duly arrived – and it looked very much like a genuine BT email. But there was still something that felt wrong about the call and the way that they were using a PIN to back up who they were. They weren't able to say what they meant by my account being hacked. After a few minutes, I hung up and called BT.

The company was able to confirm that the call hadn't come from them and there had been no hack. What's more, they confirmed my suspicions about the PIN – the point of a company sending a PIN like this (which they do on some occasions) is for the consumer to prove to BT who the consumer is – it isn't a way for BT to prove who they are. This was far and above the most sophisticated phishing attempt I've yet encountered, reliant as it was on having not just my email address but a matching phone number.

What the scammer is trying to do is to set up a new linkage in your brain. You have a set of ideas about the companies you interact with – a mental model of what it's like to, say, interact with BT. The phishing scammer was attempting to link their call with my mental image of BT messaging. Like many BT customers, I am sometimes frustrated by them – but nonetheless they occupy a box in my brain labelled 'trusted organisations'. The scammer was attempting to insert their phone call into that box.

Phishing is a very simple part of the much larger armoury of cons (short for 'confidence tricks'). At the other extreme are the so-called long cons – elaborate schemes to deceive that can be superficially glamorous. I've long been a fan of the BBC TV drama show *Hustle* that ran between 2004 and 2012, featuring a group of loveable long-con artists who were prepared to dedicate months to a single sting when the potential rewards were great.

Meet the con artists

Hustle, of course, is fiction – but the long con is a real thing. Where a phishing scam attempts to associate a particular interaction – a phone call or an email, for instance – with an existing legitimate entity in the potential victim's brain, a long con involves constructing a whole new entity and situation, gradually building a detailed deceptive model in the brain that leads the victim down the route of giving up what can be a large amount of money.

Confidence tricksters, sometimes known as grifters, have a well-established route to building a convincing worldview for their mark, applying layer on layer to the mental model to ensure that the brainjacking stays firmly in place. The stages of this process are so well-established that each is given a name. The starting point is the put-up, where a suitable victim is chosen. This can involve a considerable amount of research, digging into the individual's preferences and weaknesses. It's not unreasonable to suggest that in *Hustle*, the biggest of these weaknesses tended to be greed.

With a mark in mind, one or more grifters will then attempt to build a social bond with him or her. This is the starting point of tweaking the victim's brain so that the grifters involved become embedded in the 'trusted person' category and are able to introduce a proposition, often to make easy money, that will be accepted. This stage is known as the play. This initial contact is primarily about emotion – as we have already seen, emotion is a powerful brainjacking tool. In some cons, typically those involving romance, this may be enough to seal the deal, but financial cons then engage rational thought as well in what's known as the rope, where persuasion with a degree of logic is used, bringing in details of the scheme to make money (known as the tale).

At this stage, the new patterns in the brain supporting the trustworthiness of the con artists and the nature of the scheme aren't fixed. What's arguably the cleverest part of the whole scheme (though also the riskiest part for the grifter) is the convincer. This involves putting the apparent scheme into action in a small way, with the mark coming out on top. The convincer is at the heart of most confidence tricks of any greater subtlety than a phishing scam.

In a short con – for example the gambling game known as 'find the lady', the 'three-card trick' or 'three-card monte' – the convincer is simply a matter of letting the mark win a couple of games, so that they feel they are in control of the situation. A pattern of expectation is being set up in the brain. Find the lady is a very simple game. The con artist has three playing cards, one of which is a queen. They show the cards, turn them face down and then re-arrange them, typically by sliding the cards around each other on a table before picking up all three cards in a stack, then dropping them back down in a different order.

Once the cards are in a stack, the trick is to make it look as if the performer is dropping the bottom card, but they actually drop the top one. This is surprisingly easy to do with a bit of practice – I'm no magician, but I can do this (the process is made significantly easier by using slightly bowed cards). To make things even more convincing, the mark may well see someone else double their money and walk away with it, not realising that this was an accomplice of the operator. Once the mark has successfully found the lady a couple of times and grown in confidence, they are likely to be prepared to bet more on the exercise – only to be soundly beaten.

In the long con, the convincer is a smaller-scale version of the real thing (we will explore a particular type of long con in more detail in a moment) – which can involve the mark receiving thousands of pounds or other impressive benefits, making it clear just how good an opportunity the con is. Now, the grifters go in for the kill, but they are at their most risky point. There is nothing to stop them losing out.

A more sensible mark may, like a successful gambler, say 'enough is enough' and refuse to go any further. The grifters will lose money. To minimise the possibility, they will often add in an extra element where things appear to be going wrong – the breakdown – which still leaves a chance for a final dramatic win. So, the final stage takes place – the touch – where the mark is taken for as much as possible. In practice, with a long con there may also be final steps, known as the blow-off and the fix, which are intended to prevent come-back from the mark, who is left convinced that it is not a good idea to pursue the loss after the event, but to walk away, wiser and poorer, to avoid embarrassment or legal consequences.

Like a game of find the lady, there is often an element of gambling underlying a long con – to make the con work, the grifters are trying to establish in the brain of the mark the idea that this is indeed a gamble, but a safe one, where the chances are high of reaping a huge reward for very little risk and effort. We will look at the development of a classic con, but first take a detour into a statistical con, which illustrates well the underlying mechanism that is used to manipulate the brain of the mark.

The self-working con

This con takes us into the world of horse-racing pundits. Imagine that there is a service where you can pay a sum of money and in return will be given near-certain predictions on the outcome of horse races. If you have any sense, this is not something that you will take at face value. Anyone can claim to be able to come up with sure-fire predictions, but you would have to be particularly susceptible to take this on trust with no evidence to back it up.

However, the con-artist pundit employs the age-old sales technique of try before you buy. She will give you not one, not two, not even three successful predictions. You will be given four successful predictions in a row with no charge whatsoever. Only then, when you have a good profit and are happy with the pundit's skills, will you have to pay anything for her services. You start off tentatively, but by the fourth race you are prepared to risk a big bet – when this is successful, the payoff is extremely lucrative. This is a powerful convincer. You happily go on to pay the large sum of money required to subscribe to future predictions – and maybe you win occasionally. But before long you are losing large amounts of money.

Because it doesn't involve personal contact or large-scale effort on the part of the con artist, this is a cheap and cheerful example of a long con, but it can still be surprisingly effective. The mechanism involves very little work on the part of the grifter. Our pundit only gives predictions on races that have a small number of runners. Let's imagine they rope in 1,028 punters at the start of the process and, to make the maths easy, there are four horses in each race.

The punters are divided by the grifter into four groups, each of whom is given one of the four horses as their prediction. After that race, there will be 256 happy punters. The process is then repeated three times. When the second race is won, 64 double winners remain. We then get sixteen triple winners, and finally just four will have received a successful prediction for every race. There are 1,024 others who didn't and may have dropped out (not necessarily all of them, as some would reckon that three out of four is good enough odds). But that doesn't matter. Because there are still some who genuinely have received the correct prediction four times in a row. It would seem that their pundit has amazing inside knowledge, and a majority of punters are likely to be prepared to invest in a big way to get more predictions.

A more sophisticated version of this method, often known as a wire con, does not depend on the apparent infallibility of a human pundit. Instead, it employs whatever is the appropriate leading-edge technology of the time. After softening up the mark, the tale would involve a way to find out the result of a race while it is still possible to place a bet. The exact story behind this varies dependent on what that latest technology is (these days I'd expect something like quantum entanglement or artificial intelligence to be used as the tale), but the con dates back to a point in history when such time-bending abilities was a genuine possibility.

In the first part of the nineteenth century, it was possible to bet on a horse race after it had already been run. This was because the results from, say, a racecourse a couple of hundred miles away would not arrive for hours; those results would be carried by a horse, or later a train, to the location where bets were taken. Bookmakers would be losing good opportunities to make money if they refused to take a bet just because the race was finished, if the result was inaccessible.

When the electric telegraph was introduced, the betting industry was slow to realise that the apparent time difference between locations had disappeared. Initially, telegraph companies were induced to refuse to send messages carrying the outcome of races. But wily punters would send a message, for example asking to have a purple shawl sent up to London if the colours of the winning jockey were purple. Before long, the bookmakers had to give in and have a cut-off at the time the race had finished, wherever they were located.

The wire con gives the impression of still having the ability to bet after a result is known. This would be demonstrated to the mark by providing predictions before the end of the race, then hearing the race commentary, say on a radio, and getting the correct results. In the long con, there would be a single mark, so there was no opportunity to use the statistical approach. Instead, technology would be used to introduce a delay into the commentary, so it appeared that the race hadn't yet finished when it already had. The convincer would be to allow the punter to place a bet on one or more races and to make a reasonably large profit.* Then comes the breakdown. The grifters admit that the authorities are on to them. They can only do this one

---

* The wire con flourished before mobile internet access. Now, grifters would need a different approach, as it would be too easy for punters to check the state of a race on their phones.

more time before they are found out. Time for the mark to go big or lose out. And if they place the bet, they certainly will.

Whose truth is it anyway?

Confidence tricks make entertaining fiction, but have resulted in devastating financial blows in real life. Underlying the ability to undertake such manipulation of the mark's brain is something that comes through in a rather different way in recent years – the idea of there being more than one kind of truth. When someone speaks of 'my truth', what they really mean is 'my belief' – this can, of course, correspond to physical truth. But it can equally be totally disconnected from reality.

The con artist sets up a new belief system in the mark's brain. By going through a lengthy and potentially expensive process that is supported by plenty of personal interaction, the con artist is setting up a particular version of 'my truth' for the mark. If friends and relations find out about the con, they will probably point out the logical flaws in what is happening. Or simply that there's no such thing as a free lunch, and if something looks too good to be true, it probably is.

However, by then, it is often too late. The mark's brain has now established a pattern from which it is very hard to escape and allow rationality to return. We can see the same thing in aspects of the 'post-truth' era. A politician, for example, will make a statement of their truth: such is their conviction (or, perhaps more accurately, their apparent conviction) that the rest of us are loathe to argue with it. Anyone who does make a challenge will potentially suffer abuse. The same kind of mindset as that of the victim of a long con, or a cult, makes it impossible to counter the belief until things go wrong.

Much modern disagreement about the distinction between absolute truth and 'my truth' derives from identity politics. However, there are some attempts to distort the truth that are less naïve and a lot more cynical. This is such a feature of modern politics that it is not worth detailing in that context, but there is a major example of deliberate attempts across decades to distort our picture of what is real and to implant an alternative reality in the population's brains in the story of tobacco.

The tobacco story

We are so familiar with the concept of smoking that it can be hard to picture how strange it must first have seemed. When I was at university, I once moved into a room only to discover that a previous occupant had left a small pile of LPs (vinyl records) on top of the wardrobe. I failed to track down my predecessor, so a couple of them were added to my collection, introducing me to the American comedian Bob Newhart.

My favourite of all Newhart's sketches was a portrayal of what a phone call from England to Sir Walter Raleigh in the New World might have sounded like.* Newhart's character expresses increasing disbelief as he (but not his audience) hears Raleigh's attempt to describe what is involved with smoking tobacco. Newhart starts with dubiousness that Raleigh has bought 80 tons of a leaf: 'I don't know if you noticed last time, we have plenty of leaves over here in England.' Later he is amused after hearing about snuff, involving sticking a pinch of tobacco up your nose. But the climax is that Raleigh tells him you can shred the leaf, roll it in a piece of paper (Newhart's character suggests at this point that you might stick it in your ear) … and then you set fire to it.

* You can see Bob Newhart's phone call with Walter Raleigh at bit.ly/brainjacking9.

Initially, tobacco was treated as a pleasurable herbal concoction with potential health benefits. In 1608, for example, the English composer Thomas Weelkes wrote a madrigal clumsily entitled 'Come, Sirrah Jack, Ho' (he had presumably discovered that there aren't many things that he could rhyme with tobacco), featuring the magnificent lines:

> I swear that this tobacco
> It's perfect Trinidado ...
> It is heady, I am giddy,
> Head and brains,
> Back and reins,
> Joints and veins:
> From all pains
> It doth well purge and make clean.

Admittedly, this wasn't a universal opinion. If you take the Newhart viewpoint, it is bizarre to think that inhaling smoke would be good for you. King James I of England (James VI of Scotland) was certainly no fan. In 1604 he published his *Counterblaste to Tobacco* in which he remarked that smoking was 'dangerous to the lungs, and in the black and stinking fume thereof, nearest resembling the horrible stygian smoke of the pit that is bottomless'.

Despite James' concerns, smoking, of course, remained fashionable until well into the twentieth century. But concerns were growing as to its effects on health. Alarmed both by loss of sales and the potential for litigation, the tobacco companies fought back. Their approach is sometimes referred to as the 'tobacco industry playbook' when other bodies have attempted to use the same approach – a combination of funding research that made the scientific consensus on the dangers of smoking look less strong, lobbying governments, and using apparent third-party organisations to put forward a message that supported their needs. This was truly deception at scale.

In a 1988 interview for the Granada TV investigative journalism programme *World in Action*, Fritz Gahagan, who had worked in marketing for tobacco companies, commented: 'The problem is, how do you sell death? How do you sell a poison that kills 350,000 people per year, a thousand people a day? You do it with the great open spaces ... healthy young people ... athletes.' For a long time, tobacco companies got away with obfuscation, but the beginning of the end was work started in 1950 by English epidemiologists Richard Doll and Austin Bradford Hill for the Royal College of Physicians.

Initially, Doll and Hill had suspected that tarmac on the roads or the impact of car exhaust fumes was responsible for the marked growth in lung cancer cases, but their research highlighted the role of tobacco with the first good-quality statistical work on the subject. By the mid-1960s, especially with the publication of Doll and Hill's 1962 report *Smoking and Health*, it was no longer possible to argue scientifically against the dangers of smoking. But the tobacco companies would take decades to move away from attempts to counter this narrative.

Vaping takes the baton

It may seem that the distasteful form of deception promoting smoking is now a thing of the past, but in December 2023 *The Times* newspaper published the results of an investigation* that brought the use of such fake truths bang up to date. The report showed that tobacco companies that sell e-cigarettes (also known as vapes) were behind a number of studies that seemed designed to support the use of these products well beyond the potentially valuable use of helping existing smokers to quit.

---

* Vaping investigation by Billy Kenber in *The Times*, 15 December 2023.

Among the allegations in *The Times* report were that the cigarette manufacturers published papers downplaying the dangers of young people using vapes (reports that were then used as evidence when lobbying the government), that an NHS doctor 'who had taken millions in funding from [tobacco company] Philip Morris International' had given 'pro-vaping smoking cessation training sessions' to hundreds of British doctors and that the British American Tobacco company 'helped to run a "grassroots" campaign that presented itself as the voice of ordinary vapers and has sought to influence government policy in an apparent breach of global rules on tobacco lobbying'.

At the time, the British government, amid widespread public concerns about e-cigarettes being targeted at young people by using bright-coloured packaging and child-friendly flavours, was looking at means of reducing youth vaping.* *The Times* discovered that 'tobacco industry-linked organisations have spent years playing down the risk of young people taking up the habit and challenging measures aimed at getting vapes out of the hands of under-age users'.

Sheila Duffy, the head of the Scottish arm of the anti-smoking charity Action on Smoking and Health, refers in the report to some of the industry's activities as 'astroturf campaigning'. This is a rather cute way of describing attempts to deceptively appear to be providing grassroots opinion, which is in fact produced by a political party or foreign country, or from a company wishing to boost a product. It is part of the same breed of deception as producing fake reviews of your product.

This is a dangerous approach, as politicians are infamously over-influenced by the perception of what voters want,

* At the time of writing, in early 2024, the UK government has announced an upcoming ban in England, Scotland and Wales of disposable vapes (by far the most frequently used by young people), plus regulation of flavours, packaging and displays, but there is no date for implementation.

presumably in the hope of holding onto their seats. This can be simply frustrating – for example, at the time of writing a majority of the British public are in favour of onshore wind farms, even relatively close to their property, but for a long time MPs, particularly of the Conservative Party, thought that onshore wind turbines were vote losers and so vetoed them.

Unpleasant though astroturf campaigning may be, it is less dangerous in the long term than companies sponsoring research that is weighted in their favour, against the public good. Science is crucial to both our understanding of the world around us and to the technology that helps keep us alive. The more dubious studies that are used to make an argument, the less trust there could be in information in general from the scientific community. The fringe response to the hugely successful Covid vaccination programme demonstrates how even life-saving science can be argued against once you don't trust good-quality scientific studies.

As an example, a paper used by the tobacco-company-sponsored World Vapers' Alliance, in a submission to a British government consultation on youth vaping, was written in 2019 by Peter Lee, who according to *The Times* 'has worked closely with tobacco companies for decades', and two others, one of whom was an employee of the tobacco company Philip Morris International. The paper* concluded: 'A true gateway effect in youths has not yet been demonstrated. Even if it were, e-cigarette introduction may well have a beneficial population health impact.'

The idea of a gateway effect is that young vapers have an increased chance of moving onto cigarettes compared with their contemporaries who don't use e-cigarettes. But the alleged lack of evidence for this conflicts with an independent piece of research published in 2020 by Emily Banks, a professor at the Australian

* 'Considerations related to vaping as a possible gateway into cigarette smoking: an analytical review', Peter Lee et al.

National University.* In a press release, Banks commented: 'We found clear evidence that non-smokers who use e-cigarettes are around three times as likely to take up conventional smoking as their peers who don't use e-cigarettes ... Avoiding e-cigarettes in non-smokers is vital to keeping progress going against smoking.' University of Melbourne researcher Olivia Baneziger added: 'Our findings support concerns that e-cigarettes are a gateway to smoking, especially among young people.'

Of course, different studies can come up with opposing outcomes without there being any sinister forces involved. And not all research is of the highest quality. But deliberately misusing the process of scientific study to further a business or political aim is a particularly dangerous game.

Deception for fun

We have spent a considerable amount of time on the dark side of deception. In finishing this chapter, I'd like to dip back into another way that deception can be positive – with the potential to be a form of entertainment in large-scale spoofs or practical jokes. When I was at university, I was involved in a number of practical jokes, many of them trivial. These could be mildly amusing – a self-lighting firework display at midnight, or the organ scholar's underwear hung on a line across the front of the chapel, for example. But that's not what I mean.

I'll take a brief look at three classic examples of major spoofs, one of which I had the honour to take a small part in. One of the earliest and best-known in its day was the BBC's spaghetti harvest film.† This was first shown in 1957 when the UK only

* 'Summary report on use of e-cigarettes and relation to tobacco smoking uptake and cessation, relevant to the Australian context', Emily Banks et al.

† You can watch the spaghetti harvest film here: bit.ly/brainjacking7.

had two TV channels and when pasta was an exotic foreign food that most people in the UK had never eaten beyond, perhaps, tinned spaghetti hoops. The short film was featured on the channel's flagship current affairs programme *Panorama* and showed a family in Switzerland harvesting long strands of pasta from spaghetti trees.

This was done entirely straight-faced and without any explanation, and was a delight. Equally wonderful, though on a grander scale, was the *Guardian* newspaper's San Serriffe hoax. Like the spaghetti harvest, this was published on 1 April (in this case 1977), but with far more detail in a seven-page supplement on the (totally fictional) moving island of San Serriffe, which was shaped like a semicolon. The movement of the island was alleged to be due to coastal erosion and deposition that resulted in it moving steadily at around 1.4 kilometres (0.9 miles) per year.

The final example, in which I played a small part, was the ceremony of the Immersion of the High Professor. This was a fake ritual that was months in the planning, which took place in the mid-1970s. King's Parade in the centre of Cambridge was closed to traffic and a procession of hundreds, all in academic garb, ambled down the middle of the street (we were instructed not to be formal), through the magnificent Trinity College and onto the area of grass known as the backs that is by the river.

Here, the High Professor was presented to the crowd and stripped down to his underwear behind a curtain of cloaks. The choir, of which I was a part, chanted a Latin responsory: many years later I can still remember this couplet: '*In combinationibus stat*' (translated as 'He stands in his combinations'), and the response '*Sancta Michaelis designatus est*' ('Labelled St Michael's', which at the time was the brand of the Marks & Spencer stores). The High Professor was then slapped across the face with a fish (according to the handout for the crowd, this action was introduced a couple of hundred years ago, but no one knew why).

Finally, the High Professor was rowed off down the river while the choir sang the Palestrina anthem '*Super flumina Babylonis*' ('By the Waters of Babylon').

According to the handout given to the crowd, this ceremony celebrated the actions of a medieval professor who drowned bathing in the Cam while attempting to set an example of cleanliness to his students. He died aged 67 (I can't remember the exact number, but it was around this), and so the ceremony was enacted every 67 years. The practical joke was undertaken with the assistance of the police and Trinity College. The best bit of all came about ten years later, far from Cambridge, when someone told me the story of this bizarre ceremony he had witnessed while visiting the city as a tourist – he had been one of the large audience that assumed the whole thing was for real.

Such large-scale hoaxes really do play with the witnesses' minds. Initially the hoax may well come across simply as something strange and unusual. But when the truth is revealed, there is a mental change of gear: when the whole thing is done well, this tends to be in admiration of the sophistication of the deception.

Practical jokes are deliberate deception, as are all the examples in this chapter. But it's time to move on to a form of brainjacking that many still see to be deception, but which its advocates assure us is merely passing on useful information. The world of advertising.

6 WHO WILL BUY?

Advertising goes back as far as we have written history. A clue to its origins is embedded in the associated 'M' word – marketing. When trading was largely confined to barter, there was limited opportunity for advertising, but the combination of a physical marketplace and coinage, making products in principle available to all, made considering how to flag up your location and attract would-be buyers of far greater importance.

The silent trade

As one of the many aspects of storytelling, it's natural to think of advertising and marketing as being linked to face-to-face transactions in the days before written advertisements. But oddly, one of the earliest needs for advertising was to support silent trading. Here, the sellers and the buyers did not meet at all, because to meet face to face was to risk being attacked, killed or taken into slavery. In a strange amalgam of trust and distrust, goods were sold without contact.

The Greek historian Herodotus (himself a former trader), who wrote in the second half of the fifth century BCE, described a silent trade he was told about when visiting Carthage (located in modern Tunisia). When the vendors, typically selling knives and cloth, arrived at the coast:

> they unload the goods, arrange them tidily along the beach, and then, returning to their boats, they raise a smoke. Seeing the smoke, the natives come down to the beach, place on the ground a certain quantity of gold in exchange for the goods and go off again to a distance. The Carthaginians then come ashore and take a look at the gold – if they think it represents a fair price for their wares, they collect it and go away. If, on the other hand, it seems too little, they go back aboard and wait, and the natives come and add to the gold until they are satisfied. There is perfect honesty of both sides ...*

This is interesting in its own right as a form of trading that arguably is reflected in something like eBay or Facebook Marketplace today (though with the potential intervention of an honest broker if things go wrong). In fact, silent trading continued to be practised occasionally for centuries among a range of cultures. But from our viewpoint there are two aspects of advertising here: how the locals knew to take part in the trade in the first place, and the smoke signals, which effectively advertised a time for the trade.

It's not clear how this was originally established, but by the time Plato was writing, around 50 years after Heroditus in the first half of the fourth century BCE, he was able to point out the necessity for some form of marketing in trade and to observe the move away from barter: 'It is inefficient if a farmer or artisan brings some of his produce to a market at a time when no one is there who wants to exchange with him. Is he to sit here idle, when he might be at work? ... No! There are people

* Description of silent trading by Heroditus reported in *The Routledge Companion to Marketing History* (see Further Discovery).

who have seen an opening here for their services ... they have to stay where they are in the marketplace.'*

By being a constant presence, happy to buy or sell, the market traders or retailers provide a bridge between buyer and goods. And being able to discover their location, and when they are open, provides what can sensibly be considered the earliest true advertising and marketing. Initially this would mostly have combined the use of a central, well-known location and the deployment of street cries. Think of the 'Who will buy?' street scene in the musical *Oliver*, where various phrases are repeated to let potential customers know of the availability of roses, milk, strawberries and knife-grinding services.†

The reality of an early marketplace would have been distinctly less refined than the portrayal in the musical – a far wider range of cries, ranging from musical snatches to little more than yelling (something like the traditional town crier in action). But this was still advertising, directing would-be buyers to the relevant section of the marketplace, and was an approach found in a range of ancient civilisations, from Egypt to Greece.

Rhyming ads

We know that the more visual form of a written advertisement was already in use around 2,000 years ago because one was discovered at Pompeii dating back to around CE 79 – a verse-like ad that could also have been used as a cry:

> For eyes that are shining, cheeks like the dawn,
> For beauty that lasts until girlhood is gone,

---

* Plato's description of the marketplace reported in *The Routledge Companion to Marketing History*.

† You can see the *Oliver* 'Who will buy' scene at bit.ly/brainjacking13.

For prices in reason the woman who knows,
Will buy her cosmetics at Aescalyptos.

It is presumably a coincidence that the form of this advertising rhyme (obviously the original was in Latin, not English, but presumably it still rhymed) had distinct similarities with an enduring mid-twentieth century US roadside advertising campaign by the shaving-product company Burma-Shave. In part intended to break up the tedium of long journeys on featureless roads, these rhymes were displayed at the roadside on a series of signs a line at a time, so that the driver and passengers could pick them up as they went along. They were far pithier than the Roman original (and intended to be funny), but still, there is an echo. The sign sequences were sometimes explicitly linked to the company's products, such as:

THE BEARDED DEVIL
IS FORCED TO DWELL
IN THE ONLY PLACE
WHERE THEY DON'T SELL
(BURMA-SHAVE)

Or:

SOAP MAY DO
FOR LADS WITH FUZZ
BUT SIR, YOU AIN'T
THE KID YOU WUZ

While others simply set out to amuse, with the format so well known that association with the product was still there, such as:

DON'T STICK YOUR ELBOW
OUT TOO FAR

OR IT MAY GO HOME
IN ANOTHER CAR

And:

SPRING HAS SPRUNG
THE GRASS HAS RIZ
WHERE LAST YEAR'S
CARELESS DRIVER IS*

Or even the meta-joke of:

SLOW DOWN, PA
SAKES ALIVE
MA MISSED SIGNS
FOUR AND FIVE

The Burma-Shave signs reflect something important that has always been true of advertising, as the food critic Matthew Fort, who we will meet in more detail when we look at the brain-jacking influence of reviews, explained: 'Advertising is where I really learned my craft of writing – no one gets up in the morning and says, "I'm not going to read the news, I'll look at the ads, or fast-forward through *Downton Abbey* to get to the commercials." What advertising teaches you is you're probably trying to get people to do something they don't want to do, so you have half a nanosecond to hook someone and draw them in.' The Burma-Shave signs achieved this by being entertaining in their own right.

---

* This is a reference to a verse attributed to (or made popular by) Ogden Nash: 'Spring has sprung, the grass is riz / I wonder where the birdies is. / The bird is on the wing. / But that's absoid: the wing is on the boid.'

Physical marketplaces and tangible signs

Marketplaces, of course, still exist to this day, but historically in large towns and cities, many traders began to set up more permanent shops. One of the first ways these were marketed was by location. Rather than having the random assembly of shop fronts we typically see today, it was common for shopkeepers selling the same kind of wares to locate near each other, making it easier to identify the right place to go for, say, your bread or your meat. We can see this in some medieval street names, such as York's Colliergate, where coal and charcoal were sold, Chester's butchers in Fleshmonger's Lane (now Newgate Street), or the silver merchants of Silver Street in Cambridge.*

The establishment of dedicated shops had already started back in the days of the Pompeian advertisement, but it became heavily organised in medieval times. In Europe, this was often accompanied by the formation of guilds, which were typically groups of men with the same occupation. Although the guilds reinforced the co-location of shops selling the same kind of goods, they actively disapproved of competitive advertising. Guilds were bodies for traders to cooperate, not to compete. They fixed prices and quality standards while banning advertising or self-promotion (an approach that was retained until well into the twentieth century, for instance by the legal profession in the UK).

With many early populations largely illiterate, signage was often limited to simple, if sometimes obscure, visual clues. This approach dates back to Roman times when, for example, an image of a bush (or an actual plant) was used to indicate a wine shop. Other visual influences would be introduced in medieval

---

* York's Grape Lane is another example, but this was not a location for fruit sellers. The name is a contraction of Gropecunt Lane, a common medieval street name for a road in which prostitutes traded.

Europe. The two that can still be seen most often today are the three golden balls of the pawnbroker and the red-and-white striped pole of the barber.

The pawnbroker's sign seems to be linked to heraldry from the Lombardy region of Italy, which was so strongly associated with banking and pawnshops that European pawnbrokers were often referred to as Lombards. The barber's pole with the helical red stripe on a white background links to the way that the early surgeons were barbers: the red stripe represented the flow of blood in the common practice of bleeding a patient, and the white part was for the barber's more conventional activity. This visual aid dates back to the English Barber's Guild, which later became the Company of Barbers and Surgeons.

The other form of location advertising based on an image that flourished in Britain was the use of inn signs. To this day, it is normal for a pub to have a sign that visually identifies the name of the place (or provides an indirect reference to it), whether it's the coat of arms of local or national nobility, where the pub is, say, The King's Arms, or a tree for The Royal Oak, or a depiction of the Wiltshire smuggling activity that gives us The Moonrakers.*

It is disputed as to exactly when advertising moved from merely providing information to the stronger brainjacking modes of influence or manipulation. It has been suggested, for instance, that some Roman signage for circuses and gladiatorial combat attempted to persuade the potential punter of the positive benefits of the experience, rather than simply identifying when and where it took place – and an attempt at influence is clear in the Pompeian advert.

* The term 'moonraker' was applied to people from the county of Wiltshire who allegedly hid smuggled barrels of brandy in ponds. If caught while trying to pull the barrels out by the revenue men, the locals said they were trying to rake in the big cheese of the reflected Moon, portraying themselves as simpletons. Author Ian Fleming lived in Wiltshire for a time, hence the name of one of the James Bond stories.

The print revolution

Two requirements needed to be fulfilled for medieval advertising to catch up with Pompei in a form with more potential for persuasion: literacy and printing. The two went hand in hand, as it wasn't until the introduction of the printing press that wide-scale reading ability had any point. The printing press also brought with it the first clear examples of advertising with the intent to influence. So, for example, William Caxton, who introduced printing to England, is thought to have produced the first known English-language advertisement, which (of course) he printed.* It reads (mostly translated into modern spelling):

> If it please only man spiritual or temporal to buy any pyes of two and three commemoraios† of Salisbury use enprinted after the form of this letter which are well and truly correct, let him come to Westminster in to the almonry at the red pale and he shall have them good cheap.

The wording refers in an obscure fashion to the book it advertises: the *Sarum Ordinal*, a guide to church liturgy. The ordinal was also known as a pie or pye, perhaps because of the 'pied' appearance of its pages, as the blocks of text used were unevenly spaced. The advertisements were what would now be called flyers, pasted up on walls and doors. Following the English advert is, rather strangely, a Latin phrase meaning 'Please don't remove this notice'. We only have the eight existing copies of the advert as they were used in the binding of one of Caxton's books.

---

* See a copy of the original advertisement at the Bodleian Library: bit.ly/brainjacking5.

† Your guess is as good as mine for the meaning of 'commemoraios' – the only reference to it seems to be this advert. It feels like it should be commemorations, which could simply mean that the pyes help to make the liturgy more memorable.

Caxton's advertisement dates back to the 1470s or 80s, but the word 'advertisement' was not then in use in the current sense. It's recorded as early as 1426 as a word for the action of informing or notifying, but it wasn't until the seventeenth century that the modern usage of the word came into being. Such pasted-up handbills became increasingly common, but advertising would take off in the 1620s or 30s when it first appeared in newspapers. Within 100 years, providing such advertising had become the newspapers' main business model, to the extent that it was only in the mid-twentieth century that some newspapers' front pages began to carry anything of note other than advertising.

In this period, information still dominated the advertisement, whether about a specific vendor or to make the public aware of new products – but an element of persuasion gradually became stronger. The first known English advertisement for tea from 1658, for example, extolled its virtues, calling it: 'That excellent, and by all physicians approved, China drink.'

Printing not only helped advertisements to move on from painted signs, but as printing processes became more sophisticated, so the available vehicles for advertising multiplied. Magazines were arguably originally produced primarily as vehicles for advertising, which thrived with the birth of mail-order sales, accompanying the newly available, reliable and cheap postal service.

An efficacious compound

Influenced in part by patent medicine advertising*, and driven for the first time by trends from the US, advertisers began to use attention-grabbing means and emotional manipulation in Victorian times, around the 1860s, often trying to include a

* Patent medicine refers to commercial medications, often based on folk medicine, which were sold without any medical basis.

sense of urgency that a purchase was not only good for you but was needed *now*.

It's easy to think of early advertising as being the province of snake oil salesmen, while more established businesses would consider it beneath them. But it seems more likely that where there weren't vestigial remains of guild restrictions on advertising, it was first applied to goods where there was distinct competition. In the nineteenth century, for example, while patent medicine was up there in the top two market segments using advertising, the other big user was bookselling, which we think of as a significantly more refined trade.

However, there is no doubt about the importance of patent medicine in boosting the use of advertising – none more so than the many ads for Lydia Pinkham's Vegetable Compound. Familiar indirectly to British readers from the 1968 song 'Lily the Pink' by the Scaffold, Pinkham's story reflects the changing view of the role of advertising.

Pinkham was born Lydia Estes in 1819 to a large Quaker family in Lynn, Massachusetts. Along with her sisters, she was a campaigner for the abolition of slavery and supporter of women's rights. Pinkham married in 1843, ending a brief occupation as a teacher. Remaining in a paid job once married was then uncommon, but as part of her household duties, Pinkham produced a home-brewed, vegetable-based tonic. At the time this would have been a common activity: medical help was expensive and often limited in benefit. Provided homemade concoctions weren't positively harmful, they would at the very least have had the benefit of acting as a placebo.

The contents of Pinkham's pick-me-up were the exotic-sounding unicorn root (also known as crow-corn and white stargrass), life root (golden ragwort or groundsel), black cohosh (part of the buttercup family, with other names including black bugbane, rattle-top and fairy candle – a plant that, strangely, is not black), pleurisy root (a milkweed also known as butterfly weed), fenugreek seeds and alcohol. The importance of this last constituent should not be under-estimated: Pinkham's vegetable compound was 18 per cent alcohol, comparable with a fortified wine.

Black cohosh had been used for some time in traditional medicine for menopause symptoms, while fenugreek (which we now know is not safe for use at medicinal levels when pregnant) was thought to help when women did not have a good milk supply while nursing. Neither of these uses has been substantiated by modern medicine, but this is probably why Pinkham believed her vegetable compound to be especially efficacious for what were known as 'female complaints'.

Initially the compound was used only by the family and given out to friends and neighbours. But in 1875 (making Pinkham 54), when one of her husband's many business ventures failed, Pinkham ventured into selling her vegetable drink for profit. According to legend, a couple of strangers arrived at the Pinkhams' house and offered her $5* for six bottles of the compound, having heard of its powers. At a suggestion from Pinkham's son Dan, they began to market the vegetable compound with what would become one of the most striking advertising campaigns of the age.

The successful campaign came after Dan Pinkham had tried a whole set of imaginative but not necessarily effective measures to promote the compound. As well as handing out leaflets door to door, he scattered faux hand-written cards around New York parks, which were supposed to look like an accidentally discarded note to a friend, recommending the vegetable compound. (Finding the same note time after time might have raised a certain suspicion that something odd was going on.)

* The rise in costs since would make $5 equivalent to $145 now, while the rise in wages would make it the equivalent of $1,540 now.

Frank Leslie's Popular Monthly Magazine, Vol. XIII, No. 4, April 1882, p. 514. New York: Frank Leslie (Publisher) 'The Cooper Collections'.

Dan's younger brother Will was less imaginative, but hit on a far more effective approach of newspaper advertising, starting with the front page of the *Boston Herald*. Topped with a portrait of a stern-looking 'Mrs. Lydia E. Pinkham of Lynn, Mass.', a typical advert emphasised that the compound was a 'positive cure' for the 'worst form of Female Complaints, all ovarian troubles, Inflammation and Ulceration, Falling and Displacements, and the consequent Spinal Weakness, and is particularly adapted to the Change of Life'. The list went on to include practically every symptom imaginable.

Lydia herself was doubtful of the benefits of the newspaper advertising, but the campaign saw sales increase by an order of magnitude. Part of its success was in the kind of personal touch that twenty-first-century advertising sometimes attempts to provide. Not only did it tie the product to a real person, it invited customers to write to Mrs Pinkham for advice on women's problems. At a time when female conditions were marginalised by chauvinist male doctors this had a huge appeal. Despite including a clear sales message in her responses, Mrs Pinkham's suggestions arguably made more sense than many (male) doctors' attempts to deal with those 'female complaints'.

Let's be clear – there was no medical benefit to be had from the medicinal compound. Twenty-first century testing of similar remedies found them to be no better than placebos. Products like the vegetable compound made women feel better thanks to their psychological impact (and possibly the alcoholic content) rather than any true medical benefit. If anything, the advice obtained when writing to Pinkham was the most powerful contributor to the brand's success.

The vegetable compound's advertisements, with the special blend of brainjacking that comes from the combination of promises and the personal touch, worked for decades, but the approach was brought up short by a 1905 attack piece in the popular *Ladies' Home Journal*, written by its editor Edward Bok. His article featured a damning side-by-side pair of pictures. One was an advert urging women to write to Mrs Pinkham for advice. The other was a picture of Pinkham's graveyard monument. She had been dead for 22 years.

The Pinkham family's response was to say that there was no deceit, as the advice was not coming from Lydia, but another Mrs Pinkham, the original's daughter-in-law. Yet the advertisement still used Lydia's name in big letters. This certainly will have done some damage, though the vegetable compound suffered a more reasonable attack (along with other such remedies) for being a way that people were either accidentally consuming alcohol (and giving it to their children) or intentionally using it as a secret drink.

Making it personal

If we think about what the Pinkerton advertising was trying to do, from those early 'handwritten notes' to its newspaper campaigns, there is a fascinating modern parallel in advertising put out in 2009 for a company that was offering marketing guidance to other businesses. I am not going to name the advertiser – the company was very much focused on one individual, whom I shall call Mr X for reasons that will become clear.

Back then, I received a letter in the post containing a ripped-out newspaper cutting with an attached Post-it note, on which someone with the initial J told me, by name, that he (or she) thought I would find the cutting interesting. The cutting told me about the great success that Mr X had achieved in marketing, and how he and his company would be able to help me too. Hmm. My first thought was, Who is J? None of my friends and close business associates happened to have the initial J.

This was enough to make me take a closer look. The writing on the envelope and the sticky note were not handwritten, but in a printed handwriting font. The 'newspaper' cutting, despite its elegantly 'ripped' edge, was a fake. The whole thing was a sneaky but clever piece of advertising. I wrote this up in my blog,* and over time the blog post received page after page of comments, the most I've ever had. Many were from people who had taken the advert at face value, at least at first glance. Then things got interesting. There was an ASA† ruling against the advertisements, but it seemed to have no effect on them going out. Some of the comments were from upset people who felt that they had been deceived.

At this point, I got a cease-and-desist letter from a US law firm, complete with a printout of twenty pages of the comments, which I still treasure. According to the law firm, I was guilty of defamation of character, fraud, malicious conduct, harassment, intentional infliction of emotional distress, trademark infringement, copyright infringement, tortuous interference with Mr X's business practices, interference with prospective business advantage, solicitation of Mr X's clients and prospects, and unfair competition and business practices.

There are two things of interest in this story. One is how much you can irritate potential customers if you get your advertising wrong, however clever it may be. Just as when the dead Mrs Pinkham continued to offer to reply to letters, if advertising feels like an attempt to deceive, it results in a distinctly different impact on the brain than the intended one. The other point is the way that those who seek to undertake brainjacking can be

* My blog is Now Appearing, available with other online writing by clicking the Blog/articles link at www.brianclegg.net.

† The ASA is the Advertising Standards Authority, the UK's advertising regulator – unfortunately, they only keep rulings for five years, so were unable to provide details of it.

very sensitive when it is pointed out that the way they are doing business is potentially manipulative.

Note how the personal touch was central to both campaigns – however fake it actually was. If we are trying to influence someone else's mind it helps if the subject feels that the influence is coming from an individual, rather than a faceless company. It enables the emotional contact that the *Mr Bates vs The Post Office* TV show in the propaganda chapter produced. Just as our modern purchasing experience is riddled with 'reviews' from other purchasers, hopefully giving us a picture of what the product is really like for someone a bit like us, so anything that builds an apparent degree of closeness between the advertiser and the potential buyer is valuable. Mrs Pinkham, like the person behind the product I received an advertisement for, made her potential buyers feel that a real person was interested in them, and would reply to their concerns.

Bearing in mind the prominence of patent medicines in the development of advertising in the US, it's interesting that at least two big users of advertising made the shift from attempting to associate their products with health care to simply claming that they had an enjoyable taste. In a phrase worthy of Mrs Pinkham's products, Coca-Cola's first advertisement claimed that it was a 'valuable Brain Tonic and cure for all nerve affections – Sick Head-Ache, Neuralgia, Hysteria, Melancholy etc.' But as patent medicines lost their appeal, the company shifted its mental positioning to a simple beverage. Similarly, Kellogg's products such as Corn Flakes were originally sold as digestive aids, before switching to impressing on potential customers their role as a 'sunshine breakfast'.

Back to the Pinkham era, on the other side of the Atlantic in the UK, one of the most famous advertisements of the period illustrates the attempt to generate an emotional response by using distinctive artwork. At the time, Thomas J. Barratt was chairman of A & F Pears, a leading soap company.* Barratt is attributed with the saying 'Any fool can make soap. It takes a clever man to sell it.' It was Barratt, sometimes described as 'the father of modern advertising', who incorporated the 1886 painting 'Bubbles' into his advertising. A work by the Pre-Raphaelite artist John Millais, the evocative image shows a period-costumed boy who is blowing soap bubbles with a clay pipe.

The Pears adverts coincided with the rise of advertising agencies, and the first attempts to make something like a science out of the attempt to manipulate the potential purchaser. This is a good point to expand the concept from pure advertising to take in marketing (in the modern sense) and brands, which we will unpack in the next chapter.

* Pears soap, which was first sold in 1807, is still produced as a brand of Unilever.

MARKETING AND BRANDS 7

To get some background on the way that making others aware of a product or service's existence developed into more subtle forms of brainjacking, I asked former communications professional, Helen Carasso, about the distinction between marketing, advertising and public relations.

Marketing as seduction

Helen told me: 'The textbook definition of marketing is that you identify a need and fill it: the classic case would be the Sony Walkman. People didn't know they wanted to go around and listen to music, and Sony said, "A-ha, people would really like this, so let's produce this little box that you can put your cassette tapes in, and you can have your music with you wherever you go."* That's the extreme case of marketing: something new and different that people didn't necessarily know they wanted. Or, for example, an automatic switching-off kettle, the early Russell

* Business legend has it that the Walkman was developed when an executive came to the R&D department with a Walkman-sized block of wood and said: 'Build me something this big I can use to listen to music.'

Hobbs Forgettles,* things like that. That's the textbook definition of marketing, though people don't always use it in that way.'

This is certainly part of marketing, though I was more taken with Wally Olins's† single word definition of marketing in his book *On Brand*: seduction. Good marketing is not only about telling people about something they didn't know they wanted: it is perfectly capable of persuading people to buy something they don't want. Discovering an unfulfilled need that's already out there is certainly a marketing role, though devising a product to match it is arguably research and development. Olins went on to say: 'We should remain quite clear that what marketing, branding, and all the rest of it are about is persuading, seducing and attempting to manipulate people into buying products and services.' In other words, it is commercial brainjacking.

Helen went on: 'Also, the other thing you get, thinking of classic government campaigns, something like the seatbelt campaign was about changing behaviours, changing social norms – that's a classic government information thing when trying to change behaviours, spending quite a long time creating an understanding of that bigger social responsibility, a bit like the Nudge Unit.' (See Chapter 12 for more on what the Nudge Unit did.)

I mentioned post truth, partly thinking of American politics, but also from my viewpoint as a science writer; the university press releases often dramatically exaggerate the reality, such as the lightsaber example mentioned in Chapter 4. I asked if PR

* The British Russell Hobbs K2 kettle was the first to switch itself off automatically when the water was boiling. 'That's why it's known as the Forgettle' ran the company's advertising. My parents had one back in the 1960s, as did many British families. But no one in their right mind *ever* knew it as a Forgettle.

† Wally Olins was an English brand consultant who advised many blue-chip companies from 3i to Volkswagen on identity, branding and communication.

these days went further from the truth than it once did. 'I think it does ... I understand why people try to do it, but it's how far you go. I don't think it does you any good at all if you overdo it. The classic thing about PR is to build up relationships with journalists and you need to be trusted. You've got to be credible, otherwise people just ignore you. And the other thing is, you want to make sure that when you put out a release it really is newsworthy. You want to target it to the right people, not just to put it out to everybody, so that people know: "I've got a news release from the Oxford University press office: there's at least a reasonable chance it's worth me reading it." They understand me and my audience and they know I won't be writing nonsense.'

A unique manifestation of our times

In *On Brand*, Olins points out one novel development in the way that branding and our lives have intersected since the second half of the twentieth century, proclaiming it to be a 'unique manifestation of our time'. This is in consciously wearing visibly branded goods for a whole range of products, organisations and 'anything else for which they feel an affiliation'. There's a degree of hyperbole in this suggestion, which Olins tempers by pointing out that there have always been uniforms and ways of dressing that reflected class or religious affiliations – but suggests this was not an approach that was applicable to the population at large.

It's interesting to speculate what's happening here, whether we are talking a university-branded sweatshirt or a replica football team shirt. It feels like we have been influenced into supporting a brand (unless the branding is being worn ironically), and to feel that it's appropriate to act as a mobile billboard. Of course, the personal justification is likely to be about, say, supporting a team – but the outcome of attempting to influence others is the same.

Olins suggests that the brainjacking mechanism here amounts to likeability. As he comments: 'Some brands are successful because people love them and can't get enough of them … Other brands fail because people simply don't want them. They mean nothing to anybody. The only people you see wearing a Barclays Bank T-shirt are a few miserable people who work for Barclays and don't seem to like it much.'

I'm not totally convinced that this argument holds (at least in terms of the importance of brands for the success or failure of an organisation) because, despite any lack of love, Barclays PLC's group annual profit in the year through to September 2023 was $7.9 billion. However, brands can work their way into our affections because they seem to reflect our values – or because they provide a means to link to other people, a classic example of manipulative brainjacking. They make us feel that we are part of a team or tribe. This can happen even with unlikely products. Many years ago, we had a relatively uncommon and very distinctive little Fiat car – whenever we passed someone else driving the same model, there would be much mutual waving and smiling.

We can see how well a brand has embedded into our brains with the effectiveness of 'brand extension' – where the brand is applied to products unrelated to its original context. Virgin has reached the pinnacle of this approach – in effect, everything labelled Virgin is an extension of a record company brand where the original company is long gone.* Virgin was about a feeling of cheeky rockstar independence, a vibe which they have used to provide a similar faintly counter-culture feel to everything from an airline to a cable internet provider. But the brand extension

* The Virgin Records brand is still used by Universal Music Group in a few markets, but the company itself was sold to Thorn EMI in 1992.

approach can go too far, as demonstrated by the unsuccessful application of the Virgin brand to a failing British train company that remained thoroughly unpopular until its demise in 2019.

Many brand extensions have been trivial – take, for example, Porsche watches, which are only of interest to wannabe Porsche owners. But some extensions have taken on a life of their own that transcends the original. No one gets very excited about tyre brands. It may be true that Michelin tyres are of a high quality – but there is little in practice to distinguish them from other big names. However, appearing in the Michelin restaurant guides, and holding the coveted Michelin star rating, has become a key indicator for high-end restaurants.

From the viewpoint of influence and manipulation, brands provide a mechanism for products and services to take on some of the characteristics of a person. We recognise a familiar brand as if it were a human acquaintance. In an unfamiliar location, a brand can provide a friendly face. It can give us a faint feeling of relationship, of being part of something bigger that we get from taking part in a human gathering or event. This, arguably, is the source of their brainjacking power. Even a brand that is often disdained by the middle classes such as McDonald's can provide a welcome haven in an unfamiliar country when there isn't time to investigate local culture.*

With brands established, Olins lists a series of standardised approaches that are used to generate a 'USP' (unique selling point or proposition) for a company, brand or product, often a major tool for marketing brainjacking. The USP concept was introduced by American advertising executive

* When I gave creativity training, one of the very effective exercises was to ask how the participant thought that McDonald's would deal with their problem. When I used this technique with a group of very right-on middle-class traders some refused to even participate in anything involving McDonald's.

Rosser Reeves, who first applied it to Colgate toothpaste. The initial USP was 'beats bad breath', with advertising showing how, for instance, someone had succeeded in a job interview thanks to his great breath. Later, with greater awareness of dental hygiene among its customers, the USP was switched to 'prevents tooth decay'.

The USP is a concept that Olins disparages, saying: 'Curiously, even today, among the more credulous and naïve members of the marketing fraternity, the initials USP apparently still possess some kind of credibility.' It's certainly true that we have less focus on the USP in advertising now. It's hard to imagine the re-adoption, for example, of 'gets rid of body odour' that was used in much early deodorant advertising. Even so, it's a brainjacking mechanism that many advertisers continue to rely on in their promotions.

Winning us over

Sometimes, though, advertising attempts to go straight to the brain, not to sell a product but rather a particular viewpoint, in the manner we've already seen in the coverage of propaganda. This can be political advertising or the topic that started this very direct aspect of the advertising brainjacking business: attempts to get people to sign up for military service during the First World War. The war of influence started in 1914 with the UK's poster showing Lord Kitchener staring out, pointing at the viewer with the text:

> Britons [Lord Kitchener] 'wants you'. Join your country's army! God save the King.

Almost exactly the same approach with differing figures doing the pointing was taken up by Germany in 1915 ('You too should enlist in the army of the Reich'), Italy ('Everyone should do his duty') and the US, featuring Uncle Sam ('I want *you* for U. S. army') in 1917. Russia came to the approach a little later in 1920 (when internal warfare was raging) with 'You, have you volunteered?' In each case, the manipulative elements were strong: the implication was that 'I'm doing it, so you should too', combined with the visceral impact of the staring face and the accusatory pointing finger.

Another example of such conceptual brainjacking is often said to be the link between Santa Claus and Coca-Cola. Mythology has it that the appearance of Santa, which has now mostly replaced the visually different British figure of Father Christmas, was invented for Coca-Cola advertising (as he wears the company's corporate colours of red and white, and has been used in their advertising since the 1930s). This isn't the case, though – the merger of Father Christmas and Santa Claus had already started by the end of the nineteenth century – but there is no doubt that Coca-Cola's ubiquitous advertising has fixed the American visual appearance of Santa Claus firmly in the minds of even those who still refer to the character as Father Christmas.

The twentieth century saw advertising expand to channels that would have a more powerful impact, capable far more than print of emotional manipulation. Cinema provided the first foot in the door, but it was the ability of radio and then TV to invade homes and other private spaces that really gave advertisers a more significant power to influence, an ability that has only been amplified by internet advertising. Some of the most popular dramas on TV are still known as 'soap operas' after their origins on US radio as serials that were sponsored by soap companies, starting with Procter and Gamble's Oxydol washing powder as the name behind the 1938 serial *Ma Perkins*, which was devised not by a radio station but by the advertising agency Blackett Sample Hummert.

Deploying pester power

There was also a move around this time to make more use of insidious brainjacking in advertising directly to children, in the (often successful) hope that pester power would influence the buying choices for adults. The McDonald's fast-food company would become masters of this, while toy manufacturers were the most obvious and in-your-face examples of this approach; but even something as apparently utilitarian as breakfast cereal took the child market seriously, following the lead of Kellogg's.

Kellogg's had first advertised as early as 1906 (initially for Rice Krispies), but it was in the 1950s that their new sugar-rich products such as Frosted Flakes (Frosties in the UK) were heavily promoted to the youth market with advertising that made use of cartoon characters like Tony the Tiger, with his growling, 'They're great!' Even products that were more adult-oriented, such as Corn Flakes, were given the pester-power treatment by featuring large pictures of children on the box (initially painted by popular American artist Norman Rockwell).

The company even made reference to pester power in a large colour print advertisement that showed a boy putting piles of Corn Flakes packets featuring children's faces into his mother's shopping trolley, while she faces the other way, chatting. The text tells us with the peculiarly patronising style of the period: 'If the lady in charge doesn't turn around soon, she's going to have more Corn Flakes than Kellogg's. Her son, her pride and joy, has a good thing here, and he doesn't know quite when to stop ... It IS a good idea to have plenty of Kellogg's Corn Flakes. Somebody always seems to wake up and want them.'

Can mood trump product?

Until the internet came along, TV advertising was the definitive vehicle for reaching the minds of the public. Some campaigns have become legendary. Think, for example, of the Apple advertisement '1984', shown in the most coveted US advertising slot, during the Superbowl,* and directed by Ridley Scott, who had recently become famous for the 1979 film *Alien*. Portraying the new Apple Mac computer as a saviour breaking through the grey conformity of the corporate Big Brother's personal computing, it's a stunning one-minute piece of film.

Two things are fascinating about this ad. One is that it was hardly ever shown, yet (at least among both advertising and computing aficionados) it is very well known. The other is what the advert was trying to do to the audience. It does not sell the Mac as a way to write better documents, to calculate better spreadsheets or to create better art. It is all about personality, saying to its audience that the Mac is the way to break out of dull conformity. It will enable its users to rebel in our own way – yet still achieve success. This kind of advertising, arguably pure manipulation, can work extremely well if effectively done.

Another great example of the story-based 'mood selling' ad was a far more frequently shown and still often-remembered advert from the UK. This is the 1973 Hovis advertisement showing a boy riding his bike down the steep cobbles of Gold Hill in Shaftsbury, accompanied by a brass-band version of Dvorak's *New World Symphony*.† Although it's over 50 years old now, this ad is still widely remembered. Interestingly, this was also the work of Ridley Scott, providing an early boost for his career as a film maker. Again, it's not really about bread, but rather manipulates the viewer with feelgood nostalgia. Adverts like these remain in the psyche because they dig deep into what makes us the people we are.

Contrast these examples with another sector that attempts marketing by using feeling rather than information – car

---

* See the '1984' Apple Big Brother advert here: bit.ly/brainjacking8.

† See the 1973 Hovis advert here: bit.ly/brainjacking14.

advertising. Renault had a great success with their long-running series of 'Papa – Nicole' adverts for the Clio, which was one of the few advertising series where a continued storyline attracted viewers (another such was Nescafé's adverts featuring Anthony Head and Sharon Maughan, which featured a developing love affair between the 'Gold Blend couple'). But most car adverts are story-free, typifying style over substance. They tell you very little about the car itself, but rather try to sell a pure feeling, based solely on exciting or exotic imagery.

Helen Carasso noted in our conversation: 'Understand what you are for, what you're not for, and where you're coming from, what you are trying to achieve and why [the customer] should engage with you. You could say the brand is the story of the organisation or the product … for a long time almost all BMW's television ads you saw were for the top of the range 7 or 8 series cars that hardly anyone was going to buy. But they did television ads that were all very beautiful, and said "look at this beautifully designed German engineering", and people went off and bought a 3 series – they bought into the values they had seen in that television ad. They became part of that story of quality and design and engineering excellence.'

This makes sense if engineering is clearly featured, but many car adverts fail even to engage with this key aspect of the product. Even Audi's long-running tagline 'Vorsprung durch Technik' rarely accompanied an exploration of specific technical capability. And the sheer ubiquity of the approach when promoting cars means that they are now neither memorable nor effective in making any difference to how we, the viewers, feel about the brand or the product.

An interesting development that shows a change in attitude among advertisers to the mood-selling approach occurred in 2023 in the latest of another UK favourite series of advertisements – the Christmas adverts for department store John Lewis. The upmarket John Lewis (and its supermarket brand, Waitrose) have successfully made the release of their Christmas ad an annual event for over a decade. They started a trend that has been relatively unusual in the UK – advertising that digs even deeper than usual to gain an emotional hit.

This process started in 2011, with an advert where a small boy ignores his presents on Christmas morning because he is so excited to take a present that he has bought himself to his parents.* The manipulative approach has been underlined by using musical accompaniments featuring a rock song made more emotional by slowing it down and arranging it as an (often female) solo with a piano accompaniment. The highlight of these was probably Lily Allen's 2013 rendition of the Keane song 'Somewhere Only We Know', which made it to number one in the UK charts, whereas the original only made number three.†

This wistful, emotional approach, copied by other major UK stores, carried on for well over a decade, but interestingly in the 2020s there was a move back to a more traditional British approach to advertising, where humour plays a bigger part than powerful emotional manipulation.‡ This move was coupled with a return to the kind of advertising goal that the Victorians would have recognised. The intent was not just to make us love the brand, but to sell products – to get people into stores to make purchases.

It has been argued that the period when emotions dominated was partly due to having less individuality in the creative process and partly because humour does not translate as easily from culture to culture as does emotion. But the danger is to miss out on the actual selling power, which in the end is the point of advertising. American advertising executive Dave Trott

---

* The 2011 John Lewis advert can be seen here: bit.ly/brainjacking15.

† The 2013 John Lewis advert can be seen here: bit.ly/brainjacking16.

‡ The 2023 John Lewis advert can be seen here: bit.ly/brainjacking17.

is quoted by Sam Delaney* as saying: 'If you're anything other than the market leader, then these sorts of ads don't help you. They just remind people that it's Christmas and they need to buy presents. And then they all go on Amazon to buy them.' Whether the move away from emotion to fun (and considerably more product focus) will have the desired effect on our brains is yet to be clear.

Does product placement work?

Whatever the style, we all know what an advert looks like. Those little boxes at the side of the web page. Big posters on bus shelters and billboards, half pages in a newspaper or the breaks in commercial TV shows. But there is a more subtle type of advertising that attempts to influence our attitudes to products too. Which film franchise is instantly brought to mind by the car manufacturer Aston Martin? What computers and smartphones are in use in a particular TV show or movie? In the early days in the US, such product placement could be hilariously unsubtle, but now it is commonplace and can be close to a subconscious attempt at influence. (Am I the only one who notices that you don't see many Windows PCs or Android phones on Apple TV's shows?)

As mentioned already, this kind of influencing extends far beyond the pure advertising and marketing realm. A lot of the influences we receive visually come from dramas and factual programmes, which aren't intending to persuade us towards particular purchases, but have a brainjacking impact because all storytelling has an influence, and as *Mr Bates vs The Post Office* showed, visual storytelling on TV and in film will almost always

---

* In the *Unherd* article 'Has John Lewis killed the Christmas ad?'

be particularly persuasive. But sometimes, there is conscious product placement – or billboards for real products in an outdoor street scene.

This kind of background advertising extends into the virtual world of gaming, where it's possible to buy advertising hoardings or to place products in leading games – this is not a minor concern when you consider that the worldwide gaming market is bigger than movies, the music industry and book publishing combined. As (and if) the metaverse and AR/VR technologies* take off, so will the opportunities for this kind of influencing to increase and to leak out from the media into our everyday lives.

Lost in the metaverse

The rise of the internet certainly has already presented a huge opportunity to advertisers – potential customers anywhere in the world can see details of your products on your website – but it also presented advertisers with a big headache. In Neal Stephenson's 1992 novel *Snow Crash*, published several years before the World Wide Web made the internet available to a wide audience, shoppers of the future wandered down a virtual street in the metaverse (imaginatively called 'The Street'), where they saw advertising and shop fronts just as they did in the real world. As the internet is such an integral part of modern life, it's worth getting a feel for the context of this misunderstanding of what real online life would be like.

---

* AR/VR are technologies where we are exposed to or submerged in virtual worlds. AR (augmented reality) superimposes the virtual aspect onto a view of the real world, such as in the *Pokémon Go* phone-based game, while with VR (virtual reality) all we see is created artificially, as in *The Matrix* or the metaverse.

The internet evolved from the ARPANet, initially a US network for connecting large computers to use them remotely. Although features like email were already becoming of interest by the early 1980s, it was only with the addition of an extra layer in the World Wide Web, featuring a visual graphic interface and the ability to click links, that the internet reached a popular audience and really took off: even that took a while.* The web was made available to the world outside of CERN in 1991, a couple of years after Tim Berners-Lee developed it for the international particle physics facility. The first graphic browser for the web, Mosaic, only became available in 1993, the year after *Snow Crash* was published.

When I attended Microsoft's launch of its first network-aware version of Windows in 1995, the software giant pretty much dismissed the internet. At the time the major networks used by ordinary people were commercial ones – primarily AOL (America OnLine) by ordinary consumers and CompuServe by a more tech-savvy crowd. Microsoft wanted to add to the option with its own Microsoft Network (MSN), which had an interface based on the Windows file explorer.

Meanwhile, AOL was experimenting with an online shopping centre, and Apple had gone for the nearest thing to *Snow Crash*'s Street in its eWorld network, which users navigated through a graphic that used imagery of real-world-style streets where, presumably, the public were supposed to find the shops and services they required. Similarly, the internet-based online environment Second Life, at one time touted in the same way that Meta's Metaverse concept has been in the 2020s, featured conventional advertising and shops hosted by real-world companies on virtual streets.

---

* Although the web was the first widely used application of clickable hyperlinks to get from document to document, they had been introduced conceptually by Ted Nelson in the 1960s and were widely used in Microsoft's help systems and the Mac Hypercard program from the 1980s.

But while the analogy of a street of shops and a set of billboards works for, say, a hundred locations, if there are too many, we end up with a confusing jumble. As the internet has developed, the scale of what's on offer has transcended the imagination of everyone who was thinking about such possibilities back in the 1990s. Frankly, no one knows how many pages there are on the web, but estimates in 2023 put the count as high as 50 billion. These are housed in more than a billion websites, though apparently 'only' around 200 million or so of these are actively used and updated.

Just imagine what it would be like to navigate a virtual reality shopping district with 200 million locations that are either billboards or shops. The word 'impossible' springs to mind. To give a slight feel for the scale, on a clear night with good eyesight, you can see around 1,400 stars: this number is more than 100,000 times bigger. It is comparable with the population of Brazil.

As a result, we don't try to apply the analogy of a physical marketplace or advertising billboards to the internet anymore. Instead, advertising is driven in two primary ways – through search and with more conventional-appearing advertising on web pages. In the early days, web users were served by manually curated guides, such as Yahoo, but it soon became clear these were impossible to keep up to date, so they were rapidly displaced by search engines:* indexes produced by 'spiders' or 'bots', software that constantly travels around the web looking for new locations.

There have been many search engines: initially AltaVista dominated the landscape until the superior search algorithms of Google displaced it. Although from the user viewpoint Google provides a handy index to an impossibly large collection of

* We are so familiar with the term 'search engine' it can be easy not to notice this is a steampunkish reference to the Victorian inventor Charles Babbage's proto-computer designs – the difference engine and the analytical engine.

information, it is at heart an advertising platform – this is where much of Google's vast revenues come from, as do those of the social-media giant Facebook from its own advertising.

Internet advertising has natural advantages over everything from TV to newspapers and billboards. It is cheap to deploy and a user can be exposed to far more advertising than through other channels. More than this, though, the content can in theory be targeted to the needs of individual users. This occurs naturally when advertising is associated with a web search. The search engine knows what the user is searching for and can display appropriate advertising, sometimes difficult to distinguish from 'vanilla' search results. But it would also prove to be the case with adverts displayed on any page through more devious means. We will come back to this in Chapters 8 and 9.

Does science help advertisers?

We have seen advertising in many different forms as it has evolved over the centuries. There is sometimes a basic provision of information. 'We are here' or 'There's a new product' – though even this comes with an attempt at influence. The advertiser is not providing this information to increase general knowledge. It is done in the hope of bringing customers to the seller's door – be it a physical or virtual location.

Other advertising, as we have seen, goes further in its attempt to get into our heads and manipulate us – and this can be directly observed using modern brain-scanning technology. In a 2003 article,* Tim Ambler, Andreas Ioannides and Steven Rose noted: 'Scary as it may sound, if an ad does not modify the

* 'Brands on the Brain: Neuro-images of advertising', *Business Strategy Review.*

brains of the intended audience, then it has not worked. The response to advertising (how we encode the message) matters more than the stimulus (the ad itself) because the response is what the ad leaves behind.'

The suggestion in the article is that if managers knew how their advertising was affecting the brain, and how that impact could be used to alter brand choices, they could improve advertising productivity – as much a mystery now as when either Lord Leverhulme or John Wanamaker first made a comment along the lines of 'Half the money I spend on advertising is wasted; the trouble is I don't know which half' towards the end of the nineteenth century.

The article suggests that, historically, academic researchers have primarily focused on the rational aspect of advertising: how information is used to influence and change thought processes. Of course, the material had to be attractively presented, but it was *information* leading to a preference for a brand that had the primary impact on the brain. By contrast, advertising executives give more weight to the emotional impact of advertising, which we have associated with the manipulative aspect of brainjacking. In either case, the aim would be to build or reinforce synapses in the brain that associated certain positive memories with the brand, encouraging future commercial activity.

From Ambler et al.'s research using brain scans, it has been suggested that advertising material with an emotional impact is more likely to be remembered than the cognitive impact of reasoning, resulting in an increased likeliness of a particular product or service being chosen. However, it is worth noting that this research was originally only undertaken with three subjects fully imaged, and had a lack of controls for potentially confounding factors that could have confused the conclusions.

Having said that, it is, perhaps, hardly surprising that emotional impact provides a significant part of the sell for the right kind of product. As we saw in the propaganda section, the most notorious modern example of this manipulation is the use of tear-jerking personal tales of sadness, usually involving a sick or deceased love one, that crop up in talent shows. It has become a cliché, yet there is little doubt that such manipulation helps sell an individual to voters in the show, even though a minority are put off by what seems to be a cynical attempt to get more votes.

The study of the brain to understand the impact and manipulating potential of marketing and advertising that has arisen since the Ambler et al. study is known as neuromarketing or consumer neuroscience. This primarily uses brain scanning by fMRI (functional magnetic resonance imaging) and electroencephalograms – or monitors indicators of physiological responses, such as eye movements and heart rate.

The approach has often received a negative response from the marketing industry, in part because of the view that academics often don't really understand the field, either telling professionals what they already know or coming up with data that doesn't provide any practical benefit for marketing. So, for example, there is some evidence that markets can be better segmented by the brain similarities of potential customers – but it is hardly practical to study the population as a whole by putting them in MRI scanners. It has been suggested this approach could be used to at least get a feel for the relative size of different segments, but even this is doubtful in practice, because such studies have relatively small numbers of participants, making them unrepresentative of the population at large.

Is advertising evil?

Advertising and marketing's impact can be overstated. Rory Sutherland, then president of the Institute of Practitioners in Advertising, has said: 'If there is one thing more dishonest than dodgy marketing, it is the pretence that marketing raises no ethical concerns. The truth is that marketing raises enormous ethical questions every day – at least it does if you are doing it right. If this were not the case, the only possible explanations are either that you believe marketers are too ineffectual to make any difference, or you believe that marketing activities only affect people at the level of conscious argument.'*

But Sutherland presents us with a false dichotomy. Obviously, marketing and advertising do make a difference, but it is only as part of a wider set of influencing and manipulation that occurs as a result of us experiencing the vast array of stories that we are exposed to all the time. In their book *Badvertising*, Andrew Simms and Leo Murray tell us that 'the enabler of [a] great shift in expectations and attitudes has been the advertising and marketing industries. Advertising is selling us an imagined lifestyle – the premise is that we can only feel we are all living our best lives by flying around the world, driving ever bigger SUVS [sic], eating beef from cattle raised on cleared rainforest, and enjoying a vast array of consumer goods like there was no tomorrow.'

I am no advocate for the advertising industry, but I do think that this grants the marketers far more power than they really have. Admittedly, I do see a small amount of advertising for flying (personally, having flown far too much while working at British Airways, I haven't been on an aircraft since 1998), but I see far more indirect glamourisation of flying, and the experiences that can be gained by doing so, in factual programmes, from David Attenborough's world-spanning wildlife films and Brian Cox talking about the universe while perched on a distant mountain top, to the BBC's *Amazing Hotels* series.

* Rory Sutherland's comment on marketing is from 'We can't run away from the ethical debates in marketing', a 2010 column in *Market Leader*, the magazine of the UK Marketing Society.

Simms and Murray, who are primarily concerned about advertising as a mechanism that reinforces consumerism leading to climate change, are right about the increasing popularity of SUVs. They describe these cars as 'giant, polluting "sports utility vehicles" (SUVS) which in urban settings rove around like anti-social killing machines' and quote sales figures rising in around a decade 'from only one in ten of new cars bought to around half'. But apart from the fact that many SUVs aren't of the massive Range Rover style but are family hatchbacks with a different trim, how much of this is due to advertising? I have hardly ever seen an advert for SUVs. Instead, what I see all the time on TV is their use in dramas by the rich, the successful and criminals. I see them on the news, carrying presidents and businesspeople (and criminals). Advertising presumably has some influence, but the wider media has a far bigger role in shaping our attitudes.

As for the idea that advertising makes me eat beef from cattle raised on cleared rainforest, I have never seen advertising for beef per se, and only buy British beef – the UK is not famous for its rainforest.* Of course, this may be the case for others, and I have seen advertising for companies that sell beef, such as fast-food chains, though, for example, McDonald's claims only to use British and Irish beef in its burgers. Even so, it's a generalisation too far.

* Surprisingly, the UK *is* home to a small amount of temperate rainforest, known as Atlantic or Celtic rainforest, which is found primarily in parts of Scotland, Wales, Devon and Cornwall. This is indeed under threat, but from invasive species such as rhododendron, disease such as ash dieback and (wild) deer grazing, none of which is in any way related to advertising beef.

Seeing thousands of ads a day

One of Simms and Murray's more dramatic claims is that 'It isn't clear how many adverts we are aware of seeing, but what is clear is that they have an effect whether or not we are consciously aware of blanket online, targeted and "surveillance" advertising.'* The existence of an effect 'whether or not we are consciously aware' of the ads is stated as fact without a reference, so I am not sure why this is clear. We are also told that 'the average person is now estimated to encounter between 6,000 and 10,000 ads every single day'.

The book does provide a source for this claim: written in 2021 on a blog by Sam Carr, a 'copywriter', in a post that is strangely headed 'How Many Ads Do We See a Day in 2023'. (It was the oddity of having a source dated 2021 providing a figure for 2023 that first caught my attention.) The post itself talks (not surprisingly) about 2021 and seems to have been updated to 2023 simply by changing the year in the title. But where does the blog post get that number from? It doesn't tell us.

I highlighted this unlikely feeling number to the *More or Less* radio programme (see page 58). They investigated further, finding that there are a set of different statistics in the 3,000 to 10,000 range doing the rounds, but all seem to be plucked out of the air. Where there is limited justification, some include, for instance, seeing a cup with a coffee-chain logo on it as being exposed to advertising.

The first big numbers seem to date back to an attempt at research in the 1960s, when a marketer for General Foods tried to estimate the numbers of adverts that were experienced in the typical time spent engaging with advertising. He came up with a

---

* Surveillance advertising is a somewhat loaded term for targeted advertising that attempts to match the audience's interest – see Chapter 8 for more on this.

number of 1,500, which may have been the starting point for the bigger numbers that followed. But that 1,500 was for a family of four, not one individual, and was very specific to the US.

For the *More or Less* show, Sam Anderson, editor of the marketing magazine *The Drum*, counted the ads he was exposed to living in London in a day, and came to 93. Anderson asked others to do the same, getting a range between 26 and 154. Even asking someone to see as many as he could in a day only led to just over 500. Personally, because I never see TV adverts*, don't subscribe to newspapers and magazines, and don't live in a city, I'd put my own count, mostly from internet browsing, at well under 100. That 6,000 to 10,000 number seems entirely unsubstantiated.

Priming to purchase

It is worth investigating one of Simms and Murray's case studies in detail, as they certainly claim to be revealing massive brainjacking underway in the industry. Unfortunately, it's hard to get any certainty from the book as many assertions are made based on research that lacks scientific rigour. As an example of the power of advertising to subvert brains, *Badvertising* describes an 'experiment' undertaken by Bite Back, a 'youth activist movement challenging a food system that's been set up to fool us all'.

In the experiment, a group of teenagers were apparently exposed to the effects of priming (see Chapter 12 on subliminal brainjacking for a detailed look at the priming phenomenon), by encountering advertising for 'triple-dipped chicken' all day, both in physical adverts and online, where fake posts of influencers eating this chicken dish had been planted. The teenagers were then invited to a restaurant where they were asked to order from

---

* I avoid TV adverts either by recording the programme and skipping the ads or paying for an ad-free streaming service.

a menu of over 50 items – according to the book, every one of the youths ordered triple-dipped chicken.

Simms and Murray tells us that the young people had been 'subconsciously advertised to' and the messages about the chicken had been 'automatically absorbed by their brains even when not knowingly aware of the marketing'. As you will discover in the subliminal chapter, the effect is now considered to be relatively ineffectual. There is no evidence the experiment was properly controlled or had an effective sample size, nor that the advertising was anything other than consciously absorbed.

The message that *Badvertising* gives us in response is set in dire language – a good marker for manipulative brainjacking itself. We are told that 'Through a combination of experience and exposure advertising, connected to emotional response, brands and their logos become more "mentally available". This happens through the development of new neural pathways which are reinforced by repeated exposure.' This sounds like scary interference with our brains. Surely, we don't want our neural pathways to be hacked around by brands? But all those words come down to is a description of the way that we form memories. Memories are new neural pathways that are reinforced by repeated exposure. Is it surprising or scary that I can remember Coca-Cola, Amazon or British Airways,* to pick a few brands at random?

This kind of over-dramatisation and exaggeration of the abilities of advertisers does the understanding of the impact of brainjacking no service. Even where there is some scientific basis for an argument, it can be weak. For example, one of the studies referenced indirectly by the book showed how advertising impacted beef consumption in the UK. But when you look at the actual study, rather than articles based on it, the response of shares of beef sales to advertising was a 0.5 per cent increase.

* As I worked there many years ago, it would be worrying if I didn't remember British Airways, but you know what I mean.

This demonstrates the danger of throwing around the term 'statistically significant', which has a very particular meaning in the scientific world. This value was statistically significant in the sense that if advertising had no influence on beef market share, there would only be a 1 in 20 chance of the increase in beef consumption occurring, but that tiny 0.5 per cent increase does not show what we would think of as a significant impact of advertising on our brains.

Going for the heart and gut

One thing that is interesting from the triple-dipped chicken example, though, is that food (and particularly this kind of food) was chosen for the experiment. There is little doubt that there are certain low-level cues that most humans respond to. These are based on the essentials of maintaining human life – food, sex, preservation from danger and, perhaps to a lesser extent, a warm, comfortable environment.

Food advertising, particularly if focused on foodstuffs rich in the contents that are craved when lacking nourishment, such as fat and salt, can be particularly visceral. I hardly ever notice billboards or adverts on bus stops when I'm in a car – but one image that I find hard to ignore is a picture of a big, juicy burger, oozing cheese. I admit I have a weakness for hamburgers, but I think there is something more primal in the way that this kind of advertising can produce a desire – it seems to directly contact areas of the brain that are responsible for survival, just as much as a sudden movement in the dark can trigger a predator fear response, even if we are far from possible animal attack.

Equally, it's hardly a novelty to suggest that sex sells. At one time, this was so much an advertiser's mantra that it was taken to ridiculous lengths. I find it hard to believe that anyone ever bought a car just because that particular product had been photographed with an attractive, scantily clad woman draped over the bonnet – and yet at one point this was an everyday marketing technique. Without doubt this approach was deeply sexist – for a small element of balance I would also highlight TV adverts for Diet Coke, which for years featured hunky topless men.

This is only one aspect, though, of using sex in advertising. It is probably most explicit now in ads that are pushing cosmetics and perfumes, but it is still commonly used – and has been for at least a hundred years. Take, for instance, an advertisement from the 1920s for the American company Arrow that manufactured collars and shirts (at the time the two were usually separate items). Featuring a painting by American artist Joseph Leyendecker, the ad does, appropriately, feature a man wearing a dress shirt and bow tie. But he is dancing with an extremely attractive young woman dressed in a way that would have appeared distinctly provocative at the time.

Patterns and self-preservation

It is also perfectly possible – and more common than you might think – to use our response to attempt preservation from danger as a mechanism to influence others. We do not have to be in a real life-threatening situation to have a fear response triggered. This is because of the importance that patterns hold in our understanding of, and interaction with, the world around us. Patterns provide an essential way to simplify the complex flood of information our brains are constantly receiving, and to enable us to ever do anything practical. In another book, I've used* the example of the simple action of turning on a light switch.

* The light switch example of the use of patterns is from *Dice World* (Icon Books, 2014).

There is nothing natural about light switches – we aren't somehow genetically programmed to deal with them. Yet we can walk into an unfamiliar room and, provided we can find the light switch, we will be able to flick on the light with ease and confidence. (Until we make a transatlantic voyage and find that the people on the other side of the Atlantic mount their light switches the wrong way up.)

Contrast this with a robot that you have carefully programmed with the location of a light switch in your kitchen, plus the exact direction and the amount of force that is required to push the switch and turn the light on. Now place that same robot in the lounge and ask it to turn the light on. It will almost certainly fail.

We can succeed where the imagined robot can't because our use of patterns enables to absorb the broad principle of a light switch and how to use it. Of course, this capability wasn't developed to be able to deal with household lighting. Instead, our use of patterns enables us to take incomplete information and make a rapid judgement of the most likely outcome or desired response as quickly as possible. It's a very valuable approach when, for example, in a situation of physical danger where we need to avoid a predator.

The downside, though, is that this response is relatively easy to fool. It's better to occasionally imagine a non-existent predator and prepare for its attack rather than wait for definitive evidence, which might come too late as the fangs sink in. This is why we can jump at nothing, or see bogeymen under the bed. Failed pattern recognition isn't just about fear, of course. It's also why we think we see ghosts, or faces in unevenly toasted slices of bread. But prevention of danger is at the heart of a very strong pattern-recognising system.

When activated, pattern recognition of a potential threat triggers a series of responses in the brain. If you really like details of those squidgy bits, a part of the brain called the amygdala receives a response to stimuli from the thalamus. This then signals other parts, including the hippocampus, the prefrontal cortex and the adrenal glands, using a number of neurotransmitter chemicals, notably glutamate. While the hippocampus and prefrontal cortex are largely dealing with what to do, the adrenal glands get us ready for fight or flight by releasing stress hormones such as adrenaline and noradrenaline. When present, these chemicals result in increased heart rate, blood pressure and respiration rate.* Fear has struck.

Although advertising rarely engages the full fight or flight reflex, it can certainly use more subtle fears as part of its leverage in influencing the brain. In the next chapter we will encounter a Rimmel advert that was banned by the UK's Advertising Standards Authority, because it appeared to be playing on children's insecurities – when they suffered from fear of not fitting in, or not feeling as attractive as they were told they should be. Although FOMO – fear of missing out – is a modern acronym, the concept behind it is one that has been around as long as social circumstances have existed, and is one that advertisers have long exploited.

As we have seen, advertising and marketing go well beyond simply putting up a billboard or putting text and images in a newspaper or between TV shows. But those who wish to influence our spending – or perhaps even something as fundamental as our voting patterns – now have a powerful vehicle for their influence that many of us dip into every day. Social media.

---

* It's this kind of detail of bits of the brain that really puts me to sleep. I'll try not to do it again.

8 SOCIAL WORLD

There was a time when the name Cambridge Analytica was infamous. It may have faded by now – it sounds like an innocuous academic mathematical-analysis company – but Cambridge Analytica generated uproar when it was claimed that its work had been responsible (at least in part) for Donald Trump winning the 2016 US election.

This wasn't a matter of using numbers, say, to make clever analysis of voting districts or to produce a better poll; the suggestion was that Cambridge Analytica had such a detailed breakdown of the recipients of Facebook advertising that it was able to micro-target advertising precisely enough to swing the vote. Sometimes this might have involved appealing to a particular voter's personal interests. At other times, the company's algorithms might make use of advertising that emphasised favourite conspiracy theories. Always the advertising would suggest that Donald Trump would be supportive of the individual voter's worldview.

Adverts you want to see?

Let's take a step back before diving into the murky depths of Cambridge Analytica's work. Is there anything wrong with personalised advertising that targets individuals? As we will see in more detail in the next chapter, without doubt it can come across as downright creepy. You search online to find a good price on a diamond ring. Suddenly you are bombarded with advertising for wedding planners and venues. There's an unpleasant feeling that a virtual spy is looking over your shoulder as you browse.

On the other hand, many of us use 'free' products that are supported by advertising. Traditionally this would probably have been a TV or radio channel – but now the most widespread platform is social media. We get Facebook or Twitter/X or TikTok for free, and in return we accept that we will be exposed to advertising. We are entering into an unspoken contract with the platform – you give me the facilities that I enjoy using and I will tolerate (if occasionally getting irritated by) your regular supply of adverts.

Given that is the case, it's reasonable to ask 'Would you rather have advertising that is totally irrelevant to you, or would you like to see products and services you are likely to want?' If you go to see a film in the cinema, would you rather have the venue choose a random film, or do you want to know what's on and choose yourself? Although it can be fun to watch something totally at random – and occasionally it might make for the discovery of a new favourite – most of us, most of the time, would rather see a film we know we want to see. Why not, then, see an advert that you are more likely to appreciate?

Unfortunately, it's not so simple. If it were literally a case that we could specify which types of ad we were going to be presented with – and that was what we got – targeted advertising might well be acceptable to most of us. But in reality, there are two problems. Firstly, the social media companies don't restrict themselves to your stated preferences. This was demonstrated in a 2015 experiment.

The experimenters, led by Amit Datta, set up software agents that intentionally searched out certain topics on Facebook.* This should have resulted in these topics being visible in the ad settings available at the time for Facebook users, which were supposed to list the personal interests being used to select advertising – effectively an automatic version of stating preferences. But when the researchers checked out those interests, they did not reflect the adverts that were being fed to the agents. So, for example, when they looked up substance abuse, they were fed adverts relating to rehab facilities. When they looked at disability-related pages, they were given advertising for wheelchairs. But neither of these subject areas appeared in the agents' personal interests.

This is one degree of lacking transparency – but the problems run deeper. The attempts to maximise the influence of advertising are not limited to the platform itself. It's easy to see that searching for a topic on Facebook, or reading articles and watching videos about a particular topic, might influence Facebook advertising. But websites have been sharing information (for a price), meaning that an action you took on Facebook could be reflected in advertising on a totally different site. We'll find out more about this in the next chapter.

Influencing elections

Despite the potential benefits of personalised advertising, many of us prefer to block the information flow as much as possible and accept more generic ads. But what Cambridge Analytica claimed to have done with their micro-targeting was much more

---

* The social media agents experiment is 'Automated experiments on ad privacy settings' published in *Proceedings on Privacy Enhancing Technologies*.

than making advertising relevant to the user. Instead, the boast was that the company had influenced the outcome of an election to make Donald Trump the most powerful individual in the world.

It all started with the work of a Cambridge University academic, Alex Kogan. He had made use of a flaw in the way that Facebook allowed access to data at the time. If person X granted a third party access to his or her data, then it was also possible to drag in information on the physical location and likes of all person X's friends. Kogan had used this loophole for legitimate academic research, but then started to work with a company called SCL on a larger project to study Facebook users' personalities and likes with political aims in mind.

As Kogan told mathematician David Sumpter: 'A lot of what I study is emotions and I think if we had thought about whether people might feel weird or icky about us making personality predictions about them, then we would have made a different decision.' Kogan and his new team used a major customer survey to gain access to Facebook profiles – seemingly as a simple part of the questionnaire process. As a result, they got direct access to around 200,000 US profiles, which, with Facebook's then provision of access to friends' information, gave them data on around 30 million individuals.

Of course, political messages have always been tailored to the platforms they were put out on. An ad on, say, the right-wing Fox News would be very different to one on the more left-leaning MSNBC. But until Cambridge Analytica was formed as a part of SCL, the targeting was crude – based on the self-selection of the TV channel you watch, or basic socio-political distinguishers such as socio-economic status, age and gender. But with access to the greater detail in the Facebook data, there was the potential to be far more nuanced, picking out detailed policy aspects or concerns that might appeal to a selected personality type. No longer would there be a broad, hit-or-miss message. These ads would tell every individual exactly what they wanted to hear.

At least that was the theory. But when Sumpter recreated the approach used by Cambridge Analytica he found that the real abilities of such an algorithm lagged far behind the capabilities that had been claimed for it.* Sumpter points out that there are a number of flaws. Firstly, it's easy to assume that correlations work two ways when they don't. An example he gives is that Democrats were more likely than Republicans to give a Facebook like to a Harry Potter page. But this doesn't mean you can deduce that someone who likes Harry Potter will be a Democrat supporter. Secondly, a model can only make effective predictions if there are sufficient data points – but many individuals on Facebook stick to interacting with friends and don't like sufficient numbers of pages to draw any conclusions.

Perhaps most damningly, to be useful in the way that Cambridge Analytica was supposed to be able to deliver, the algorithm had to be able to place individuals on the major scales used in personality tests, typically agreeableness, conscientiousness, extroversion, openness and neuroticism. It was by positioning a user on these scales that the Cambridge Analytica algorithm was supposed to select the appropriate individual message for them. When Sumpter tested his model, on all the scales but one, he found it was only slightly better at assessing relative values than picking at random. (The one scale that was better was openness, where the algorithm was right about two thirds of the time.)

Of course, Sumpter didn't have the details of the proprietary Cambridge Analytica algorithm, but he knew the limitations of the data available and the kind of approach that could have been

* For details of Sumpter's work, see the Cambridge Analytica entry in Further Discovery

taken. And his conclusions were confirmed by Alex Kogan from his own analysis using different data sets.

The story has a twist. After claiming to have influenced the successful 2016 election of Donald Trump using personality information gleaned from Facebook to target advertising, Cambridge Analytica then dropped all mention of this. It came out that Facebook had told them to delete their data *before* the election campaign. The company later said that it had not used Kogan's data, nor was such personality-targeted advertising deployed. Instead, they had fallen back on the tried and tested basics of location, age and gender. By mid-2018, Cambridge Analytica had faced a torrent of allegations and the company folded. Yet many of those who do remember the company's existence probably still believe its exaggerated role.

Meet the influencer

However strong the impact of personalised advertising, social media has brought us a particularly insidious type of paid endorsement in the work of the online influencer. These individuals are given freebies and paid to pass on recommendations for specific products. But their videos are designed to build up a false sense of relationship with their viewers. It feels to their followers that they are not getting recommendations from a complete stranger, but from a friend. Unfortunately, many of these recommendations are based not on the quality of the product, but as a response to receiving a payment.

In this sense, influencers act like celebrity endorsers in conventional advertising. I've never understood the apparent value of these, perhaps because I don't hero worship sports stars or Hollywood actors. Most of us surely know perfectly well that George Clooney is probably not a particular fan of Nespresso coffee, and that sports stars would endorse any trainer they were paid enough to say was great. But still the advertisers love to make use of those celebrity faces.

A follower's relationship with an influencer, though, is far closer to an ersatz friendship than a viewer's with a superstar endorser in a TV advert. And this makes influencers particularly dangerous. Ranvir Singh notes that until recently this relationship was open to misuse: 'On Instagram not so long ago they made it policy that you had to put #Ad because often what was happening was people would go, "Oh my god, I've just had this new tea and I've lost a stone, I can't believe it!" Famous people were doing that. And then there was a huge push to label it with #Ad – that was a sea change in how people viewed influencing online.'

Helen Carasso echoed this: 'Advertising should be made clear: we've had all this stuff with social media influencers where they now have to make clear, "This post is supported by ... whatever I'm wearing, or whatever" – such advertising is an absolutely direct open link from the product to the potential consumer, or the person you want to receive the message.'

Despite labelling often being applied, marketing departments consider influencers to be a significant part of their armoury. Pat Fallon, the chairman of the Fallon Worldwide agency, commented a few years ago:* 'By letting people participate in a brand's public persona, a marketer can trigger infectious word-of-mouth goodwill ... It's time to embrace the public as co-marketers of brands. The brand, as David Ogilvy once pointed out, exists insides the minds of consumers, but now they have the means to show and tell the world their version of it.' There can be no doubt that brands see influencers as a prime tool in this type of brainjacking exercise.

* In *A History of Advertising* – see Further Discovery.

Reaching the young

Perhaps the biggest concern raised by social media influencers is their ability to have an impact on young people, who are both more susceptible to manipulation and more likely than the general population to get their information from social media. A clear example is the way that beauty products are now being marketed to a young audience. In 2023, the UK's ASA banned an advert by Rimmel London which carried the tagline 'Get ready to slay this back-to-school season'.

The Facebook ad included a video of a 25-year-old influencer, Lana Jenkins, applying Rimmel London makeup. According to Coty UK, the company behind Rimmel, this was not 'communicating a need to wear makeup' but rather 'was intended to refer more generally to the period of time starting in September for anyone going back to work including, for example, university students, mums and teachers'. It was, according to the manufacturer, 'intended to motivate and build confidence, rather than prey on young girls' insecurities'.

In response, the ASA said that 'the words "back-to-school season" in this ad, in conjunction with the vibrant pink colour scheme, the books and star emojis and the fluffy pink pen held by Ms Jenkins in the video, would primarily be understood by viewers as referring to the time of the year when students return to senior school or sixth form college after the summer break and would be perceived as speaking to that age group, and would have appealed to them', and that 'the use of the word "slay" in the claim "Get ready to slay this back-to-school season" implied that girls or young women were more likely to succeed or do well when they went back to school if they wore make-up'. In conclusion, the ASA determined that the ad 'had the effect of playing on young girls' insecurities about their appearance and therefore [we] concluded it was irresponsible'.

Journalist Kristina Murkett noted:*

> Up and down the country, children and pre-teens are not asking for Barbies and bikes for Christmas this year; instead, they're requesting toners, serums, cleansers and moisturisers ... "kid-preneur" influencers like Haven Garza (who is 7 years old and has nearly 5 million TikTok followers) are reviewing skincare products to sell to other children their age. Penelope Disick, the 11-year-old daughter of Kourtney Kardashian, posted a video of her skincare and makeup routine that has over 8 million views on TikTok. A skincare range by 19-year-old actress Millie Bobby Brown is particularly popular with teenagers, while skincare companies such as Drunk Elephant are being endorsed and followed by children as young as eight years old.

Are they stealing our focus?

One further influence on our brains that is often suggested as being thanks to social media is a reduction in human attention spans. This concern was brought to the fore at the beginning of 2022 when the previously disgraced Scottish-Swiss journalist Johann Hari published his book *Stolen Focus: Why You Can't Pay Attention*. This was a clear assertion of darkest brainjacking – not only, it was suggested, was social media reducing our ability to concentrate on a topic for any length of time, companies such as Meta were doing so intentionally: they were *stealing* our focus.

In an *Observer* newspaper article based on his book,† Hari recounts a visit to Graceland in Memphis, Tennessee, with his

---

* Kristina Murkett: 'Rimmel: the latest brand to prey on children's insecurities', unherd.com.

† 'Your attention didn't collapse. It was stolen' (2 January 2022).

nineteen-year-old godson, 'Adam' (the name was changed). Hari describes Adam as 'lost', having dropped out of school at fifteen and spending 'almost all his waking hours alternating blankly between screens – a blur of YouTube, WhatsApp and porn'. Not only does Adam break a promise to keep his phone switched off during the day, Hari is appalled when visitors to Graceland spend time scrolling through features of the building on an iPad they are given, rather than looking at them directly.

Horrified, Hari goes on to interview experts, and tells of a small study of college students that found 'they now only focus on any task for 65 seconds'. Another study of office workers found that 'they only focus on average for three minutes'. Hari asserts that this isn't happening because we all individually became weak-willed: 'Your focus didn't collapse. It was stolen.' He goes on to describe the 'switch-cost effect', where a tendency to keep switching between tasks, encouraged by social media, results in time being wasted on refocusing.

To demonstrate this, we are told of a study at Carnegie Mellon University's human computer interaction lab where 136 students are given a test. They are split between having their phones off, or on with intermittent text messages. On average, the students getting the messages performed 20 per cent worse. Hari muses: 'It seems to me that almost all of us are currently losing that 20% of our brainpower.' He tells us we need to fight, that we need to reclaim our minds 'just as the feminist movement reclaimed women's right to their own bodies'.

Strong stuff. But there are some significant doubts about the science behind these assertions. In their excellent podcast *The Studies Show*, Tom Chivers and Stuart Ritchie point out that, for instance, there are issues with the description of that Carnegie Mellon study. This was not a published study that underwent peer review – it was commissioned for another book (*The Plateau Effect* by Bob Sullivan and Hugh Thompson). And even the description of the study is not accurate. In reality, there were three ways the students were split. Some had phones off, some phones on but didn't receive texts, and some had phones on and did receive texts.

Crucially, the students who received texts were told that the content of the texts was important for the test – undermining any suggestion that there was an inherent problem in using mobile phones. It is hardly a surprise that participants did less well in a test if part of the time allocated for the test was taken up by an activity they were told was part of the process. When the need to read those text messages is part of the test, they can't be said to have done worse overall. And to add insult to injury, apparently the trial was run twice – and only in one of the two runs was there a deterioration in outcome.

Overall, the lack of logic demonstrated is remarkable. Hari goes from a small, low-quality study that said people did 20 per cent less well in a specific test when repeatedly interrupted to the generalised statement that 'almost all of us are currently losing that 20% of our brainpower'. Even if the study had been a high-quality, peer-reviewed example, where the texts were pure distraction, we can hardly deduce from its results that most of us are mislaying a fifth of our brainpower. There is simply no connection.

On average ...

Are social media companies really intentionally engaged in destroying our attention span? The assertion seems to be based on the not-unreasonable idea that by doing so, they will make sure we get exposed to more advertising, which, in the end, is their reason for existence. They want us to keep scrolling. But over and above the concern about some of the studies mentioned above, there are bigger-picture problems with the way that this is presented.

The office worker study that Hari mentioned said that on average the participants only focused for three minutes. But this is a highly misleading statement. Averages are very useful mathematical methods, but like all statistical tools, they have to be deployed carefully or then can mislead in a big way.

One problem here is that 'average' isn't a mathematical term. It is usually a synonym for the mean – the value produced by adding up a set of figures and dividing by the number of figures. So, for example, the mean of 2, 3, 4 and 5 is 14/4 = 3.5. This is often an effective measure, but it can be highly misleading. If Elon Musk is in a room with nine other people who have the typical UK net worth of around £125,000, the average net worth of the people in the room (as of 2023) is over £19.2 billion. This doesn't help us in any way to understand the population being studied.

Because of this limitation, statisticians often use an alternative type of average called the median. This ranks individuals in order and picks the middle value. So, the median net worth of that group is a far more representative £125,000 – though now it is as if Mr Musk has disappeared. The lack of clarity over which type of average is being used can cause confusion. We often see, for example, a figure given in the press for the 'average' house price in the UK. If this referred to the mean, it would be highly misleading, because the vast majority of houses in the UK are worth less than the mean, due to a small number of very expensive houses (the equivalent of Elon Musk in the example above).

I took this up some while ago with Robert Gardner, then the chief economist of the Nationwide Building Society, which is one of the organisations that provide these figures. He kindly took me through what they called an average. This turned out to be far more complex than a mean or a median. It was the result of stratifying the price data according to region, type of house and a number of other factors, then producing a weighted figure that they could perhaps have called a *typical* value, but that was not an average in any traditional sense.

When it comes to calculating an average attention span, we are dealing with an extremely fuzzy concept that is not susceptible to taking a meaningful average. Our attention spans are highly dependent on the activity undertaken. Attention is an entirely different thing when flicking through social media posts than it is when watching an absorbing film or driving a car. There is little doubt that social media is devised to reduce how much time we spend with individual posts – but we can't deduce from this that we are unable to apply attention for longer periods where appropriate. Arguably, we don't give very much attention to social media posts because they don't deserve being looked at for any longer.

Attention vs memory

The nadir of attention-span pseudoscience came with a frequently quoted 'paper' from Microsoft published in 2015* that claimed that digital media had such an impact on our attention span that on average it had dropped from twelve seconds in 2000 to eight seconds in 2013. This data was not derived from a published paper, but from a website called Statistic Brain, which gave no source for the information.

One of the most unlikely aspects of the Microsoft attention span document was that it said that, by dropping to eight seconds by 2013, humans now had less than the 'average attention span of a goldfish', which was given as nine seconds. There is a real oddity here. What appeared to be referenced as if it were fact was the old chestnut that goldfish have a very limited memory

* 'Attention Spans – Consumer Insights', Microsoft Canada (2015).

(the figure is not consistent: it can be given as any one of three, five or nine seconds). This assertion has no basis in science and is easily disproved.

Anyone who has kept goldfish in a pond knows that they can remember a pond-side activity that precedes feeding from day to day, heading to the appropriate spot when it occurs. For that matter, in 2003 the TV show *Mythbusters* demonstrated goldfish remembering routes through mazes for at least a month, adding to a string of papers that had demonstrated the incorrect nature of the three, five or nine second memory that dates back at least as far as 1908. Even if the assertion had been true, though (and it's not), the claim about goldfish refers to a measure of memory retention, not of attention span. They aren't the same thing. No one has ever suggested that humans have been reduced to having an eight-second memory.

Social media addiction

If social media really is designed to shorten our overall attention span just to increase our exposure to more lucrative advertising, though having little impact on our attention elsewhere, it is still a distinctly evil level of brainjacking – but some claim there is something even worse happening. According to a BBC article from 2023,* 'hundreds of families are suing some of the world's biggest technology companies – who, they say, knowingly expose children to harmful products'. Specifically, social media companies are being blamed for creating addiction in their users.

The article quotes an American woman called Taylor Little, who says: 'I literally was trapped by addiction at the age of 12.

---

* https://www.bbc.co.uk/news/technology-67443705.

And I did not get my life back for all of my teenage years.' The article takes the existence of this addiction as a given. The allegation that Little and her co-plaintiffs make is that social media platforms are designed to foster addiction.

Part of the legal case is straightforwardly clear and has already been acknowledged by a US judge – that platforms like Facebook and TikTok do not have useful age verification or effective parental controls. But the particular assertion of addiction is a difficult one to justify. *The Studies Show* podcast points to a paper in *Behavior Research Methods* from 2020* that casts doubt on the methods used to demonstrate that social media provides a dangerous mechanism for addiction.

The paper points out that the measures used to detect social media addiction are focused on the motivations for absorbing social information online, which are exactly the same as the motivations for seeking social information in traditional offline circumstances. The paper's authors take social media use scales and reword them so that they apply to 'spending time with friends': they discover that 69 per cent of those tested are addicted to spending time with friends.

As the paper's abstract puts it: 'We question the extent to which connecting with others can be considered an "addiction" and discuss issues concerning the validation of new "addiction" measures without relevant medical constructs. Readers should approach our measure with a level of skepticism that should be afforded to current social media addiction measures.' Of course, as human beings we have habits, and we like to do things that we enjoy – but it is surely an insult to addicts who are struggling with a disease to describe social media activity as addiction.

Beyond doubt, social media has had an impact on our personal storytelling circles. Traditionally, we would have asked

---

* 'Development of an Offline-Friend Addiction Questionnaire (O-FAQ): Are most people really social addicts?' by Liam Satchell et al.

friends and relations to, say, recommend a good plumber, and might be influenced in everything from food we eat to our thoughts on political issues as a result of interaction with those real-world social networks. Such physical networks might typically have included around ten individuals in an inner circle, with each giving access to about another ten, meaning that our social sphere contained around a hundred people. But on social media, the apparent equivalent, whether we are considering friends or influencers, could stretch into many hundreds or even thousands.

Again, in a traditional physical social network, we would choose how much exposure we got to any particular individual. But on social media, it is unseen algorithms that decide how much information we receive from whom. This artificial, data-driven setting can result in the easy formation of echo chambers where we get locked into polarised views, as well as allowing companies to apply influence as if they were part of our real-world networks.

Whether or not you agree, for instance, with J.K. Rowling's views on the need for safe spaces for women, the mechanisms of social media platforms make it easy to develop a bifurcation of opinion, with millions loudly supporting her and millions of others vehemently insulting her. This seems to be the influence of social media on the way that we approach issues: it goes far beyond rational debate, to hatred and death threats being flung towards anyone who disagrees. In this sense, social media certainly does provide a vehicle for dark brainjacking.

It's also true that we don't carry our real-world social networks in our pockets – if you don't turn alerts off (and you should), social media can be far more intrusive on everyday life. This, I would suggest, is why it can be so pernicious for children, rather than addiction. Any trouble they might experience face to face, such as bullying, is amplified massively by the constant pinging of social media alerts. In the UK at the time of writing some are arguing for bans on either smartphones or social media up to, say, the age of sixteen. While the practicalities make this unlikely, finding some way to mitigate the pressure of social media on the young is well worth exploring.

Social media companies are in the data business in a big way – and attempt to gain greater influence and the ability to manipulate by giving the appearance of being close to their users. But this is just a small part of the way that data about us is used and shared to gain brainjacking abilities. Systems that know us, or make use of what they think we like, or how we behave, have proliferated as the use of the internet has become ubiquitous. There's a battle on over what we share, who can access it, and what can be done to us.

9 KNOWING ME, KNOWING YOU

When verbal storytelling was the only source of brainjacking it was a one-way street. Information came from the storyteller and, by hearing or experiencing it, the recipient would think differently. It might then develop into a discussion, but basic storytelling has a clear direction of flow. Now, though, as we have seen with social media and tailored advertising, the sharing of stories can be far more of an interaction. The ability to influence our thoughts and actions can be driven by data – and there has never been a time when so much data is available, not just about the world in general, but about us as individuals.

Staying private online

Data-driven influence is why some major IT companies like Apple have made such a big deal of the degree to which their systems provide better user privacy. As an Apple user, when I sign up to a service, I don't have to use my own email address – I can ask Apple to provide a fake address that has no external connection to me. When I am on the web, the browser prevents information being passed from one site to another (something that at the time of writing, Google has just added to its Chrome browser too).

If I pull up the 'privacy report' on my browser, I can see that in the last 30 days, 28 different trackers have been prevented from profiling me – and over half of the sites I visited contacted such trackers. Somewhat surprisingly, given their reputation for being customer-friendly, the most invasive site I used for attempting to engage trackers was that of the John Lewis department store, which contacted nineteen trackers. As well as the almost inevitable Google and its offspring (according to the report, google.com was prevented from profiling me across 98 websites), the tracking sites John Lewis attempted to pass information to included Microsoft's search engine Bing, Facebook, Snapchat, Twitter, Yahoo and a number of monetisation sites.

Similarly, Apple now gives iPhone users the option to prevent apps from sharing information. Of course, advertising providers would tell me that such data sharing was all done for my benefit, so that I can receive the most appropriate ads. Why would I want to receive ads for cat food if I don't have a cat? This costs the advertiser unnecessary money, and also irritates me. Yet, as we saw in the previous chapter, the way that this information is obtained and used feels manipulative. It's not just a matter of appropriate advertising, but rather the way that adverts can insidiously attempt to get inside my mind and act in a way that maximises the chance of me making a purchase.

Big data systems, working invisibly behind the websites I visit, enable this profiling and tracking to spread information in the background without my knowledge. And there can be little doubt that the intention – again, often using the defence of doing something useful for me – is to maximise influence. If you don't have this kind of tracking under control – as wasn't possible until relatively recently – the result can be quite unnerving.

Back in 2016, when writing my book *Big Data*, I noted that I had been talking to my wife about a Christmas present for one of our daughters. A couple of days later, I went into Facebook and the first advert I saw was for the specific brand of perfume that we had discussed. This was a shock – I hadn't searched for it online. At the time, we had Amazon's Alexa-based Echo smart speakers, which are always listening to what's being said. Could they somehow have informed Facebook of our discussion?

In reality, such Big Brother-like possibilities weren't necessary – though the always-on nature of Echo speakers has in the past (after some legal wrangling) been used to collect evidence from crime scenes. It turned out that, after our discussion, my wife had used my computer to search for the perfume, so there was a more conventional tracking opportunity.

Although my browser now prevents information passing from one website to another, it can't stop tracking happening within a website such as Facebook. And this provides an example of one of the most frustrating aspects of targeted advertising for the user. If you click on an advert in Facebook, you are likely to be bombarded with adverts subsequently for the same product. This even occurs if you buy the product, but it is particularly frustrating if you look at it and decide not to buy.

Even with the protection offered by the likes of Apple and Google, at the time of writing this process is still being expanded. In January 2024, Meta, the company behind Facebook and Instagram, announced what was described as a customer user-experience improvement. Their apps would now store link history for 30 days – so users could go back to pages they had visited in the apps' built-in browser for the last month. The catch is, as Meta admitted: 'We may use link history information from our browser to improve your ads across Meta technologies.' This 'experience improvement' was really about enabling more targeted advertising.

There are also examples where targeted advertising misfires in a big way. In her book on big data,* Timandra Harkness mentions a woman who flew to Florida to take care of her aging mother, who was ill. After some online browsing relevant to her mother's needs, the next day she started to get adverts for local funeral services. With such a tragic misfire, the only brainjacking that occurs is to turn the purchaser against whichever website served up the offensive advertising. But when the targeting has been effective, it seems very likely that purchasing decisions can be influenced.

We'll tell you what you want

A slightly more beneficial-feeling process is the way that Netflix or Amazon make recommendations, based on what you have already looked at, watched or bought, and rated. This is an attempt to get inside your head, to understand your preferences and to influence your choices. Again, you can see this as a problem or an opportunity. The likes of Netflix and Amazon have a vast database of products to choose from. There can be too much on offer to be able to make a sensible selection. Sometimes their suggestions might be beneficial, but they can also provide a useless rabbit hole of information.

Of course, on a small scale, recommendations have always been one of the features of shopping in conventional stores. A big bookshop, for example, carries tens of thousands of different titles. If you had to look at each book individually to find something you wanted to buy, you would rapidly become overwhelmed. In response, the bookshop offers two vehicles to assist. Firstly, they have topic sections, separating, say, biography

---

* See big data in Further Discovery for details on Timandra Harkness's book.

from science fiction, or children's books from cookery. If you know what *type* of book you are interested in, you can cut down the choice to a few hundred titles.

Secondly, as bricks and mortar bookshops try to better their online rivals, they have ways of highlighting certain stock. There may be shelves for new releases in different categories. There will be tables, highlighting a small proportion of titles, some with special offers. And 'shelf talkers' – labels on the shelves with personal recommendations will be used to pick out certain books. For that matter, you can always ask a human bookseller.

These approaches give the shop a chance to manipulate customers' decision making. Even the categories influence our purchasing patterns. The UK's biggest bookshop chain Waterstones, for example, has (at least in many shops) moved crime from being a separate category into general fiction, and subsumed popular science into a wider 'smart thinking' category, which presumably is intended to increase sales, though those of us looking specifically for crime and popular science titles find it frustrating. But even more so, what goes on the tables or in the window, what gets its own display case and those shelf-talkers will influence the minds of customers.

I was party to a small example of the power of this approach to influencing when I knew a senior manager at WH Smith, the UK's biggest stationery store chain, which is also a significant bookseller. Smith's offered publishers the chance to pay to have a new book featured front and centre in their stores. One sales period, no one had purchased the slot. In response, as an experiment, the management simply chose a book that wasn't particularly promising to see what would happen to it. It ended up on the national bestseller list. Of course, it might have done that anyway – but that wasn't the expectation of the experienced booksellers at the company.

Online at Amazon, the potential stock to look through is far greater. The same applies to a streaming company like Netflix with a vast catalogue to choose from. And so, as well as using categories, such websites make personalised recommendations. The algorithms behind these recommendations are opaque. We don't know why they made their decisions. Like the WH Smith featured book, it could be that in some cases this is not really a matter of what would work for the purchaser, but rather what would be financially beneficial to the website. And once big data is involved, the companies can go beyond recommendation to commissioning products based on user preference.

Netflix, for example, is known to have commissioned series based on viewer preferences. Rather than adopt the traditional broadcasters' approach of commissioning a pilot and using the response that gets to decide whether or not to go for a whole series, Netflix has used data from its subscribers to decide whether or not a new series is worth taking a risk on, and as a result commissioned a number of series from scratch. And that data also allows them to provide several different trailers depending on user preference.

Big data has also got another way to influence our decision making: the comparison site. The personal benefit from sites like this is easy to recognise when the purchaser has a specific product in their sights. The first comparison site in the UK searched the online bookshops and found the cheapest place to buy a particular title. This site, BookBrain, was briefly successful, but the commissions involved in book sales are small, and such sites are now relatively rare.

Commission is, after all, the only source of revenue for a comparison site, and so they have flourished where commission opportunities have always been far greater – notably in the insurance business. Comparison sites dealing with insurance still offer the user something positive – there are far too many individual insurance companies to check them all, and the amount of information you have to provide each company is lengthy. But the comparison sites can manipulate the user's decision towards suppliers that maximise their income, primarily by making each offering subtly different in what it provides, making a realistic comparison harder to make. Canny users will also check a handful of insurers that are not on the comparison sites.

A company like Amazon is straightforwardly attempting to manipulate customers into spending money. It is not there to educate or to inform. But Amazon has also led the way in another way that big data can influence customers – by providing customer reviews. And reviews provide a whole extra layer of brainjacking opportunity.

The critic at work

Reviewing has a long, and mostly useful, history. Even before the slew of products we now have to choose between, for centuries there has been a need to help those with the money to spend to make wise choices. If there are twenty plays on in your city, which would be best for you to see? Which book should you pick up, or which restaurant should you eat at? If you subscribe to a newspaper, magazine or a review site like the UK's *Which?*, you may benefit from guidance from professionals.

To explore what professional reviews are attempting to do, I spoke to the last of my *University Challenge* teammates, Matthew Fort. Matthew started out in advertising but came to fame by reviewing restaurants for the *Guardian* newspaper and as a judge on the BBC TV show *Great British Menu*. He emphasised the need for a reviewer to build a relationship with their readership: 'If you are writing for a newspaper and you want people to turn to you every week you have to create a relationship – first of all that people are interested enough in what you want to write, and secondly they've got to trust you when they've read what you do. Tone of voice is absolutely critical: who are you, why open the *Guardian* and read Matthew Fort reviewing the Fat Duck? It's like creating a relationship, sitting across the table and you're chatting away and this is the story I've got to tell.'

This seem particularly true where a review is standalone. It's probably less the case where a newspaper publishes a whole list of reviews of books or films pulled together from different people, but applies where it involves something like Matthew's restaurant reviews, or Mark Kermode and Simon Mayo's film and TV review podcast *Kermode & Mayo's Take* – or even in a small way my own popular science and science-fiction book reviews.*

In a sense, although professional reviewers would probably not like to think it, there is a similarity with the social media influencer – they also build a relationship with the viewers, though arguably while both include an element of entertainment, the good professional reviewer incorporates expertise and experience where the influencers often rely entirely on personality.

As Matthew noted, some reviewers' style majors on entertainment – he picked out the late A.A. Gill among food critics, and the same could be said, for example, of Jeremy Clarkson's car reviews – but Matthew aimed primarily to be seen as an informed friend and raconteur. He pointed out a letter he received that said: 'I'm an OAP and I'm pretty much housebound and the height of my week is when the Saturday *Guardian* arrives and I read the travel section because I can go to Antarctica or America or Argentina or wherever it might be, and then I go to the food page: I'm never going to go to these restaurants but thanks to you I can go and see what it's like.'

---

* My popular science and science-fiction reviews can be found at www.popularscience.co.uk.

Whether feeling like a friend or an entertainer, the brainjacking involved often strays into social manipulation, good or bad. But for those looking for a recommendation for a restaurant to book, it is rather different. Matthew again: 'Obviously you do want to influence people, but first of all you have to entertain people to some extent: they have to want to read it ... whether they go to the restaurant or not is up to them. There are degrees [of influence] I suppose: if it's an absolute corker of a restaurant I want people to go there – I would probably actually say everybody should go there.'

Having said this, Matthew was doubtful of the power of reviews: 'I've lost count of the number of restaurants I've praised to the skies only for them to disappear a month later. And I've lost track of the restaurants where I and a whole lot of others have put the boot in with full vigour only to find them doing flourishing business decades later. The classic case was the Fat Duck – I reviewed it for the *Guardian* and gave it 19½/20, the only time I ever did that. Heston [Blumenthal] said, "Why only 19½?" I said, "Because I want to keep you hungry." But the fact is everyone who reviewed it said it was fantastic – yet it was going bust! Until it got its third Michelin star, which then established it beyond the parochial level of British cuisine, establishing that it was an international place to visit and that saved him from bankruptcy.'

However, sometimes there was clear influence – even if the outcome wasn't the expected one. Matthew again: 'Emily Green wrote for the *Independent* and one week we both reviewed the same restaurant. I gave it quite a warm welcome and she gave one of the most excoriating reviews I've ever read in my life – absolutely virulent, it was, and I was a little taken aback. Anyway, I rang them up a few days later and said this, and I hope it hasn't affected business. They said, "We've never been busier" – people couldn't believe it was that bad, or if they did believe, wanted to experience how bad it actually was.'

I began professional writing with software reviews for magazines. My first big review article, taking the magazine cover, was for a new spreadsheet package called Excel. Although it's not a 100 per cent guarantee, we can assume that most professional reviews provide an honest assessment of the product or service covered, and are written by someone who knows what they are talking about. It's not an absolute guarantee, of course – there can be fraudulent bias. When I wrote reviews for computing magazines, I was once approached by a representative of a US software company and asked how much it would cost to ensure that their new product got an effusively good review.

This might seem to contradict the suggestion that such reviews are honest – but I have written thousands of reviews and this has only ever happened to me once. Admittedly, I've occasionally had people or companies complain that they didn't like my review, but that is a different proposition. Incidentally, I didn't take up the offer of a considerable bribe, amounting to what I earned in around three months, but I can remember how shocked I felt after the phone call.

Ask the customer

It's likely that professional reviews do exert influence on those who read them – but the majority of potential buyers for a product or service at any one time will never have read a conventional review. And such reviews can only ever cover a small sample of the overall market. These days, far more of us are likely to use something like Tripadvisor to get guidance on restaurants, if only because it provides what appears to be a more complete view. Customer reviews have become the go-to source for many when making a purchasing choice. The idea is simple: make it easy for us to provide feedback on our purchases, which will help others make a choice. It's a big-data equivalent of asking friends and relations to recommend something. Customer reviews can also have a big effect, so much so that it didn't take manufacturers long to look for ways to manipulate the outcome.

Initially, this manipulation was just an extension of what happened with professional reviews. When I reviewed software back in the day, or when I review a book now, I mostly haven't paid for it – I am provided with a review copy, but still expected to produce a fair, unbiased review (as, indeed, I do). I have also professionally reviewed hardware, such as laptops and TVs – but those you don't keep. However, manufacturers, particularly from China, soon began to bombard those regularly writing customer reviews with emails offering free or discounted products in return for reviews.

This soon took a turn for the worse. Manufacturers would not only ask for a review, but would require a five-star review. This crosses the line from beneficial brainjacking to the malicious variety. As we've seen, it's not that it never happens with professional reviews, but it is rare. As online stores like Amazon have tried to prevent this happening, the dodgy manufacturers have introduced indirect means to try to avoid detection, for example asking paid reviewers to buy the product themselves and then refunding the price, plus a premium. Now it's more a matter of trying to detect patterns of excessively enthusiastic, often short reviews from the same customer.

I admit that when I give a particularly bad professional review, I tend to send an apologetic email to the PR person who has been my contact – but to date they have always been very positive about this, emphasising that people value my reviews because I am prepared to give bad ones. If I always gave five stars, my reviews would be devalued. Having said that, one magazine stopped using me as a book reviewer because I sometimes gave negative reviews – oddly, sometimes the publication itself wants always to appear positive about the products it covers. The only time I have ever had a publicly negative response to a bad review was on Twitter from the author, not a press office – and that only happened once when I was rather negative about a maths-based adult colouring book.

As with all information sourced online, while customer reviews remain very useful in their ability to shape our opinions, we need to approach them with caution, looking out for the signs of paid-for or sloppy reviewing, such as very short five-star reviews, or those that give limited information about the product, often with similar terms to those used by the manufacturer.

Star rating

With the introduction of big data information systems and businesses built around them, the approach of rating products has spread to both people and services. Like customer reviews, this has its origins in personal recommendations, or job references. But the modern twist is the ability to give a quick, often star-based review to a service just as you would for a product. Once again there is the opportunity here for both good and bad brainjacking.

We get a feeling of reassurance, when, for example, Tripadvisor tells us that a restaurant or hotel is excellent, and we can read a series of glowing reviews. But there is more danger here of malicious reviewing deployed by competitors. Admittedly, this has occurred for products, notably when academics have used 'sock puppets' – fake accounts – to excoriate fellow academics' books. In 2010, for example, Orlando Figes, a professor of history at Birkbeck College, admitted to having used sock puppets to give positive reviews to his own books on Amazon and to attack those written by fellow historians. But there is a lot more potential financial benefit for a bad actor who, for instance, owns one of two competing restaurants in a small town and wants to win the business from his or her rival.

Organisations such as Tripadvisor claim to police this kind of abuse of the system, but there have been well-publicised examples of businesses being ruined by a targeted campaign of fake reviews, when business owners have found it difficult to have fake negative comments reviewed or removed. This is an example* of a complaint to Google headed 'i own a business that is being destroyed by a disgruntled customer who is using fake reviews':

> i have a disgruntled customer who despite breaking the contract that he signed has left me a terrible google review. i understand that that is his perogative even though it is a blatant lie, the problem is that he is using his friends and family to post one star reviews often with no comment, there are several and he does it regularly this has been going on for a couple of months , my revenue is down 90% as a direct result of this hate campaign ... i can prove 100% that these posts are fake as all of my bookings go through a booking service provider and not one of the people have ever used my company and several of them are not even in america. PLEASE HELP ME BEFORE I HAVE TO CLOSE MY BUSINESS DOWN

I have no evidence whether or not this particular complaint is genuine, but it gives a flavour of the frustration that can result from such insidious brainjacking. Matthew Fort commented: 'They are ruthlessly manipulated: ever since Tripadvisor from the word go you had no control ... you could tell half of the stuff was written either by disenchanted restaurateurs themselves about their competition, or in praise by members of their own family. It was ludicrous. But that's perhaps why restaurant critics

* Example of complaint about fake reviews online found at bit.ly/brainjacking10.

have hung on in newspapers because in the end the newspaper becomes a guarantor of the authenticity of the reviewer. Online, anyone can write anything and there is no recourse ... But why do people trust it? Even if genuine, the reviews are written by people who are ignorant about food, service or indeed anything else.'

According to an article in the *Metro* newspaper from 2022* that highlighted the dangers of fake reviews, 'the average UK household spends around £900 each year that's directly influenced by online reviews'. That's around £25 billion of spending in total – lots of opportunity for those who are able to manipulate online reviews to make money from doing so.

What do ratings mean?

Another problem is that the way a rating system works can be interpreted differently by those doing the rating and those making use of the ratings, whether they be potential customers or the company that set up the system in the first place. Amazon, for example, does not give guidance on how to choose the number of stars customers give to a product.

On my popular-science book review site, I make the star ratings explicit with a published marking scheme:

> * – Just doesn't work for us
> ** – Has some interesting points, but not for everyone – check the provisos in the review
> *** – Good solid book, well worth reading if you are interested in the topic
> **** – Excellent book that any science fan would want to read
> ***** – One of the best popular science/science-fiction books of the year

* The *Metro* article on fake reviews can be found at bit.ly/brainjacking11.

Rating confusion can be particularly prevalent when the ratings directly affect outcomes, as is the case, for instance, with the taxi/rideshare service Uber. Here customers rate drivers, and drivers rate their passengers. The same is the case on the online auction site eBay, where both ends of the transaction rate each other. There's a dangerous-feeling circularity in this mechanism that can lead to false ratings being given to avoid negative outcomes.

There can also be significant cultural differences in the way star ratings are viewed if there is no guidance available, especially when those designing the system don't understand the people who are going to give scores. Those filling out satisfaction ratings in the UK, for example, are less likely to use the most extreme ratings than US customers, avoiding both the absolute worst and the absolute best. This means that in normal circumstances, four stars ought to represent a 'good' or 'very good' level of customer satisfaction. However, Uber has stated in the past that the minimum acceptable average rating is 4.6.

With lower scores, drivers could lose their position on the Uber network. Every apparently 'good' four-star rating drags them down. It's also possible that personal prejudice plays a role. Uber's data hasn't been made available for study, but when companies with a similar rating system, such as accommodation rental company Airbnb, have opened up their data, it has been found that this can happen. In one 2016 US study, people with African-American-sounding names were 16 per cent less likely to be accepted as guests in Airbnb properties than customers with European-American-sounding names.*

In Charlie Brooker's TV series *Black Mirror* (shown on the rating-obsessed Netflix), there is an episode called 'Nosedive'

---

* 'Racial Discrimination in the Sharing Economy: Evidence from a Field Experiment' by Benjamin Edelman et al.

which features a near-future society where everyone rates everyone else at each interaction. The central character has an argument that spirals into a collapse of her ratings, leading to the discovery of the freedom that comes from being unrated. Such rating of behaviour may seem like pure science fiction, and yet something not dissimilar is happening for real in China, a country with a very different attitude to personal freedoms than is the case in much of the West.

The Chinese system is an explicit attempt to shape minds using a 'social credit' scoring system, based on 'trustworthiness'. Depending on their social and financial rating, citizens are rewarded with access to benefits and treats such as the ability to make a restaurant reservation or book a flight, or to get access to online dating – or punished by a lack of access. As well as more familiar personal data like financial credit scores, input to this system is intended to include everything from helping others to playing music too loud, jaywalking or fare dodging on public transport.

According to the Chinese state, this system is intended to increase freedom, though those from different cultures are likely to see it as quite the opposite. It's a bit like the old criminal justice system mantra of 'if you've done nothing wrong, you have nothing to fear'. If you act in a trustworthy manner, the system will reward you. But act in a way that runs counter to maintaining a 'harmonious socialist society' and you will suffer. Break trust in one place and you will be restricted wherever you go.

The Chinese state believes that such a system is necessary to get on top of an out-of-control economy where fraud and bribery are common, and all too often companies sell inedible food or dangerous fake medicines. And there is no doubt that adequate monitoring should be able to help with these kinds of problems – but the scale of this proposed system, and its brainjacking intent of shaping attitudes and behaviour, will take in far more than the fraudsters.

This is a Big Brother attempt on a massive scale – too massive to be practical even with today's technology, given China's population of over 1.3 billion people. First revealed as a concept in 2014, as of 2023 it was still only being trialled on a voluntary basis in some regions, and may never come to full fruition. Should the system ever go fully live there, it is hard to imagine that all the potential problems with bad data and poor assumptions will be predicted and prevented. Here, simple errors in information could destroy people's lives. Those who are blacklisted could face ruin. We've seen how something similar happened to British sub-postmasters – but this would apply to every citizen. It's a scary prospect.

Pushing an outcome

Sometimes, the manipulative aspect is not so much how the data is used, but how we are steered by websites and apps into certain ways of thinking and interacting. This often surfaces when a subscription service is coming to the end of a payment period and we want to shut it down. I have in the past subscribed to two different newspapers through their online services – the *i* and *The Times*. Subscribing was very simple in both cases. I gave my card details and was given immediate access to the online papers with a couple of clicks. But the experience of ending the subscription was very different.

To leave the *i* subscription was no harder than joining up. All I had to do was click on a button saying that I wanted to end the subscription, then confirm it. But when I went to my account page on *The Times* website there was no obvious means to end the subscription. After spending some time searching for an unsubscribe button, I discovered that the only way to do so was to ring the company up. At the time of writing, the UK government was looking into requiring an easier process: making it much easier to join than it is to leave is more the kind of approach you'd expect from a cult than a respected newspaper.

Another example of attempting to influence by making something unnecessarily complicated has been Amazon's Prime subscription service, which offers a number of benefits, from streaming TV to free delivery. The US Federal Trade Commission (FTC) took out a lawsuit against Amazon, alleging that the design of their website was manipulative when it came to getting out of the Prime service. It's very easy to sign up for Prime – an offer of a free trial is front and centre when checking out with a purchase. But getting out required what the FTC described as a 'four-page, six click, fifteen option' sequence.

This was changed by Amazon at about the time the lawsuit was filed, though it still required five clicks on the desktop, or six if doing so on a phone. At the time of writing, the suit was due to go to trial in February 2025.

Much of what has been covered in this chapter has been as a result of the collection of large amounts of data. Once such data in collected, it gives opportunities to a new kid on the brainjacking block: artificial intelligence.

ARTIFICIAL INTELLIGENCE 10

Artificial intelligence (AI) has been big news since the introduction of 'generative' AI, such as the text-writing ChatGPT or the image-producing DALL-E. We have seen headlines, international conferences and dire warnings from AI creators about the dangers the technology presents to humanity. For many of us, this reaction generates a sceptical response, as far as the more dramatic predictions are concerned. But there is no doubt that AI has plenty of potential to interfere with what we think – as a tool for brainjacking it is highly impressive.

The origins of AI

You might think from the buzz that has grown around AI in the 2020s that it is a new concept. Instead, the idea (if not the practicality) of artificial thought has been around far longer. In ancient times, for example, Homer's *Iliad* and *Odyssey* featured a number of autonomous artificial devices, some of which had intelligence. This was, of course, fiction, as was the case of the talking brass heads attributed to medieval clerics such as Gerbert of Aurillac, Albertus Magnus and Roger Bacon – although these intelligent automata were at least given real people as their creators.

Science-fiction writers went on to devise many robots and other intelligent devices, some friendly, others deadly. And as soon as computing technology had been devised there was speculation that it should be possible to embody intelligence in the machine. The theories on which the first practical artificial intelligence techniques, expert systems, were based had already been developed in the 1930s. At the end of the 1970s, Japan commissioned a three-year study into expert systems, known as fifth-generation computing. There was widespread reaction to this. In Britain, a government-industry body called the Alvey Directorate* was established to investigate AI applications.

Back in 1986, when I was working at British Airways, I made a short film about expert systems, which the airline had just begun to investigate. Note that this was only five years after the IBM PC was launched, two years after the Mac and five years *before* World Wide Web technology was taken up outside of CERN.

In the film, I interviewed James Alty, then professor of computer science at the Turing Institute of the University of Strathclyde. He said: 'I think it's important that we put artificial intelligence into perspective. The word "intelligence" has unfortunate connotations. It tends to raise the expectations far beyond what workers in artificial intelligence intend. AI is concerned with automating thought processes, and this is an incremental process, just like computer science or engineering … Already we've been successful in certain limited areas. If British Airways, or another organisation, thinks that the techniques of

* The Alvey Directorate (sounding impressively like the title of a thriller) was named after its chair, John Alvey, an executive at the British telecommunications company BT.

artificial intelligence can solve all their problems, though, then they're misguided.'

The AI revolution

BA would continue working with AI, but expert systems did not live up to their original promise. Part of the problem was that they relied on humans to codify their expertise. Not only was it very difficult to do this effectively, many experts were reluctant to take part, as they could easily be doing away with their own jobs in the process. It took three components to enable AI to take off: much faster computers, the availability of very large amounts of data (particularly from the internet), and machine-learning algorithms that could improve the quality of their performance with limited human interaction.

Such machine learning was also key to artificial intelligence having a significant role in brainjacking. Expert systems required manual extraction of expertise and painstaking codification of it. But given vast quantities of data, and the use of neural networks, it became possible for an AI system to, at least in part, handle its own learning without consuming expensive expert time.

Neural networks were originally designed to mimic the structure of the brain, assuming this would enable computers to produce human-like thought. This concept failed. But neural networks have re-emerged as the processing hubs of machine-learning systems. A neural network consists of a set of input values (referred to as nodes), linked to several layers of other nodes before producing output values. Each link between nodes has a weight, which determines how much a particular input will influence the value in the next node in the chain.

The power of neural networks is that the weight on each of the links is modified as data is fed into the system. If an outcome is incorrect, the system tweaks the weights to produce a better outcome. Initially, most of this learning process was supervised manually. However, to achieve the big leap forwards that would come in the twenty-first century, machine learning benefited from being self-guided. This is how, for example, it was possible to produce the AlphaGo AI, which was able to beat all comers at an ancient game.

Go is an ideal game for artificial intelligence to play because the rules are very simple, but playing is hugely complex because of the combinatorial explosion of possible layouts of stones on the board. AlphaGo triumphed not by learning Go strategies as a human might, but by a two-stage process. First, it analysed vast numbers of games, looking not for strategies, but patterns in the data which it could reproduce. It then played randomly using those patterns and was rewarded for winning. As the weights built up in its network, the software was eventually good enough to play against itself, testing different approaches, learning even more in the process.

It is worth stressing that this did not make AlphaGo intelligent in the human sense. Ask it to draw a picture or play a different game and it would fail miserably. It was totally focused on that role – and it did not know it was playing a game. It was simply looking for patterns in data. Although game playing is not of great value in itself, the approach taken could then be reused, starting from scratch and training the software up in a different field. The biggest success to date has arguably been AlphaFold, which looks at the different ways that complex protein molecules can fold up in three dimensions. The resultant shape has a major influence on many biological processes and the software has the potential to speed up many biological and pharmacological investigations, though as yet it is better at acting as a filter on what to look at in more detail than producing absolute results.

Let's have a chat

The next step forward was the development of generative AI. The most familiar examples of these are so-called chatbots, such as ChatGPT and Gemini. The term chatbot originates from software written to emulate human-like responses when having a (text-based) chat with them. This may seem a limited application, but the amount of effort put into the field reflects the Turing test for machine intelligence. This test, based on a paper by the computing pioneer Alan Turing, requires human interlocuters to decide whether the responses they receive remotely are coming from a human or a computer.

Chatbots have been around since the 1960s, when software called ELIZA was developed. This is a very simple program designed to act like a psychoanalyst, giving it the opportunity to turn back a lot of what you say to it as questions. You can try out a version of ELIZA at bit.ly/brainjacking12 – it only has around 400 lines of code, but can still handle a simple, if often frustrating conversation. Far more sophisticated versions have been developed since, but none came close to the capabilities of ChatGPT and its competitors.

In practice, the modern 'large language model' chatbots (LLMs) do far more than have a convincing chat with the end user. Because they have the whole of the accessible internet to call on – something that has raised significant issues of copyright misuse that at the time of writing have not been settled – the LLMs are able to respond convincingly to requests to write material, whether it is an essay for school or university, an article for a magazine or a section of a book (see page 194). They are also able, for instance, to check software code or to write poetry on a given topic in any style.

How deep is your fake?

Perhaps the biggest brainjacking concern that current AI presents is the ability to produce fake political material, whether to help win an election or to support a particular cause. As we saw in the social media chapter, there is limited evidence that hyper-targeted advertising has had much real effect on election outcomes. But could the same argument be applied to a video showing a political candidate committing a deeply offensive act? Or recordings of Hollywood stars supporting a policy that in reality they totally oppose?

The speed with which AI has progressed in the third decade of the twenty-first century means that for the first time it is possible to produce such 'deepfake' videos or audio cheaply, quickly and in a highly convincing form. And there is no doubt that there are malicious actors, whether they be foreign powers or supporters of extreme politics, who would be prepared to use such material to sway voters' opinions.

In 2023, the UK's National Cyber Security Centre, part of the electronic security service GCHQ, published its annual review.* One of the case studies in the report looks at the ways in which Russia presents an 'acute and chronic cyber threat':

> It is no secret that Russia seeks to weaken and divide their adversaries by interfering in elections using mis- and dis-information, cyber attacks, and other methods. The UK government assesses that it is almost certain that Russian actors sought to interfere in the 2019 general election. In the coming months [of 2024], with UK and US elections on the horizon we can expect to see the integrity of our systems tested again.

---

* www.ncsc.gov.uk/files/Annual_Review_2023.pdf.

A second case study in the report is particularly relevant here. It looks at 'Defending our democracy in a new digital age'. This identifies a number of potential threats from AI, noting that 'rather than presenting entirely new risks, it is AI's ability to enable existing techniques which poses the biggest threat'. AI makes what was previously a difficult, highly expensive task – which meant it was only ever occasionally used – trivial to achieve.

Partly this refers to the products of large language models like ChatGPT. Their ability to generate realistic and persuasive text makes it far easier to flood social media, pour out emails and generate more convincing propaganda material. Similarly, we have seen fake images from PhotoShop in the past, or bogus audio apparently of well-known individuals provided by impersonators. But AI's ability to produce deepfake videos and audio recordings that are extremely convincing is not just better than what came before – it is also far cheaper and easier to produce.

Small-scale examples of audio deepfakes occurred in 2023 – in the UK, for example, clips were circulated in September in which Labour Party leader Sir Keir Starmer appeared to be verbally abusive to staff, while in November a bogus recording of London mayor Sadiq Khan was shared in which 'he' said that Armistice Day (the anniversary of the end of the First World War on 11 November) should be moved to make room for a pro-Palestinian march.

Both of these clips could have been produced in the past by using impersonators. But the AI versions sounded more distinctively real – and were far easier to produce. In both cases, the clips were immediately denounced as fakes, but this didn't stop millions from hearing them – and for those who get their news solely from social media, it is entirely possible that they never realised they were listening to facsimiles, because they would not have been given any context.

Close to an election, such fake audio or video can have much more leverage, as there may not be time for anyone to register that this is an AI creation rather than the real thing. Something like this happened in 2023, when an apparent recording of Michal Šimečka, who hoped to become prime minister of Slovakia, emerged in which he appeared to discuss rigging the election. While it's not certain that Šimečka's party would have won the election without the recording, there is no doubt that it would have damaged his standing, released as it was immediately before polling, with no time for the media to discredit it.

Taking it to the next level

In his book *The Coming Wave*, Mustafa Suleyman, a co-founder of DeepMind, the company behind AlphaGo and AlphaFold, suggests that AI deepfake-based disinformation will be a significant threat, both in straightforward politics and also in the propaganda produced by terrorists. He points out that videos of radical preacher Anwar al-Awlaki 'inspired the Boston Marathon bombers, the attackers of Charlie Hebdo in Paris, and the shooter who killed forty-nine people at an Orlando nightclub'.

Al-Awlaki is dead, but his videos continued to inspire would-be terrorists after his death: Suleyman suggests that AI could be used to 'uncover' new deepfake videos that continue to spread al-Awlaki's message – and that as AI develops, the potential for such dark manipulation becomes far worse. Suleyman notes:

> Soon these videos will be fully and believably interactive. You are talking directly to him. He knows you and adapts to your dialect and style, plays on your history, your personal grievances, your bullying at school, your terrible, immoral Westernized parents. This is not disinformation as carpet bombing: it's disinformation as surgical strike.

The nightmare scenario that Suleyman paints is that as AI gets more effective, it will also be able to create a full backstory for fake events and messages, planting information online in ways that would back up these fakes, making them virtually impossible to accurately check out: 'Individual citizens won't have time or the tools to verify a fraction of the content coming their way. Fakes will easily pass sophisticated checks, let alone a two-second smell test.' Whether these attempts come from terrorists, malicious state-sponsored attacks or politicians looking for an edge, AI has the potential in the future to make the truth far harder to determine.

Fighting the fakes

We aren't there yet, though – and for the moment there are still some possibilities for defence. Countering deepfakes requires a degree of trust on behalf of the public. In the 1960s a political scandal rocked the UK, involving Secretary of State for War John Profumo and Lord Astor. At a subsequent trial, Astor denied having an affair with a key witness, Mandy Rice-Davies. She famously remarked: 'Well, he would say that, wouldn't he?' It feels quite natural to agree.

If you are a member of the public who is suspicious of the establishment (a trait that is far more common now than it was in the 1960s), you may well have a similar response when the claim is made that an embarrassing video or audio recording is fake. At the very least, though, it is important that awareness of the abilities of AI are widespread and that checks on fakes come from more trusted sources than politicians alone.

We have already seen (see page 49) the rise of fact-checking websites, but they only tend to be used by those who already suspect something is wrong with a media story. Meanwhile, governments are attempting to counter deepfake brainjacking by a combination of legislation and education. Efforts to regulate online information are very difficult to enforce – but, for instance, in October 2023 the US put forward proposals that included the need for AI-generated material to be watermarked so that it can be clearly identified. Legislation has also been proposed to make it illegal to create a 'digital depiction' of a real person (whether alive or dead).

Both the EU and the UK also have legislation on the way that attempts to control the output of AI – but, as has been the case with social media, it is much easier to put forward suggested controls than it is to deploy them. There is no doubt that this kind of legislation would limit the use of amateur deepfakes, produced using commercial products, but it wouldn't make a difference when, say, rogue states are using their own homegrown technology.

In discussing the potential impact of deepfakes in upcoming elections, the BBC quoted the director general of MI5, Ken McCallum, as saying that awareness and checking for deepfakes may make those attempting to influence the outcome of elections use a different approach: 'So I wouldn't want to make some sort of strong prediction that [deepfakes] will feature in the forthcoming election, but we would be not doing our jobs properly if we didn't really think through the possibility.'

The same report* suggests that AI could influence us by putting together more effective spear phishing emails. We have already seen in Chapter 5 how fraudsters make use of phishing emails – spear phishing refers to a particularly sophisticated version of such an email that is more personalised to the individual, making use of data that is stolen or gathered from the internet to encourage a response.

This careful form of attack might seem to counter the idea that many phishing emails are deliberately poor quality to catch out the gullible. But here the intent is often different. A

---

* The BBC report on AI and election interference is www.bbc.co.uk/news/uk-politics-67518511.

fraudulent phishing email that results in a long conversation with, say, a Nigerian prince, and requires money transfers to be able to release locked-away millions, may well benefit from a credulous recipient. But spear phishing emails often require just a few clicks to enable malicious software to infect a computer. As such it is far more important that the email looks authentic.

What AI brings to bear here is the ability to pull together information about an individual from a wide range of sources, making it possible to tailor the attack so that the recipient is more likely to click on a link or an attachment. Such an AI-driven attack cannot be prevented by legislation. All that can sensibly be done is a combination of better anti-attack software monitoring emails and education to prevent users clicking on links and attachments without checking them out (just as education is essential about the ease with which images, videos and audio recording can be faked).

Such education will only ever reach a percentage of the population, though. And in the right circumstances even a careful individual can slip up. Generally speaking, I don't click on any links in emails without first hovering the mouse cursor over them and seeing where the link points to. (This means never clicking a link on a phone, where this isn't safely possible.) Similarly, in the rare cases that I get an email from an unknown source with an attachment and still want to open it, I first check it out with my antivirus software.

Checking the destination of a link reduces the threat from many dubious emails. However, I did once get an email just after making a payment to the online auction site eBay. The email queried a payment I had just made – so I clicked the link and logged in. But the login failed. Now suspicious, I checked the link, and with a sinking feeling discovered it was fake. I'd just given my eBay password to someone else. Within seconds I then changed the password, and had no comeback as a result. But it was a close call because of the coincidence of the timing of my

ChatGPT's opinion

It seemed appropriate to ask the generative AI tool ChatGPT about the potential danger of generative AI for elections. Incidentally, I asked for references, which I haven't given here. Most of the references were legitimate, but at least one was made up by the software, which as yet is a distinct failing of generative AIs. Here's ChatGPT's response:

Introduction

In recent years, the rise of generative artificial intelligence (AI) has brought about numerous advancements in various fields, but it has also raised concerns about its potential misuse, particularly in the context of elections. Generative AI, capable of producing realistic and convincing content, poses a significant threat to the integrity of electoral processes worldwide. This article delves into the potential dangers associated with the use of generative AI in elections, exploring its impact on misinformation, deepfakes, political manipulation, and the overall trust in democratic systems.

Misinformation and Manipulation

Generative AI, equipped with deep learning algorithms, has the ability to generate realistic text, images, and even videos that are indistinguishable from authentic content. This capability raises the specter of widespread misinformation campaigns during elections. Political actors with malicious intent could use generative AI to create convincing fake news stories, social media posts, and other content designed to deceive voters.

Such misinformation can influence public opinion, sway voter preferences, and ultimately undermine the democratic process. The challenge for election officials and platforms is to differentiate between genuine and AI-generated content, as the latter can be crafted to mimic the tone, style, and context of legitimate sources.

Deepfakes and Candidate Manipulation

One of the most concerning applications of generative AI in elections is the creation of deepfake videos, where AI-generated content replaces the likeness and voice of real individuals. Candidates could be targeted with manipulated videos that portray them making false statements, engaging in inappropriate behavior, or expressing opinions contrary to their actual beliefs.

The potential impact of deepfake videos on elections is substantial, as they have the potential to tarnish a candidate's reputation and credibility. Voters may be misled by these sophisticated manipulations, eroding trust in the electoral process and casting doubt on the authenticity of political discourse.

Amplification of Political Polarization

Generative AI can be programmed to exploit existing political divides by generating content that caters specifically to certain ideological groups. This targeted approach may exacerbate political polarization by creating and disseminating content that reinforces pre-existing beliefs, amplifying echo chambers, and deepening societal divisions.

The consequence of this polarization is a fractured electorate that is less open to dialogue and compromise. As generative AI contributes to the creation of content tailored to specific political demographics, it poses a threat to the democratic ideal of fostering an informed and engaged citizenry capable of making independent and well-informed decisions.

The erosion of trust can have far-reaching consequences, affecting voter turnout, political engagement, and the overall health of democratic institutions. To address this challenge, election authorities must invest in robust strategies for detecting and countering AI-generated content while educating the public about the potential dangers and vulnerabilities associated with generative AI.

Conclusion

Generative AI presents a double-edged sword in the realm of elections. While its potential applications for positive contributions are vast,* its misuse poses significant threats to the integrity of democratic processes. From misinformation campaigns to deepfake videos and the amplification of political polarization, the dangers associated with generative AI in elections demand urgent attention.

Addressing these challenges requires a multi-faceted approach, involving collaboration between technology developers, election authorities, policymakers, and the public. Striking a balance between innovation and regulation is crucial to harness the benefits of generative AI while mitigating its potential risks.† As the field of AI continues to evolve, safeguarding the democratic foundation of elections becomes paramount to ensuring the continued trust and participation of citizens in the political process.

---

* It's hard not to believe that ChatGPT's assertion that generative AI's 'potential applications for positive contributions [to elections] are vast' feels a little defensive. I asked what they were and they amounted to improved voter engagement (by doing the same thing described above as amplification of polarisation), improving election systems and better analytics.

† As Mandy Rice-Davies might have said, it would say that, wouldn't it?

action and the email that apparently came in response to that.*

AI may well enable this kind of apparent coincidence to happen more often – I certainly have never trusted any email of this kind since.

We know what you're thinking

So far, we have been considering AI's potential to change our opinions and thoughts. However, it is also worth considering if AI can turn the tables, not so much telling us what to think, but telling other people what we are thinking – which has a huge potential to then be turned around for brainjacking purposes. We have already seen the overblown threat of neuromarketing (see page 136), but there are wider potential possibilities.

A 2023 *Times* article by Rhys Blakely was headlined 'AI will read your mind sooner than you think' and described AI-based approaches to gaining direct access to our brains' activities. This has long been a desire, not so much for Big Brother monitoring (though if it were possible to undertake remotely, it's hard to imagine that such mental snooping wouldn't be the key application), but to provide medical support for people who have lost the ability to interface with their body, or the wider world, as a result of brain or nervous system damage.

The newspaper headline was sensationalist, but there was a small factual core to the story. Researchers at the University of California, Berkeley claim to have been able to reproduce a rock song that people were listening to, with AI

* The possibility of having a password harvested, as happened with my eBay password, is why it's essential not to use the same password for multiple sites.

software recreating the song from brain activity. Using Pink Floyd's very distinctive song 'Another Brick in the Wall', the team led by Ludovic Bellier and Robert Knight claimed that in one test with a single subject, their models 'provided a level of spectrotemporal details high enough to recognise the song'.

In another example they claimed 'we retrieved partial vocals e.g., in P15, "all," "was," and "just a brick" were the only recognizable syllables'. After checking out the study, this seems worryingly like self-deception. You can no more hear words in their samples than you can in a keyboard solo. The audio they produced is available to listen to online.* I'm a big fan of Pink Floyd, and I can say with some certainty that it is totally impossible to recognise the song from the synthesiser-like noise produced. And bear in mind, to test this possibility the listener should not know what the song is: I couldn't recognise it even though I knew what it was supposed to be. It is worth noting, though, that in another experiment, AI software was able to make a (significantly better) visual approximation to what someone was looking at from MRI scan data,† though there isn't enough evidence to be sure how fine-tuned the approach used was to enable image reproduction – and MRI is never likely to be available as a wearable accessory or to scan remotely.

This reflects a big proviso that makes that headline of AI reading your mind soon seem far less likely. Neither of the examples above involved anything as unobtrusive as a helmet or array

* The paper is 'Music can be reconstructed from human auditory cortex activity using nonlinear decoding models' by Ludovic Bellier et al. You can access the sample with the claim that the song is recognisable at bit.ly/brainjacking2 and the version with the claimed recognisable words at bit.ly/brainjacking3.

† You can see the reconstructed images at the researchers' website sites.google.com/view/stablediffusion-with-brain.

of sensors placed on the head, let alone some means of remote detection of brain activity. An MRI scan is hardly subtle surveillance. And to allegedly reproduce parts of the song required probes to be inserted into the brain. Enthusiasts for this kind of technology usually wildly underplay the difficulties of getting a good connection to what's going on inside your skull.

The chances of *Matrix*-style sockets in your head ever being commonplace are low. All physical interaction with the brain involves a risk to the participant – it literally *is* brain surgery. And the human body is not enthusiastic about such intrusion. Most implants' effectiveness deteriorates over time as the body attempts to reject them. For that matter, the benefits obtained from surgical implants over and above external linking through the conventional senses would have to be immense before direct brain wiring was accepted by the general population.

There are, though, concerns inspired by these ideas of human–computer linkages that require less invasive action. In 2023, the UK's Information Commissioner's Office (ICO) released a report called *Tech Futures: Neurotechnology* on the potential for the use and misuse of our brain data. The report suggested that within a few years' time, brain-scanning helmets or other safety equipment might be used to measure how much attention an employee is giving to a task, and what their focus is.

The reasoning for deploying such technology would be given as safety – meaning that it would typically be used in high-risk environments – but there is inevitable concern that it may lead to a dystopian level of monitoring of worker activity, building on supervision that is already considered intrusive in some call centres and warehouses. The ICO is responsible for protecting personal data in the UK and points out that since this 'neurodata' is subconsciously generated, people don't know what is being revealed, and so cannot give informed consent for that data to be released.

While AI is currently oversold as a tool of manipulation, there is no doubt that it takes the advertisers and influencers to a whole new level of sophistication and will continue to be increasingly powerful. But some research suggests that this approach may be unnecessarily heavy handed. Why put all that effort in if we could just change people's minds, manipulating their intentions and ideas with a subtle nudge?

11 INCREMENTAL DISPLACEMENT THEORY

On 8 April 2008 one of the most influential books of the early twenty-first century was published. If it had been an academic work, it might have been titled *Incremental Displacement Theory* … but this was popular psychology, so it was called *Nudge*. In full, the title was *Nudge: Improving decisions about health, wealth and happiness*, by a pair of US writers, economist Richard Thaler and law professor Cass Sunstein.

If it sounds like yet another self-improvement book, that is probably the market the authors had in mind – but it was treated as an instruction manual for subtle brainjacking on a large scale. In 2010, the UK government set up the Behavioural Insights Team based on the concept and widely known as the 'Nudge Unit'. They were not alone – the notion of nudges became an international phenomenon after the publication of the book. The thesis the authors presented was that it's possible to design the way we provide information to avoid the recipient making mistakes and to steer them towards the right choices. To indulge in subtle brainjacking.

Design for life

Designing to influence choice is not an original concept (even though Thaler would win the 2017 Sveriges Riksbank Prize in

Economic Sciences in Memory of Alfred Nobel for the work that *Nudge* is based on). For example, in his classic book from 1988, *The Design of Everyday Things,* American design engineer Don Norman pointed out a number of cases where design had been driven by aesthetics, without consideration of usability. In his book, Norman noted that some totally impractical designs 'probably won a prize'. In other words, design is too often assessed on how attractive something looks, rather than thinking about how its design helps us avoid making mistakes by steering us towards the right choices.

Let's take two simple examples given by Norman. One is the design of cooker hobs. Most hobs have four rings, each requiring a control. Often, the designer puts the controls for the rings in a straight line, because that makes for the most elegant design. However, it's then not obvious which control is responsible for which ring. As a result, the controls have to be labelled to show you their function – and that means wasted time and effort peering at those little icons, trying to work out what they mean.

By contrast, when the (rare) thoughtful designer lays the four controls out in the same orientation as the rings, there can be no doubt: there's no need for the icons. It is entirely obvious, for example, that the top left ring is turned on and off by the top left control. Just rearranging the way the controls are displayed makes the cooker easier to use. I just had a look on a major retailer's website: most of the hobs still have their controls in a straight line. (On a couple of fancy high-end devices, the touch controls were so subtly marked you could not even see them, itself a design issue.)

A second bugbear of Norman's was the use of glass doors with concealed hinges. Quite often in modern commercial design, a door is one of a range of glass panels on the front of a building. Aesthetically speaking, it looks particularly smart if the door is visually identical to the surrounding panels. Thankfully, it is often narrower than the window panels, which makes it easier to find. So, what's the problem? Which side of the door to push to open it. As Norman pointed out, by making the hinges visible, it is obvious which side to push – but when the designer hides the hinges (as is often the case), building users have to resort to putting signs on the relevant side of the door, to avoid causing confusion.

A much more common design fault along the same lines comes when a door needs to be pushed from one side and pulled from the other. There is a very simple way to indicate what to do. You put a pull handle on one side, and a push plate on the other. The user of the door gets it right every time without any effort. But all too often, a designer obsessed with symmetry puts a pull handle on both sides.*

I worked at British Airways at a time when we had moved into a new headquarters building, and I noticed that the designers had done exactly this on the entrance to each of the bathrooms. I spent a happy afternoon monitoring one of these. The way the doors were constructed, to get into the toilet area you had to push the door – but there was a pull handle on the outside as well as the interior. As a result, time after time, someone would walk up to the door, pull the handle, realise it wasn't working and then push it. Hardly anyone ever pushed the handle when they first arrived at the door.

That was many years ago, so you might assume that the lesson has long since been learned. But in my neighbourhood a nice new independent coffee shop has recently opened. I've noticed they've had to put signs on the door saying PULL and PUSH because they too have pull handles on both sides of the door. And even with the signs, around half of the customers

* The true minimalist designer might be tempted to put a push plate on both sides of a door that only opens one way, but in that case the problem caused would become significantly more severe.

try to open the door from the outside incorrectly. This is presumably because they see a pull handle and (rightly) don't feel that they need to read instructions in order to open a door.

Making it easy to deal with a door may seem trivial, but what having a push plate on one side and a pull handle on the other does is to nudge people into taking the correct action: they would avoid wasting time and making mistakes (which leaves them feeling irritated) and be gently prodded into the right choice. It's a subtle influence that is so easy to deploy – yet judging by all those double-pull-handled doors that are still out there, it's also so easy to get wrong.

Interface influences intelligence

Norman was highlighting issues with what computer people call user interface design – the interface between an object and the person who uses it. This has become a major industry with our interactions with computers and phones. If you are old enough to remember using one of the early PCs, working with the operating system DOS involved knowing what to do when presented with a prompt that looked something like:

C:\>

This was the computer's invitation for you to type an instruction (obvious, isn't it?). But unlike typing into a search engine, using plain English would get you nowhere with DOS. You needed to know the exact wording to use to, for example, make a copy of a file or list the contents of a directory (as folders were called back then). Moving to a modern computer or touchscreen phone interface, things have become a lot more intuitive. If a user is confident enough, they can usually find their way around without instruction.

Sometimes visual interfaces can be easy to pick up thanks to a degree of skeuomorphism, the user-interface design term for making elements of a computer program look or act like real-world objects. So, for instance, on the Word software I am using to type this, there is a 'home' button that looks like a house, and a 'print' button that looks like a printer.*

At one point skeuomorphism was taken to ridiculous extremes by some companies – for instance, making a contacts list look like a physical address book, down to the faux leather binding. We have (thankfully) largely moved away from such over-dedication to real world parallels – but there are still plenty of skeuomorphic cues that enable us to undertake an action without making a mistake or needing to be told how to do it.

If, for example, I have a file on the desktop in Windows or on a Mac, I can drag it to the waste bin or trash basket and it disappears. The DOS equivalent would have required me to type something like:

```
DEL C:\desktop\filename.ext
```

And it would only work if I got the spelling and punctuation exactly right. Another example where doing what comes naturally is derived from the real world is dealing with tabs in a web browser. Based on the tabs on filing cabinet folders, most users are aware that they can click on a tab to look at the website

* One danger of designing software controls to represent real-world objects is that the object could become obsolete. The 'Save' button on Word looks like a 3.5-inch diskette, often called a floppy disk after its flexible 5.25-inch predecessors, even though it is rigid. Such diskettes have rarely been used in a couple of decades.

that it 'contains'. But a while ago, I had several tabs open in a browser and wanted to get one of the websites open in a separate window. No one had ever told me or showed me how to do this, but it seemed natural to drag the tab out of the browser window, which opened another window featuring just that tab. The interface designer had anticipated what made sense to a user, making it possible to intuitively use it correctly. I was nudged in the right direction.

Using choice architecture

This, then, is where nudges came from: and their appeal rapidly became apparent. According to Thaler and Sunstein, a nudge is the result of a 'choice architecture' – setting up a situation so that people are more likely to make the choice you want them to choose, without forcing them. It's what the authors (somewhat cringemakingly) call 'libertarian paternalism' – libertarian because we aren't limiting choice, but paternalistic because we are encouraging them (indeed, brainjacking them) to be more likely to make the choice that we decide is best. The authors suggest that the approach involves nudging people towards choices that make their lives 'longer, healthier and better'.

Thaler and Sunstein add in a couple of extra requirements (without justifying them) for their brainjacking attempt to be a nudge. It should 'alter people's behaviour in a predictable way without forbidding any options or significantly changing their economic incentives'. This means, they claim, that nudges must be both easy *and cheap* [my emphasis] if they are to remain libertarian. It's not a nudge if there are fines or subsidies involved.

The poster child for nudging, both from its position in the book and its apparent brilliance, involves organ donation. Around the world, countries and healthcare systems have struggled to get sufficient donor organs to meet the needs of potential transplant recipients. According to Thaler and Sunstein, one step towards making the system better was a subtle but hugely effective nudge. Some systems are opt-in. Individuals have to tick a box if they wish to be organ donors. Other countries go for opt-out. You are presumed to be a donor unless you specify otherwise. And that simple switch of the action generated by the tick box has the potential to make a big difference to take-up of organ donation.

To give Thaler and Sunstein their due, they did say that while the nudge makes a significant difference to those saying that they are willing to donate, it isn't sufficient to improve the rates of donation. Where the switch has been made, there has not been a significant difference in the number of transplants as a result. To make that happen requires a major change to the healthcare system to match potential donors to recipients and to make it possible for the transplant to successfully take place. Usually, these system issues are much more expensive to solve and provide the biggest hurdle – they certainly aren't susceptible to nudges. There is no doubt that opt-out results in more *potential* donors, but it's hard to believe the assertion in the book that switching to opt-out saves thousands of lives.

There are a couple of provisos to bear in mind when making the leap from the organ donor problem to the wider policy applications of nudges, and to deciding that nudging is a useful form of brainjacking. Firstly, the reality is that the move to organ donor opt-out involves an unusual form of decision. Most decisions that a government, or a business, would like to sway are not as simple as choosing whether or not to tick a box. Secondly, many of the issues where nudges have been considered may not be immediately attractive to the general population. Governments, for example, may want to nudge voters towards an unpopular policy. But very few people think that organ donation is a bad thing. They may decide not to do it, but they are still able to see the potential benefits to the population at large.

For organ donation, the move to opt-out was not a useful nudge in its own right. But a better demonstration where the concept of moving from opt-in to opt-out can be effective was the UK's 2012 move (inspired by the Behavioural Insights Team nudge unit) to require workers to opt-out of workplace pensions, rather than to opt-in. Like the organ donation situation, most agree that pensions are a good thing – but a good number of workers didn't get round to it when it was opt-in. Because the infrastructure to make this happen was much simpler, the nudge here created by switching to opt-out was far more successful.

Another example that Thaler and Sunstein use involves an (imaginary) director of food services for a school group. With guidance from a consultant who works with supermarkets, the director, Caroline, experiments by placing, say, desserts first or last in the servery, and by choosing whether to put, say, French fries or carrot sticks at eye level. The authors suggest that Caroline is a 'choice architect' who has considerable power. She can engage in brainjacking by deciding how to place the items and shift behaviour – whether it is towards healthier food, or to generate more profit.

The important lesson we can draw from this example is that there is no such thing as being neutral. Anything that involves design, for example, has an element of brainjacking, whether it is intentional or accidental. Whichever way the food is presented and arranged in a supermarket or canteen will have some influence on choice. While it seems likely that nudge supporters overplay the extent of that influence, there will surely be some.

Is it really a nudge?

Perhaps the most bizarre example Thaler and Sunstein give in framing an action as a nudge comes in the form of daylight saving or summer time. This is the idea of moving clocks forward for summer and back for winter to better match the working day to daylight hours. According to *Nudge*, 'surveys reveal that many (though by no means all) people think that daylight saving time is a great idea'. Yet I've never come across anyone who likes it and many countries are thinking of moving away from it. The authors describe daylight saving as something that nudges us into waking up an hour earlier. But by their own definition, this isn't a nudge, as you don't have a realistic choice. Not putting your clocks forward, for instance, isn't an option when that means you will be late for work every day, will miss every timed event and generally will fail at life.

The outcomes of nudges sound very impressive in the book – until you examine them in a little more detail. We've already seen that moving organ donation to opt-out, rather than opt-in, has had hardly any effect alone on the rate of transplants. Another of the book's apparently impressive examples features an anti-littering campaign in Texas.

Faced with a serious litter problem, rather than trying to persuade people it was their civic duty not to litter, the campaign designers opted for a combination of a zippy slogan – 'Don't mess with Texas' – and a TV campaign where players for the Dallas Cowboys American football team crushed cans and menacingly uttered the slogan. According to Thaler and Sunstein, the result was the amount of litter dropping by 29 per cent, while visible roadside litter dropped by 72 per cent. 'All this happened,' they tell us, 'without the use of any mandates, threats or coercion but rather via a creative nudge.'

Except. What is omitted in the story, but is highlighted in Michael Hobbes and Peter Shamshiri's podcast *If Books Could Kill*, is the way that the state put up signs along the highways saying there was an 'up to $2,000 fine' for littering. That sounds ever so much like coercion by threat. It's also not mentioned that Texas introduced a programme where volunteers did regular litter clean-up days – relying on exactly the kind of civic duty we're told wouldn't do the job without the nudge. When there's less litter already, there is good evidence that people drop less. The overall campaign can hardly be seen as a nudge by the book's definition.

Another example where nudges seemed to be given far more weight than they deserved was in an experiment in the US state of Minnesota to see if a change in wording would result in greater compliance to tax collection. They tried four different messages, each used on a separate group of people. One message pointed out how taxes supported education, the emergency services and so on. A second described the punishment that came with non-compliance. A third told how to get help to fill the form in correctly, while a fourth made it clear that more than 90 per cent of Minnesotans complied in full with their tax obligations.

If you are at all familiar with the way nudges are supposed to work, you won't be surprised that we are told that only the last approach had a significant effect. But there are problems here. One is that the definition of a nudge is so vague that as long as it's not an enforced choice or results in a large penalty (despite their aversion to fines, the authors give examples of nudges that involve losing or gaining money), practically anything done to elicit a change of behaviour can be described as nudge. Only one of the four tax examples mentioned a penalty. At the very least three of the approaches could be called nudges – the only reason that the fourth message was picked out seems to have been that it could be said to have had a 'significant effect' on compliance.

The other problem is that the data supporting this isn't great. Bear in mind that in scientific language a 'significant' effect does not have to be a large one – it can be tiny, as long as it seems statistically likely to hold. What is usually meant by a significant effect in psychology studies is that if we assume the null hypothesis – that the effect we're studying doesn't exist – there is only a one in twenty chance that you would get the result that is recorded. But it says nothing about the size of the effect.

The fourth tax message saying '90 per cent complied' produced only a tiny change in what was wanted: the size of the tax revenues. And in some parts of the experimental sample, the threat produced far greater revenues than the compliance argument, while in others the '90 per cent complied' approach reduced revenues. Nudges are sometimes portrayed as universal solutions, but they clearly aren't – and depending on the population distribution they can have an overall negative effect. To be fair to Thaler and Sunstein, they do say 'Populations are not all alike' – but it does seem that in trying to portray the power of nudges they then ignore their own statement.

A tradition of behavioural insights

As we have seen, as a result of the book, the concept of nudges has been taken up by governments in a number of countries – after all, what government would have a problem with the idea of brainjacking their population in a way that's cheap and non-coercive? In the UK, the government's Behavioural Insights Team was set up in 2010 to take a nudge-style approach. In his book *Inside the Nudge Unit,** behavioural scientist David Halpern, who headed up the team, gives examples of nudges that occurred in history before the concept was labelled as such.

Halpern points out, for example, that in the early days of motoring many accidents were caused by cars cornering too quickly, resulting in them cutting across the road and getting in the path of an oncoming vehicle. Painting a broken white line down the middle of the road reduced this tendency by nudging drivers without any enforcement. More recently, this idea has been extended to protect villages on high-speed country roads.

---

* See Further Discovery section.

To keep speeds down, the section of road through the village is painted red, with white stripes down each side of the road that make the road feel narrower than it really is: this does seem to encourage motorists to take more care.

We've already seen the benefits of a nudge in workplace pensions – but others of Halpern's bigger attempts have had a more mixed outcome. In his book, Halpern describes how effective e-cigarettes – what we now often call vaping – had been as a way to help people quit smoking. Arguably the vapes could be considered a nudge because they weren't forced on the smokers in any way, but made it easier to move away from cigarettes.

However, vaping demonstrates the danger of applying nudges to a major issue without thinking through the potential consequences. The very fact that they were a nudge, rather than, say, a medically prescribed alternative (with the associated controls and balances), has made e-cigarettes a thorny issue. Halpern comments: 'One concern was that e-cigs might pull in non-smokers, but again the numbers did not suggest this.'

This might have been true when Halpern's book was published in 2015, but he was reckoning without the e-cigarette manufacturers' realisation that they could undertake a nudge of their own. As we saw on page 95, by making vapes with all sorts of sweet-like flavours and packaging them like toys, not surprisingly, they found that a big market opened up for teenagers to start using e-cigarettes. At the time of writing, the UK government is planning to take action to prevent this, but no legislation has yet been produced. Perhaps nudges are best left to circumstances where they don't have the potential to cause harm.

Cheap and cheerful – but effective?

Arguably, examples like painting lines on roads are genuine and effective example of nudges (that didn't need the book to make happen) – there is no enforcement, but they do change behaviour. However, it seems likely that, like many of the *Nudge* book examples, the benefits reaped by the UK government's nudge unit often had small impacts, if any. There is indubitably an argument that as it can be very cheap to do, even a small beneficial change makes nudging worthwhile, so there is no reason not to do this – it's just that nudges have been hyped beyond their capabilities.

The nudge theory has also spread to some local councils. In *Nudge* we are told that 'in the Royal Borough of Windsor and Maidenhead, a London suburb,* citizens could sign up for a rewards program in which they earned points depending on the weight of the material they recycled. The points were good for discounts at merchants in the area. Recycling increased by 35%.' The UK government was excited about this, and in 2010 praised the scheme and said that the (then newly elected) coalition government would be 'encouraging councils which want to get involved in such reward programmes'.

It never happened. There have been a few half-hearted schemes launched, but no big roll out. A 2016 review† found that 'Overall, schemes did not experience a sea change in recycling tonnage, participation or claimed behaviour.' On a wider scale, a study of schemes in the US, UK and Canada‡ found 'the effectiveness of the reward or incentive schemes in promoting domestic waste recycling is doubtful'. The scheme hasn't operated in Windsor and Maidenhead for years, which itself is suggestive of the way such schemes can have a brief benefit

---

* I suspect most residents of Windsor or Maidenhead would be more than a little affronted to be told that they lived in a suburb of London.

† The 2016 review of recycling reward schemes by Brook Lyndhurst is available at randd.defra.gov.uk/ProjectDetails?ProjectId=18513.

‡ The study of schemes in the US, UK and Canada by Yung Yau is referenced at www.circularonline.co.uk/opinions/recycling-rewards-scheme-chips/.

when trialled that rapidly evaporates if the nudge is made a policy.

Bear in mind bias

The whole idea of nudges as presented by Thaler and Sunstein is inspired by the biases that we naturally exhibit. Over the years, the fields of psychology and behavioural economics have bombarded us with a long of list of these biases. Being biased sounds inherently to be a bad thing, but these biases often reflect the shortcuts that we use to deal with the world around us. In a dangerous world, there isn't always time to sit down and patiently weigh the pros and cons of how to act. We have to rapidly assess the situation, make a best guess of what to do and act quickly.

This is fine, but it does mean applying a whole lot of assumptions about the environment, our situation and our capabilities that may be incorrect. Our mental wiring to come up with these snap decisions means that in some circumstances we can fail. For example, recognising faces and objects is so important to dealing with the world around us that we tend to see patterns that don't really exist, a phenomenon known as pareidolia. This is behind many ghost sightings, and the discovery of what appeared to be a giant face on the surface of Mars, which totally disappeared once more detail was available for the image.

Similarly, psychologists have come up with many cognitive biases that we apply in aspects of decision making. For example, there's confirmation bias, where we take more notice of information that confirms our existing opinions; implicit bias, where we apply stereotypes and generalisations; and overconfidence bias, where we overrate our own abilities. Another favourite bias is loss aversion – the idea that we are more influenced by losing something of a particular value than we are by gaining something of the same value.

However, we can overstate the importance of biases. For example, a frequently used example of overconfidence bias is that the majority of people think they are better than average drivers. This isn't a great example, as it is very likely that more than half of people *are* better than average, assuming that by 'average' we mean the mean. It is far more likely that a subset of drivers are really bad than it is that a subset are unusually good. This will drag the mean well below the median, meaning that indeed more than half of drivers are better than average.

Nudges are designed to make use of biases to produce a touch of sneaky brainjacking. If we understand biases, we can present information and design environments in a way that users will be nudged by those biases towards the desired outcomes. There is a problem here. Many results produced by experimental psychology in the period relied on by Thaler and Sunstein have proved impossible to reproduce in what has been referred to as the replication crisis. Huge numbers of the studies involved too small a sample of individuals, had poorly designed protocols or manipulated the data to produce invalid statistical significance. And this applies to much of the research supporting biases. For example, Thaler and Sunstein tell us that 'the prospect of losing something makes you twice as miserable as the prospect of gaining the same thing makes you happy' – but this isn't borne out by reliable studies.

The other issue with nudges, as we have seen, is that those who favour them can label any action that produces a positive result a nudge, while anything that doesn't is excluded from consideration, a scientific no-no known as cherry picking. In the book *Nudge* we are told of a Yale University study where students were given information about the importance of having a tetanus jab, but only 3 per cent took up the vaccination. Another group got the same talk, but were given a map with the location of the health centre, were asked to check their weekly schedules, make a plan for when they would go (which could have encouraged them to add a visit to their calendar), and asked to decide the route they'd take.

Thaler and Sunstein tell us uptake in this group was 28 per cent (still rather low to my mind). 'Notice,' they say, 'that this manipulation was very subtle.' In essence, they are saying, this was a nudge in action. Really? Telling them where to go, getting them to check their diary for a good time – this isn't a nudge, it's how you book a meeting or get a student to a lecture. There is nothing subtle about it. Similarly, the authors describe a warning buzzer that sounds when you fail to fasten your seatbelt as a nudge – but surely alarms are too heavy-handed to be a nudge? When an alarm goes off, it makes it pretty well impossible to proceed without doing something. This is not choice architecture.

The concept of nudges is not worthless. They do appear to have some effect. We do have biases, and nudges can influence us in small ways. But their impact is far smaller than the nudge industry has sold it to be – and that's if we also accept that nudges sometimes need supplementing, whether by the whole surrounding system that lay behind improved organ transplants, or the financial penalties that in reality made other apparent so-called nudges viable.

Nudges are designed to be subtle attempts to influence – but there are some potential aspects of brainjacking that are so subtle that we are not supposed to even be aware that anything is happening. It's time to get subliminal.

12 SUBLIMINAL

What do the words 'subliminal advertising' bring to mind? Perhaps a devious villain persuading individuals to act against their will by flashing secret messages onto a cinema screen. Or, if we widen that to subliminal influencing, what about the abilities of the hypnotist to persuade victims to perform a ridiculous act without their knowledge, or the psychological technique of priming, which is said to be able to influence our decisions without any conscious awareness of it happening?

It would be a good start to unpack that Victorian-feeling word 'subliminal'. It dates back at least to the 1880s and refers to something – a sensory stimulus or influence – that is below the limits of conscious awareness (*'limen'* is the Latin word for a threshold). It is, if you like, unnoticeable or unnoticed brainjacking that nonetheless changes the way we think or behave. Unlike other examples of brainjacking it is arguable that subliminal forms are always manipulative, though some are self-inflicted.

A flicker in the film

We can pin down the term 'subliminal advertising' very precisely to 1957, because the concept emerges from a single piece of work.* This archetypal example of subliminal advertising involved inserting very short prompts into a cinema film, which were on screen for too short a time to be noticed as anything more than a flicker. Despite this, it was claimed that those prompts modified the audience's behaviour.

The way moving pictures work is a subliminal illusion in itself. A film or video does not consist of truly continuous motion but rather a series of still images, each shown for a very short period of time – typically between 30 and 60 of these 'frames' are displayed per second. The effect was familiar from toys predating moving pictures, such as the phenakistiscope and zoetrope, dating back to 1833 and 1866 respectively, which used a slit to get brief views of still pictures on a rotating disc or drum.

In the nineteenth century, the explanation for this illusion was 'persistence of vision', a concept that is still regularly mentioned today, although it has long since been dismissed scientifically. The suggestion is that the brain retains one image long enough to overlap with the next, simulating the effect of motion – but in reality, imposing one image on another just produces a visual mess. As we saw in Chapter 5, the reality is that the eye/brain systems do not work on what is seen as a whole entity, but build a picture up from various features. And it is the way that these mental systems analyse the makeup of the information coming from the optic nerve that gives the impression of movement from a series of still images.

Replacing a couple of frames of the moving pictures with something else – text or imagery – will appear as a slight glitch

---

* There is a claim that subliminal advertising had previously been used in a 1947 Daffy Duck cartoon. This features a rapidly rotating statue, whose shield shows the words 'Buy Bonds' in an attempt to increase buying of war bonds, but it's arguable this isn't subliminal as it's obvious it is happening; it's just not clear what the words say without slowing the cartoon down.

in the video or film, but the viewers will not be consciously aware of the content. However, the principle behind subliminal advertising is that such an intervention produces a brainjacking effect, changing the viewers' feelings or needs. Such was the concern from the 1957 article on subliminal advertising that making use of such messages was made illegal in a number of countries, such as the UK, and carefully controlled in others, such as the US, where it is considered unfair practice.

What happened in 1957 is often described as an experiment, but more realistically it could be called a publicity stunt. The 'scientist' behind it was James Vicary, a market researcher. In a piece in the marketing industry magazine *Advertising Age*, Vicary claimed to have tried out subliminal images on over 45,000 people in a movie theatre in New Jersey (not all at once), as a result of which he found that there was an 18.1 per cent increase in sales of Coca-Cola and a 57.5 per cent increase in sales of popcorn. Impressive stuff.

There is no doubt that managers of cinemas have attempted manipulation of their audiences in various ways to make more money. My father was friends with the manager of one of the cinemas in my original hometown of Rochdale back in the 1950s and 1960s. At this time a visit to the cinema usually included an interval, when most food and drink was purchased. The manager confessed that, half an hour before the interval, they used to crank the heating up to full, in the hope of increasing sales of ice cream and drinks.

However, Vicary was claiming something far more specific and focused than fiddling with the thermostat – the ability to influence sales of a specific product with his hidden messages. However, this was not a properly run scientific trial – we are not even sure it was undertaken at all. Vicary gave no description of how the comparison was made with sales without the subliminal messages, nor was there any detail of his methods. Inevitably, there were many attempts to reproduce Vicary's results – it appears that the only certain brainjacking here was the brief increase in clients enjoyed by Vicary's company.

Prime viewing

If there was any impact from subliminal advertising at all, it would be due to a psychological theory known as priming. This is a suggested effect where participants in studies appear to act differently if they have been subliminally primed by more or less subtle mentions of the subject beforehand. This sounds a lot more promising than the crude nature of subliminal advertising, but there is a sting in the tail of priming, as we will discover.

Priming features in the work of someone we have already met, TV and stage magician Derren Brown. In a TV episode called 'How to Control the Nation', Brown claimed to use priming to change subjects' viewpoints and also to create a short film with subliminal prompts that would leave the audience glued to their seats – not literally (no glue was involved), but preventing them from being able to stand up when they attempted to do so.

In the show, Brown started with a couple of relatively simple demonstrations of what he claimed was priming. For example, he asked an audience member to choose one of ten blank cards – and it turned out to be the only one that said 'Lose' (as opposed to 'Win') on the other side. Brown claimed this was due to subliminal priming, as that card had 'pick me' written in invisible ink on the back, which he later made visible with ultraviolet light. It's just about possible that this was sufficiently on the edge of visibility to be subliminally noticeable, but it's worth bearing in mind that Brown uses psychological pseudo-explanations to increase the impact of traditional conjuring tricks – and forcing a particular card on an individual is one of the oldest in the book of stage magicians' standards.

Brown then took the process to the next level. A subject was brought into the five-storey toy shop Hamley's in London's Regent Street. After passing through the store accompanied by Brown, the participant was asked to mentally select any toy from the thousands available without saying anything. She chose a cuddly giraffe. Subsequently, Brown demonstrated that he had pre-selected this item in suitably dramatic fashion with an enormous stuffed giraffe arriving outside the store. We are then shown a series of priming opportunities that were encountered in the initial tour. Remember, priming is supposed to bias someone by subliminally exposing them to prompts. The most obvious of these to viewers was a wall panel with a giraffe pattern, but Brown pointed out that he mimed a giraffe while talking about 'various spots' around the store. He also said 'did you have a favourite toy' by running the words 'did you have' together so they sounded a little like 'giraffe', they passed T-shirts with giraffes on, and so forth.

Is this credible? It's arguable there was some pre-selection. The subject was a young woman – at one point on her tour both she and Brown called the items on one level 'boy's toys' – it's arguable that a similar-aged man would not have chosen a cuddly giraffe. While it's quite possible that the priming had some influence, we have to bear in mind that magic tricks work by misdirection – it is much more likely that the trick had a totally different mechanism. And this certainly wasn't a scientific take on priming. But is there real evidence for its existence? We'll see in a moment.

In the finale of Brown's show, we get to the video that supposedly contained subliminal messaging. Brown claimed this would fix the audience in a viewing room and at home in place, unable to stand up when requested. We were first shown six 'trial' scenes where individuals were apparently exposed to different variants of the special video, with different effects on their behaviour. (Brown claimed there was no collaboration in the part of his act involving audience members, but the individuals in the test videos did look suspiciously like actors.)*

There is no doubt that the dramatic way the 'test subjects' reacted in the videos helped prepare suggestive viewers. Brown emphasised that those who got stuck in the main experiment would have the 'best talent to respond' – suggesting it was a good thing to get stuck. The audience were given a whole string of instructions to encourage them to stay in position, then shown a minute of rotating lines on the screen with some sound effects. These did feel mildly hypnotic, but I did not get stuck. After the effect had already taken place, Brown showed a very obvious (hence not) 'subliminal' image of someone tied to a chair. This was never mentioned in the script.

Thinking old

Let's focus first on the concept of priming, which Brown used as the explanation for his first tricks. Unlike subliminal advertising, priming originates in the field of psychology rather than public relations. Priming typically makes use of associations between words, concepts, images and more to make a change to a subsequent choice or action. It's a concept that features strongly in one of the most famous works of popular psychology, Daniel Kahneman's 2011 book *Thinking, Fast and Slow*.

Kahneman details a whole string of experiments where priming was shown to produce a subliminal manipulation of mental state. Perhaps the best known was made using a group of New York University students, mostly aged between eighteen

* In his book *Tricks of the Mind*, Brown says that he never uses stooges in the sense of people in the audience who appear to be innocently experiencing his tricks but are actually part of the act. But he does admit to deception and the 'trial' videos were part of the trick's setup, not using audience members.

and 22.* The students were told that their task was to make four-word sentences out of collections of five words. Some students got word sets that included terms associated with the elderly: Kahneman tells us that these included 'Florida, forgetful, bald, gray or wrinkle'. The other students didn't have such words.

The students were then told to head down the corridor to another lab for a second part of the experiment. In reality, heading down the corridor *was* the second part of the experiment. The experimenters measured the time the students took to make the walk – and as the scientist behind this experiment, John Bargh, predicted, the students with the 'old people' words took longer to make the walk. The suggestion was that being exposed to the age-associated words primed them for thinking about being old, and this in turn primed them for walking more like an old person.

It's worth pointing out in passing that many psychology experiments, like this one – perhaps even the majority of such experiments – involve brainjacking as part of the experimental design. The scientists involved routinely lie to the participants about what they are doing in an attempt to avoid biasing the students' behaviour. It is arguably a necessary deceit to make the experiment work – but it definitely does involve manipulation.

Note the purely subliminal nature of what happened here. Old age was never mentioned. The idea was that, without being aware of it, the way the students acted was influenced by being primed with the concept of being old. Kahneman even claimed that reading the sentences above should have been enough to prime you – and should you now get up and get yourself a glass of water, you would do it slightly more as you think an old

* Psychology experiments often use university students as guinea pigs, because they are both readily available and cheap. This shortcut has proved problematic in some cases, as they are not typical of people at large.

person would. (It appears Kahneman did not expect to have any old readers.)

I'm not going to go through all of Kahneman's priming examples, but here are a choice few. He emphasised the result of priming for money, whether using money-related terms as was done with old age, or taking the kind of approach that Brown does with a giraffe in the alleged priming experiment at Hamley's – for example by leaving a pile of Monopoly money lying around in the room. Apparently, the effect here was to increase self-reliance and to reduce how much help was offered to someone who dropped a pile of pencils. Those who were primed with money sat less close to others and were more inclined to want to be alone. (Just as we're told that the love of money is the root of all evil, it appears that priming with money is the root of at least some antisocial behaviour.)

The chapter on priming finishes with an example from an office kitchen at a UK university, where according to Kahneman 'members of that office had paid for the tea or coffee to which they helped themselves during the day by dropping money into an "honesty box"'. So far, so normal. But over a number of weeks, a poster was displayed over the price list. Sometimes the staff were primed with pictures of flowers. At other times they saw a pair of eyes, staring at them.

Thanks to the priming, it appears that in weeks when there were eyes watching, donations went up. When there were flowers, payments plummeted. There is an interesting echo here of what seems to be a medieval attempt at priming. In the seventeenth-century Kedermister Pew at St Mary's Church in Langley, Berkshire, the nobility who used to occupy it were screened from the rest of the congregation. Presumably to prime against potential misbehaviour during services, the inside of the pew is painted with large eyes in the ceiling – the oculus Dei, or eye of God.

We don't have a study of the effects of the eyes in the pew, but according to Kahneman, when the eyes were on display by the drinks, 'average contribution was 70 pence per litre of milk' – with flowers displayed, this dropped dramatically to an average of around 15 pence per litre. This is a remarkable difference, though it's slightly odd that the metric for consuming coffee and tea was the amount of milk used – presumably those who had their drinks black were excluded from the experiment.

The need for blinding

These are remarkable assertions for the subliminal power of priming. However, there is a major problem here that now applies to many of the psychological studies that have contributed to an apparent understanding of effects like priming. As we have already seen, a large number of the experiments were poorly designed, had inadequate controls, too few participants, and misused statistics to generate apparently significant results from data that did not support these conclusions.

It doesn't help that most of us come across this kind of study in a passing reference in a book like Kahneman's – popular-science books rarely say anything about the quality of the study, simply reporting the results as fact. But it's also true that the scientific community was slow to respond to criticisms of their research, particularly in the social sciences like psychology. It was around 2011, when Kahneman's book had just been published, that things started to fall apart – and at the heart of the criticism was the study that Kahneman deemed an 'instant classic': Bargh, Chan and Burrows' 1996 paper 'Automaticity of social behavior: direct effects of trait construct and stereotype-activation on action'* – the elderly priming study described above.

* Psychologists do sometimes come up with very snappy titles for their papers ... but not always.

Any scientific study has the potential for flaws – and because of the issues that were common in psychological studies, the field had a particularly strong potential. Where this is the case, it's important that a piece of research is replicated using better protocols than the original. The experiment should be undertaken again, ideally several times and by different groups, to see if the results are the same. In 2012, Stéphane Doyen, Olivier Klein, Cora-Lise Pichon and Axel Cleermans published 'Behavioural Priming: It's all in the mind, but whose mind?'

In this study they did two things. First, they duplicated the initial study, but with a larger group of participants and using automated timing for the speed of walking (the original study relied on manual timing with a stopwatch, which is potentially subject to experimenter error). The result: no outcome. The supposed priming had no effect in this improved replication. The second part of the study was arguably more interesting still. This time, the unwitting subjects were not the participants, but the scientists performing the experiment.

In this second stage, if researchers were given the expectation that participants would walk slower, they recorded an effect from priming. But if they were expecting to find no priming effect, there wasn't one. This echoes a famous 1963 study involving super rats.* Two groups of researchers were given rats to time in maze-solving trials. One group had normal rats, the other had specially bred super rats with advanced maze-solving capabilities. Not surprisingly, the super rats trounced the ordinary variety. It was then revealed that the animals in both cases were identical. The only difference was the observers' expectations.

It might seem that there is little opportunity in an experiment like the super rat study for observer bias to corrupt the results. It was just a matter of recording how long it took for

---

* The 1963 super rat study was 'The effect of experimenter bias on the performance of the albino rat' by Robert Rosenthal and Kermit Fode.

the rats to get around a maze. And there was no suggestion that the scientists testing 'super rats' were consciously cheating. However, expectations can still lead to incorrect results. The super rats were given better treatment and more handling than the run of the mill variety. When it was borderline whether or not the rat truly completed the maze in a time limit, the super rats were more likely to be treated as succeeding. And there is always the danger of cherry picking. For instance, if there was a loud noise in the lab while an experiment was running, an experimenter might decide that a super rat was put off, and leave a failure out of the statistics – but an ordinary rat would not be given the same leeway, as it would be assumed to have failed anyway.

This effect is not subliminal in the usual sense, but it certainly is brainjacking. If a scientist has expectation of an outcome for an experiment and knows which group the trial subjects she is working on belong to, there is a strong tendency where there is any leeway for interpretation by the observer for them to be biased in favour of the expected outcome. It can happen with any scientific study, and has sometimes been observed even in hard sciences such as physics. This has led to double blinding being used: for example, in gravitational wave experiments, where part of the interpretation requires subjective input. But there are far more opportunities for this kind of error when living participants are involved, and experimenter bias has proven to be rife in both psychology and medicine, where double blinding has not been used.

The double-blinding process means that, for example, in a clinical trial where some participants are given a drug on test and others are given a placebo, neither the participants nor the researchers know which of the participants have taken the active drug. Making a study double blind takes extra effort and is not always easy to build into the experimental procedure – but when the approach is not used it becomes far easier to get dubious results in psychological studies.

The aspect of the elderly priming experiment that caused particular suspicion was that a good number of subsequent experiments suggested the need for conscious awareness of the priming – it wasn't a subliminal effect – and the stimulus had to have some relevance to the participants, something that clearly was not the case with the original student subjects. Those attempting to replicate the study weren't totally dismissive of the original. They point out that the person timing the walks was effectively blinded – they didn't know if the person they were timing had been primed. But the person giving the task to the participants did know, and that proved sufficient to modify the observer's behaviour.

The replication crisis

Despite this blow to the veracity of priming, the authors of the 2012 failed replication paper were enthusiastic not to be seen as dismissing priming entirely. They conclude: 'Although automatic behavioural priming seems well established in the social cognition literature, it seems important to consider its limitations.' But bear in mind this was only an early step in the discovery of how many such experiments were dubious.

Over the next few years, many attempts to replicate findings failed. Some were due to failures in experimental design. Many were the result of so-called p-hacking and other ways to manipulate statistical results, fudges that were commonly used at the time, particularly in the social sciences where researchers were less familiar with probability and statistics than the more mathematical disciplines. P-hacking involves chopping up a set of data in multiple ways until you can find a hoped-for statistical relationship. With a big enough data set, it is easy to find spurious correlations where one factor appears to be related to another, but that apparent relationship is purely coincidental.

Remember that to be statistically significant in psychology experiments usually requires that if the null hypothesis is true (the effect does not exist), the results should only occur one in twenty times or less. When p-hacking, each different cut that is made of the data gives another chance of a one-in-twenty event occurring. The 'p' in p-hacking refers to p-values, which for the common one-in-twenty measure would be 0.05. Many have argued that a one-in-twenty chance of error allows too many false results through, but despite much debate, it is still the measure used to establish statistical significance in almost all social-science studies.

The scientific community is now very aware of these problems (though they do still regularly crop up). A well-designed experiment will now decide ahead of time exactly how the data will be analysed, preventing this kind of manipulation. But there is no doubt that this problem, and many other issues, were rife in the studies that were used to justify unconscious priming. By 2015, an article in *Nature* had concluded: 'Don't trust everything you read in psychology literature. In fact, two thirds of it should probably be distrusted.'*

Subsequently, a 2017 analysis of the studies Kahneman featured on priming in his book showed very low replication of results across the board.† Kahneman responded by agreeing that he had 'placed too much faith in underpowered studies'. He also agreed that there was a worrying absence from the reporting of experiments. Given that the results only just achieved significance, it should be inevitable that some non-significant results would be observed – but non-significant events were never published

* The *Nature* article saying 'don't trust everything' was 'First results from psychology's largest reproducibility test' by Monya Baker.

† The 2017 analysis of the studies on priming used by Kahneman was 'Reconstruction of a Train Wreck: How Priming Research Went off the Rails' by Ulrich Schimmack et al. on the Replicability Index website.

in the priming literature: with weak effects this is a key indicator that researchers are cherry picking what they publish, p-hacking and dismissing negative outcomes that don't fit their hypothesis.

Kahneman concluded: 'I still believe that actions can be primed, sometimes even by stimuli of which the person is unaware … but I have changed my views about the size of behavioural priming effects – they cannot be as large and as robust as my chapter suggested.' Others are less generous and suspect that the kind of unconscious priming that Derren Brown purports to be using in his Hamley's giraffe trick have no effect whatsoever.

The failure of much psychological research to meet acceptable scientific standards does not, of course, mean that we can dismiss all examples of brainjacking. We know that many of the more explicit mechanisms work and have been replicated many times. However, particularly when faced with apparently subtle influences such as priming, we do need to raise a sceptical eyebrow at the very suggestion that it has any significant effect. Certainly in Derren Brown's case, it's likely that what we were seeing was a conventional magic trick, dressed up to make it more impressive in the clothes of a psychological phenomenon. We will come back to his claim to glue participants to their seats with a subliminal video a little later.

So far, most subliminal brainjacking we've covered has been problematic – and even if it were possible, it would surely be an unpleasant and dangerous form of manipulation – but what about the more positive idea that we can get through the tedious business of learning something new without wasting any conscious effort on it? Can we gain knowledge subliminally?

Learning in your sleep

The ultimate would be to have Trinity's ability to become a helicopter pilot in seconds, shown in a *The Matrix* scene that featured in the opening chapter – but we know that this is pure science fiction. However, something that was taken seriously in the last century was the concept of sleep learning. The brain is, after all, not inactive during sleep, but rather is functioning in different ways from normal waking activity. Why not harness some of that sleep time to be able to subliminally learn new facts, or to pick up a language without all that boring work of committing vocabulary to memory?

Also known as hypnopedia, the hope of sleep learning was that just as it was possible to give (some) people suggestions while hypnotised that would result in later action or recall (more on this in a moment), so something similar could be undertaken while sleeping, a state that seemed to have some relation to the hypnotised state.

Early attempts at sleep learning involved placing a loudspeaker under the pillow, while it's now possible to purchase sleep-learning smartphone apps which play suitable suggestions during the night. Initially, there was no doubt this was the brainjacking equivalent of aspects of medical practice that aren't evidence-based – it seemed reasonable that it should work, but there was no scientific verification of its benefits, and no research to support it.

This started to change as early as 1956, when Charles Simon and William Emmons made use of a then trendy piece of technology to investigate sleep learning for the semi-governmental US organisation the Rand Corporation.* The new equipment was the EEG, or electroencephalograph, a device used to record electrical activity in the brain. These detectors date back as far as the 1920s and led to the introduction of the concept of brainwaves – repeated fluctuations in electrical brain activity, with a range of characteristic frequencies.

---

* The 1956 Simon and Emmons sleep learning study was 'Responses to material presented during various levels of sleep'.

Brain waves seem to have been named at random – they are represented by Greek letters and come in the order delta, theta, alpha, beta and gamma,* roughly equivalent to D, TH, A, B and C or G, in that order. Delta is the lowest frequency, below 4 hertz (cycles per second). The middling alpha and beta waves are 8 to 12 hertz and 13 to 30 hertz respectively, with gammas at 30 to 80 hertz.

Simon and Emmons discovered that when a subject recalled anything 'taught' during sleep, that information had been presented when there was alpha-wave activity, which typically occurs in waking or near-waking states during the night. In effect, participants were simply remembering something they had heard while conscious – and there was no improvement in learning over simply hearing a piece of information when fully awake.

There is reasonable evidence, though, that part of the role of sleep is to give the brain a chance to consolidate memories, getting them properly organised in long-term storage. A couple of experiments (with the proviso we've already met that these may not be high-quality studies) have suggested that it is possible to give the brain a helping hand in fixing memories in place to make them possible to recover in the future.

Of all the senses, smell appears to be the easiest to stimulate during sleep – perhaps surprising, given the way that sound is more likely to warn of impending danger. A 2007 study† found that if a subject was exposed to a particular smell while attempting to learn something during the day, and then was exposed to that same smell when asleep, they managed to retain the information better. In 2014, researchers found the same result

---

* There are also mu waves, which occupy the same frequency range as alpha, but relate to motor neurons.

† 'Odor cues during slow-wave sleep prompt declarative memory consolidation' by Björn Rasch et al.

from playing music while learning, then playing the same tunes during sleep.*

An earlier piece of work from 2004† made use of 'transcranial stimulation', where a (small) electrical current is applied to the skull and indirectly to the brain. This appeared to enhance the electrical activity in the brain during memory consolidation and gave some evidence of improvement, though perhaps due to its suggestion of unsettling practices such as electroshock therapy, this seems not to have been taken seriously as a way forward.

We do have to be particularly aware of the proviso about the quality of studies, though. Sleep research requires a lot of laboratory space, and takes up a lot of the subjects' time. As a result, it's not unusual for sleep experiments to be undertaken with only a handful of subjects. The 1956 experiment, for example, involved only 21 'normal, adult male‡ subjects'.

Not learning, but reinforcement

There is one glimmer of hope, though, for those who struggle with learning, particularly something that is very structured in small units, such as vocabulary when learning a language. In the 2015 paper 'Boosting vocabulary learning by verbal cueing during sleep', Thomas Schreiner and Björn Rasch took a larger (though still not huge) mixed-sex group of 60 individuals and split them into four subsets, so there were fifteen undergoing any particular experience.

---

* 'Targeted Memory Reactivation During Slow Wave Sleep Facilitates Emotional Memory Consolidation' by Scott Cairney et al.

† 'Transcranial direct current stimulation during sleep improves declarative memory' by Lisa Marshall et al.

‡ It's an uncomfortable reality that early research on human subjects rarely used a balanced set of male and female participants.

The subjects here were German speakers who did not know Dutch. At 10pm they were taught a series of German–Dutch word pairs – and it was noted which words appeared to have been recalled by each subject at this point. Two of the groups were sent to bed an hour later and left to sleep until 2am. The other two groups were prevented from sleeping while Dutch words were played to them – one group undertook other tasks while the words were played, while the other paid full attention to the words being played.

For 90 minutes between 11pm and 1am, all groups except the control group, who were left to sleep undisturbed, were cued by repeatedly playing 90 Dutch words – 30 that had been recalled, 30 that hadn't been recalled and 30 new words – playing each word ten or eleven times. No German translation was given during this process.

The results, which are better than borderline statistically, showed two interesting things. Firstly, both groups allowed to sleep retained significantly more than those who weren't. The awake groups had similar performance on Dutch words that weren't cued, but interestingly those who were paying attention to the words being played did *worse* on those words than they did on words that weren't played. Paying active attention to the words (without the German translation) seemed to make them harder to recall.

The awake group that was concentrating on other activities while the words were played did do marginally better on words that were cued. As we have seen, neither awake group did as well as the control sleep group. However, the sleep group with Dutch words cued during sleep did perform significantly better at recalling the vocabulary than any other group.

This does seem to highlight that there is some benefit from giving the brain a nudge in the right direct while undergoing the consolidation processing parts of sleep. Unfortunately, we don't know if there is any benefit from playing the words at random times during the night. The researchers carefully avoided REM (dreaming) sleep and times when the sleepers were close to waking. This is less easy to do when you aren't in a sleep lab, though some smartwatches do have a limited ability to monitor sleep conditions.

Before we get too excited, though, remember that this experiment only measured the improvement of recall over a few hours – how much it would help with long-term retention of vocabulary is not clear. What it certainly doesn't show is that true sleep learning with no daytime work is possible. There remains no evidence for this. But it does give a hint that we can help the brain with the consolidation process for something that it has already learned, to increase the chances of retention in long-term memory.

You are feeling sleepy ...

We have so far skipped over the area of subliminal manipulation that is both most widely accepted and yet also most heavily questioned – hypnotism. Derren Brown, who we recently encountered through his use of priming, is also an experienced hypnotist* and relies on the power of suggestion that goes hand in hand with hypnotism in his more dramatic stunts.

Part of the strange status of hypnotism is that it has been used both medically and as a stage entertainment. Its origins include the entirely discredited practice of mesmerism (an eighteenth-century phenomenon based on a non-existent concept of 'animal magnetism'), but there seems no doubt that the

* Brown doesn't like to be described as a hypnotist, because of the connotation of bad stage hypnotism, which can sometimes seem like abuse.

techniques of hypnotism can have some effects on attitude and behaviour that are not purely conscious.

A real problem in describing how to think scientifically about hypnosis is that there is only limited agreement over what it really is – or whether, in the way that hypnotism is often portrayed, it exists at all. The version we get from old movies tends to feature someone waving a watch in front of their client and telling them they are feeling sleepy. The victim (sorry, patient) goes into a trance state where they can be told what do, sometimes after a significant delay, and they obey without question. One thing that is certain is that whatever we label as being 'hypnosis' is really not like that.

While some consider that hypnotism involves putting a subject's brain into a special state – a bit like changing the settings on your phone – the more widely held and, for me, the more scientifically likely interpretation is that the term covers a collection of normal human behaviours and responses to suggestions that don't require a special brain state. It's hard to see what the biological or evolutionary function of such a special state would be, while the interpretation that reflects more a combination of behaviours and responses seems far more likely – if less showy and dramatic.

In his wide-ranging book *Tricks of the Mind*, Derren Brown makes a useful analogy between hypnotism and (stage) magic. He suggests that just as we accept that the term 'magic' is used to cover a whole collection of different techniques, from physical manipulation of props to misdirection and psychological manipulation of the audience, so hypnosis consists of the manipulation of a range of behaviours and of responses to suggestions. Magic, Brown says, 'is the final effect when those methods are combined to form a particular type of performance … I think it is rather the same with hypnosis'.

Hypnotism appears to depend on the expectations of the subjects and a combination of relaxation, suggestibility and inclination to conform. This comes across strongly in the more dramatic aspects of stage hypnotism. For well over a century, entertainers have influenced audience members to act like chickens or to carry out a delayed suggestion, much to their apparent bewilderment. It has been suggested that many of these demonstrations rely as much on the need to conform as they do to suggestibility. Some feel very strongly that they don't want to stand out as a 'difficult person' and so, whether totally consciously or not, they go along with the command.

This brings to mind the American psychologist Stanley Milgram's experiments in the 1960s.* These were inspired by Nazi atrocities in the Second World War, aiming to provide an insight into how ordinary people appeared to set aside their moral compasses when ordered to undertake unspeakable actions on others. Subjects in Milgram's studies were told that the research they were participating in involved a teaching experiment, to see if punishment would assist with learning.

The unfortunate subjects were individually put in charge of a 'learner' who supposedly had to memorise some text. The learner then repeated the text – each time they got something wrong, the teacher was told to administer an electric shock. The punishment aspect of the experiment was totally faked – there was no electrical system, and the learner was an actor. As the learners continued to fail, the teachers were bullied by the researchers to give more and more powerful shocks, using a control that went up to a deadly sounding 450 volts.

The expectation was that only a few of the subjects would go all the way, but the researchers found that 65 per cent would (mostly very reluctantly) be pushed to the 450 volts level – and all made it as far as 300 volts. There has been considerable resistance to the findings, but they have been reproduced several times with reasonably similar outcomes to the Milgram original.

* 'Behavioral Study of Obedience', Stanley Milgram.

It's hard to argue that human beings don't have a significant urge to conform with expectations, resulting in behaviour under pressure that would not otherwise be typical – something that is also true in stage hypnotism shows.

The alleged ability of hypnotists to force people to act in a way they wouldn't otherwise is at best exaggerated and in some cases is pure fiction. In a fascinating 1998 experiment at Macquarie University in Australia,* researchers hypnotised a group of people and implanted the suggestion to send a postcard (from a pile provided to them) to lead researcher Amanda Barnier every day. They duly complied. But a second group were simply asked to send the cards in – and also did so. In fact, they sent more.

In the interest of balance, as I've expressed some doubt over studies elsewhere, I ought to say that this falls solidly in the 'unreliable' period for psychological research. The Macquarie experiment involved two groups, one of sixteen and the other of nineteen individuals (unusually for the period, in both cases more participants were female than male). The p-values were mostly better than the 0.05 level. But we still need to exhibit a degree of scepticism.

A mix of reactions

When we watch stage hypnotism, it can seem that what's on show is far too dramatic to be based purely on a willingness to go along with the crowd and responsiveness to suggestion. Many stage hypnotists, for example, get people on stage to accept that the hypnotist is invisible: the subjects then appear shocked when things are moved around by the 'invisible' person. It feels

* 'Posthypnotic responding away from the hypnotic setting', Amanda Barnier and Kevin McConkey.

unlikely that someone can be made to disappear without hypnotism involving a special trance state. But remember how fake our view of the world is. It's a construct of the brain that is regularly and reliably fooled by optical illusions. Why is it so surprising that, for some individuals, it can also be fooled by suggestion? We can never know exactly what those people do and don't see – but it no more requires mystical powers and trances than does the chessboard illusion on page 75.

Derren Brown notes that when he has used hypnosis to 'make himself invisible' on stage, he found afterwards that there was a range of responses to his act. Out of, say, ten responsive subjects, two would clearly be able to see him, two genuinely thought he was invisible, but the remainder were aware that it was Brown moving the objects. However, Brown writes, they 'could only act *as if* I were invisible'. (Italics in original.) He suggests that in their case he did not influence their visual perception, but rather manipulated their responses to what was happening. The gasp of shock some gave was produced by suggestion, not the rendering of the performer invisible.

With this view of what hypnotism is, we can see that Derren Brown's 'experiment' that apparently locked viewers in their seats, supposedly as a result of watching a subliminal video (see page 221), was nothing to do with subliminal messaging. His inclusion of clearly visible 'subliminal' imagery after the event was classic stage-magic misdirection. In reality, those in the audience, both physically present and watching from home, were undergoing hypnotic suggestion.

The only thing that the swirly video contributed to this was the associated relaxation: the real effect was generated by the lead-up to the video, where the audience was eased into accepting that they *would* be rendered immobile (a strong part of this was those almost certainly faked 'test' videos). What the show demonstrated very well was the power of suggestion in action.

Response to suggestion

Because we are considering hypnosis to be a collection of behaviours and responses rather than a single phenomenon, it's important to stress that not all those undergoing hypnotism, from those who eat onions on stage as if they were tasty fruit to those undergoing minor surgery without anaesthesia, are consciously going along with what they are told, like the participants in the Milgram experiments. Suggestion as a process is significantly more than just conscious conformity.

Some subjects do appear to have a strong subliminal response to suggestion and as a result exhibit striking behaviour and responses. Perhaps the surgery aspect is most dramatic, but even this is not as surprising as it sounds. Much of the sensitivity to the pain of cutting in surgery comes from the skin – which is usually deadened with local anaesthetic during surgery under hypnosis. We know that pain can be reduced by placebos – sugar pills with no active content, as is also the case with homeopathic remedies. Even the pain reduction of products such as paracetamol appear to include a strong placebo component. If someone who is particularly susceptible to suggestion and is thoroughly relaxed seems not to suffer much pain during minor surgery under hypnosis, it is not entirely surprising.

Hypnosis is now well-established in some medical circles, with detailed clinical research supporting its use in managing some medical symptoms. It is well known that there is a wide variation in response to hypnotic suggestion and this has been associated with 'atypical brain connectivity profiles',* suggesting that the 10 per cent or so of the population who have a high response may have greater connectivity in part of the corpus

* See, for instance, the 2017, 'New directions in hypnosis research: strategies for advancing the cognitive and clinical neuroscience of hypnosis' by Mark Jensen et al. for more on medical use of hypnosis.

collosum (the bundle of nerve fibres that links the two brain halves) and in medial prefrontal and anterior cingulate cortices (areas of the brain above and in front of the corpus collosum), and also may be supported by reducing activity in the prefrontal cortex. This may be linked to levels of neuromodulators and neurotransmitters, notably dopamine and GABA, which can have that inhibitory action on areas of the cortex.*

It has been suggested that hypnosis bears some similarities to experiences many of us have in everyday life. Most drivers, especially when following a familiar route, can lose conscious awareness of part of the drive. I have experienced this on my regular morning walk – I can struggle to remember which route I took on sections where I have a number of alternatives. Similarly, we might get carried away when reading a book, or in the creative process known as 'flow', where awareness of time disappears. I find this happens regularly when I am in the process of writing a book – a couple of hours can fall out of my conscious awareness, because I am totally engaged in what is happening. Flow is self-imposed brainjacking.

Detached from the association with stage performances and magic tricks, hypnosis seems far less mysterious – but it still remains one of the more dramatic examples of brainjacking. If most attempts at subliminal manipulation are at the subtle (if sometimes non-existent) end of the spectrum, in the next chapter we will see some entertaining speculation about highly brainjacking-influenced advertising by taking a look at science fiction. At the same time, we will see how technological advances such as the use of drone swarms can put brainjacking influences where we least expect them.

---

* Sorry, I said I wouldn't do this again, but couldn't resist here.

MERCHANTS' WORLD 13

By comparison with the US, advertising in the UK has mostly been restrained and far less in your face. This made the impact of Frederik Pohl and Cyril Kornbluth's 1953 novel *The Space Merchants* even stronger on me than it would have been on its US audience.

Meet the future merchants

Alongside a story of horrendous life under the thumb of massive corporations, *The Space Merchants* is what amounts to a compact handbook on how to take the principles of advertising and marketing, and amplify them to generate extreme brainjacking where anything goes. We are taken inside the Fowler Schocken Associates advertising agency to see the development of their campaigns in action.

Some of the earlier ideas are relatively subtle, if devious. One of their clients, a company called Starrzelius Verily, makes a range of products aimed at children. Realising that school lunches will always be unpleasant, the company packages their 'soya-burgers and regenerated steak' in green, because this is the corporate colour used by their main competitor, Universal. However, they put their more enticing options, such as the 'Kiddiebutt cigarette ration' in their distinctive corporate shade of red. This way, the consumer will be subtly influenced to think of the competitor's green as bad, and their own red as good. As their 'Industrial Anthropology' expert puts it: 'When those kids grow up ... According to our extrapolation fifteen years from now Universal products will be broke, bankrupt, and off the market entirely!'

As I've already mentioned, the intention of science fiction is not to predict the future. It is a way of exposing characters to speculative science and technology to see how they would react. But having said that, it's quite shocking just how much this vignette reflects aspects of reality more than 70 years after the book was first published. It's not just that the soya-burgers (which raise a collective shudder from those present in the book) are not uncommon these days (I had one for lunch) and are likely to be used in schools – but more horrifyingly, the way that e-cigarettes are presented in bright colours with child-like flavours such as bubble gum. Quite clearly appealing to children, these are all too close to those 'Kiddiebutts' (if more subtly named).

Even in the imagined future of the novel, the government imposes some limitations. The agency men (this was written in the advertising age portrayed so engagingly in the TV show *Mad Men*, so it definitely is men) bemoan the way that 'the safety cranks' have been able to persuade the government to stop advertisers from 'projecting messages on air-car windows' for reasons as trivial as avoiding crashes, though they hope to fight back by developing the technology to project advertising directly onto the human retina.

It's likely that Pohl and Kornbluth were reflecting the battle put up by the tobacco companies to counter the 'safety cranks' who suggested that such an all-American activity as smoking could be bad for you. But there's an element of genius in the idea that advertising could become so obtrusive that it could endanger the lives of drivers (extended here into the futuristic concept of air-cars) by making it difficult to see – and for that matter presenting ads in a fashion that would be nearly impossible to avoid.

One of the ways that science-fiction views of the future can be particularly interesting is when the imagination of the SF writers *couldn't* stretch to the realities of what would happen. Few SF writers from the 1950s, 60s and 70s realised that physical media would be replaced by electronic media, whether provided through a wired network or wirelessly. Time and time again, SF stories featured information being accessed from standalone storage. Look, for example, at the original series of *Star Trek*, where Mr Spock was always plugging in data stores, rather than accessing information online. Even more extreme, Isaac Asimov's 1954 novel *The Caves of Steel*, set 3,000 years in the future, features data-processing technology with the mercury delay-line computer memory that was in use in the 1950s, no more a sophisticated method for humans to access information than wire recorders and microfilm.

Getting to us differently

Because of this limitation, what was also largely missed in science fiction was the way that advertising would end up struggling to keep up with how we consume information. If you think of the way that advertising might reach a consumer in the second half of the twentieth century, it would largely have been through TV and radio, newspapers and magazines, and billboards. But think of the typical day of someone like me who works primarily from home. I don't see billboards. I don't subscribe to newspapers and magazines. Admittedly, when I do take the occasional trip on the train, I may be exposed to both forms of advertising media, but in practice I am so used to not having them that I simply don't take the adverts in. If I read a newspaper, 90 per cent of the advertising will never even register with me as existing.

I do watch TV and listen to the radio. But even here, my ad consumption has collapsed compared with my youth. Ever since digital video recorders, when watching TV channels with advertisements cannier consumers have tended to record the programme and skip the advertising. Now, much that we watch is streamed from services without advertising. Admittedly, I can't avoid having internet advertising appear when I'm looking something up online – but my browser blocks the more obtrusive popups and generally speaking I don't look at the on-screen advertising. It may be, of course, as suggested in *Badvertising* (see Chapter 7), that I am unconsciously influenced by advertising that I am not aware of, but I am yet to see evidence of this.

This is being reflected in the bottom line of UK media. In the nine months to the end of 2023, the company behind the *Guardian* and *Observer* newspapers reported a 16 per cent drop in advertising revenue across a combination of print and online. Channel 4 TV's chief executive Alex Mahon said that they expected a 14 per cent drop in 2023. Although some forecast increases in TV advertising revenue in 2024, it feels a little like confident predictions from gas lighting manufacturers that they would recover by building a better gas light towards the end of the nineteenth century. As more of us switch TV viewing to streaming, and pay to avoid ads, the industry is likely to see a significant decline in its traditional sources of income.

It will be interesting to see whether explicit advertising as a concept goes the way of film cameras, where, apart from specialist use, the new technology of digital photography has made the older version extinct. This doesn't mean that marketing will disappear – just that the means by which the word is spread will be transformed. We have already seen this with the growth, for example, of social media influencers. Online advertising will clearly continue – but it's likely that advertisers will need to find new ways to grab our attention.

The Campbellian reflex

Meanwhile, back in the world of *The Space Merchants*, and its sequel *The Merchants' War*, the underhand means of influence were being stepped up. To tie consumers into a brand of instant coffee, 'each sample of Coffiest contains three milligrams of a simple alkaloid. Nothing harmful. But definitely habit-forming. After ten weeks the customer is hooked for life. It would cost him at least five thousand dollars for a cure, so it's simpler for him to go right on drinking Coffiest – three cups with every meal and a pot beside his bedside every night, just as it says on the jar.'

It is certainly true that some early products – intentionally or otherwise – contained addictive substances. Tobacco is the obvious example, though infamously Coca-Cola is so named because it originally contained extract of the addictive coca leaf (the source of cocaine). Coke was initially introduced as a temperance drink, providing a non-alcoholic alternative to the manufacturer's alcohol-rich nerve tonic Pemberton's French Wine Coca, which also contained the extract. Surprisingly, Coca-Cola contains coca extract to this day, although from 1904 it used so-called spent coca leaves from which the cocaine had already been refined, and since 1929 has been able to use a totally cocaine-free extract.

Apart from products linked to existing sources of addiction, such as vapes, it is highly unlikely that with modern consumer-protection laws a company could get away with introducing Coffiest. What is more interesting is the approach taken to achieve an even greater product dependence in *The Merchants' War*. Here, the main character has recently returned to Earth from a space colony and isn't aware of the latest approaches to marketing.

Similar to the way that we now have locations where public smoking is allowed, such as in a pub garden or smoker's shelter, so Pohl (Cyril Kornbluth had sadly died by the time *The Merchants' War* was published in 1984) imagined 'commercial zones', which you entered at your peril. The character walks into such a zone where he is subjected to what's described as a 'Campbellian reflex', giving him a deep-seated urge to drink a product called Mokie-Koke, which is apparently a 'refreshing, taste-tingling blend of the finest chocolate-type flavoring, synthetic coffee extract and selected cocaine analogues'. Without even realising he is doing so, the character goes on to repeatedly order and drink Mokie-Koke.

Leaving aside the hat-tip to Coca-Cola's origins in those cocaine analogues, the 'Campbellian reflex' refers to the twentieth-century English neurologist Herbert James Campbell, who the novel describes as the 'inventor of limbic-pleasure therapy'. Campbell was a real person, though any papers he produced seem largely to have disappeared. He did, however, write a popular science book called *The Pleasure Areas*, published in 1973, which was likely to have been Pohl's inspiration.

According to Campbell, human beings were largely driven by pleasure, whether sensuous, intellectual or spiritual. He believed that the repression of pleasure damaged human evolutionary potential and made people ill. Although Campbell's work was to some degree driven by science, he appears to have had something of an obsession with pleasure. The 'limbic' part of Pohl's comment refers to the limbic system, a part of the brain dealing with, among other things, emotion and behaviour. There seems limited scientific support for the guaranteed nature of Pohl's manipulative marketing.

However, this doesn't mean that manufacturers don't do something similar on a less dramatic scale. As we have seen, we are naturally attracted to fatty foods, sugar and salt, because on a restricted diet, fat and sugar give a quick energy hit, while salt can be missing from a plant-based diet. Food manufacturers have always used these ingredients to increase the attractiveness of their foods. On the whole, this is more a matter of attraction than addiction – but it's no surprise, for example, that burger adverts tend to feature a stack of meat, dripping in cheese.

It is unlikely ever to be used in marketing, but a 2018 study* suggested that male consumers who were exposed to the hormone testosterone were more likely to have a preference for luxury goods, possibly because testosterone increases our awareness of social status, which tends to be associated with such items. A modern version of *The Merchants' War* might envisage department stores adding testosterone to the air-conditioning in sections selling high-priced items. We do, however, need to apply the usual warning to this kind of research. The subjects were 243 males, 217 of whom were students. The testosterone was applied to much of the upper body using a gel (which is hardly a practical approach in a shopping environment) and no purchases were involved, simply an expression of preference.

The shop window knows you

Much science fiction takes current US outdoor advertising and makes it dramatically bigger or bolder. Think, for example, of the huge video billboards and three-dimensional holographic imagery featured in *Blade Runner* and its sequel. But one example

* 'Single-dose testosterone administration increases men's preference for status goods', G. Nave et al.

that really stretched the boundaries for future advertising was the movie *Minority Report*. Coincidentally, like *Blade Runner*, this was based on a story by American author Philip K. Dick.*

The central theme of *Minority Report* is pure fantasy, featuring as it does 'precogs' who can see what is likely to happen in the future unless the pre-crime police intervene. However, there is a more feasible aspect of the storyline in the personalised advertising the movie features. We are already familiar in everyday life with biometric identification on our phones, whether using fingerprints or facial recognition. *Minority Report* links advertising to an alternative biometric approach of retina scans.

This is a perfectly legitimate means of biometric identification – the retina of the eye has as unique a pattern as fingerprints, though there is some likelihood of change over time as eyes deteriorate with age. And it is true that the approach has been used occasionally for high-security identification. But in real life, it is verging on impossible to scan the retina of a distant moving eye. Even if it were possible, facial recognition – particularly if it is accompanied by sophisticated technology using lidar† as well as image recognition – is far less invasive than retinal recognition, so the *Minority Report* scenario we are about to explore would almost certainly be executed with facial recognition.

The movie cleverly combines the intrusive marketing of *The Space Merchants* with the kind of targeted advertising we see on the internet. As characters walk down the street, they are

---

* *Blade Runner* is extremely loosely based on Dick's 1968 novel *Do Androids Dream of Electric Sheep?*, while *Minority Report* is somewhat closer to Dick's 1956 novella *The Minority Report*.

† Lidar is not unlike radar, but using lasers rather than microwaves to sense the location of objects by reflection. Lidar is used in the facial-recognition systems of smartphones, as well as to help self-driving cars to scan their surroundings, but there may be health concerns in using powerful enough lidar for long-distance recognition.

scanned and recognised, and then screens, speakers and even whole windows of shops pump out personalised advertising, addressing individuals by name. While personal privacy legislation such as GDPR makes such an approach unlikely in Europe, there is every possibility of having as much targeting this way, as happens when browsing a website – with one serious problem to be overcome.

There is a big difference between what a smartphone does in identifying its owner and what personalised street advertising would require. When you unlock your phone, it says: 'Here is what my owner looks like – is this the same person?' To identify someone at random in the street, the software has to say: 'Here's a face in [say] New York. Who is it likely to be?' That's a much harder problem. A lot of effort has been put into facial recognition, but it is still relatively flawed, and in most countries the data is highly protected and not available for commercial applications. It might enable the authorities to solve a crime, but it is unlikely to be available to would-be advertisers.

It's possible that it's far easier to identify someone from their technology. Many of us carry some sort of sophisticated electronics most of the time, whether it's a smartphone, smartwatch, laptop or tablet. Many of these devices can interact with nearby devices without direct contact. Think, for example, of the Covid-19 apps that were widely used during the pandemic. Here, two smartphones would interact with each other and flag up a contact. Exactly the same thing could happen between individuals and advertising devices they pass.

In practice, once again, the personal privacy laws in many countries would prevent this happening without the owner of the data giving permission. But it is certainly not inconceivable. At a much cruder level, some companies, such as the coffee chain Starbucks, already have apps that can tell you where the nearest store is if you come relatively close to it, while the

McDonald's app will detect how close you are to their store when you pre-order food, getting it prepared when you are in the vicinity. Such examples are very much opt-in.

Selective vision

One relatively low-tech approach to personalising street advertising that has been successfully deployed already is lenticular printing. This is a mechanism for producing images that appear to move or that modify content as your viewpoint changes. Two (or more) images are interlaced in strips on a poster, which is then covered with a special lens that itself has a series of bands that change the direction light rays travel from the images. The result is that from one direction you see one image; from another direction the other is on show. As you move, one image fades into the other.

Usually, this approach is used to make an advert more eye catching by appearing to feature movement. But in a Spanish street campaign it was used to deliver tailored selective advertising. When the posters were viewed from adult height, they provided information on ANAR Foundation, a child-protection charity, showing a picture of an unblemished boy and the text 'Sometimes child abuse is only visible to the child suffering it'. But when the same poster was viewed by someone under 1.34 metres in height, they would see a picture of the same boy's face with a bruise, a hotline number and: 'If someone hurts you, phone us and we'll help you.'*

Reach for the stars

Because many conventional advertising routes are becoming less effective, there have been several attempts to provide more

* You can see the ANAR Foundation lenticular advert in action at bit.ly/brainjacking4.

in-your-face mechanisms. Historically, one way to do this was to fly an advertising banner behind a light aircraft, though the coverage from these was always doubtful, as they are only visible from any particular location for a short period of time. Such banners have been responsible for a number of fatal accidents when they interfere with the plane's control surfaces, but are still used in the US and parts of Europe. Advertising balloons and blimps have also been deployed with limited success.

In science fiction, sky-based advertising has been more dramatic, with vast billboards supported by some undefined new propulsion technique that seems to come as standard in most future city portrayals. Building-sized air cars are unlikely to become a reality for practical reasons, but there are a couple of ways that real sky-based advertising has been proposed. The most dramatic, if most unlikely, is sometimes given the cringe-worthy name of 'moonvertising'.

The Moon is, of course, the largest body visible in the night sky, and for decades lasers have been powerful enough to be beamed to the Moon and reflected back. For a long time there have been rumours of the potential to project a laser-based image onto the surface of the Moon, making it visible when the Moon is in the night sky. This would take the kind of advertising that is projected onto the side of a building to a whole new level – but there are three huge issues to overcome.

The biggest one is that although the Moon is indeed the largest and brightest object in the night sky, the size we see the Moon as being is pretty small – it's hard to imagine squeezing much of a readable advert onto it. But the reality is far worse. If you've ever taken a photo of the Moon with your phone without using a telephoto setting, it seems ridiculously tiny – but that's its true visible size. The Moon as seen from Earth is about the same size as the hole produced by a hole punch, held at arm's length. The apparent size when you look at it is due to an optical illusion that isn't fully understood.

Unfortunately, the optical illusion doesn't mean you can see detail with the naked eye any better than you would through that hole. So, we're talking about fitting the advertising spiel into that hole-punch hole held at arm's length. Such advertising could not get a message across directly – it could only ever be a publicity stunt, where the advert would actually be seen as a result of photographs taken through telescopes. This would probably work for the first couple of times, but the novelty would swiftly wear off – and it would be easy to fake.

The second problem is that the Moon is a poor projection screen. Firstly, it's big, the size of a small planet. From edge to edge it is just under 3,500 kilometres (2,175 miles) across. To call it widescreen is an understatement. There is no technology we currently have that could project such a big image. To make matters worse, the white appearance of the 'screen' is another optical illusion. When we see the Moon in the sky it appears very bright. But most of the surface is a dark grey, making for poor contrast. The apparent brightness is just relative to the night sky. And, of course, most of the time the surface is only partly visible, with the rest in shade. All of the side of the Moon that faces us is always visible when it's in the sky, but that's a huge contrast difference at the terminator between the dark and light parts to cope with.

Finally, the Moon is a long way away – on average about 384,000 kilometres (240,000 miles). The strength of a projection drops off with the square of the distance. So, for instance, an image projected from the Earth to the Moon is about 148 billion times dimmer than an image projected to a screen that is one kilometre distant (itself an impressive projection range). Realistically, the only way of producing such a projection would be from a lunar satellite, making it an extremely expensive venture. And all these problems are without even considering the huge negative reaction that would arise from spoiling a view of natural beauty. Think how people would respond to sticking a billboard on top of Mount Everest – and multiply it many times.

Satellite selling and drone displays

If the Moon is an unlikely vehicle, let's get closer in the sky, where things become more practical. In 2022, the Russian journal *Aerospace* carried a paper* on using formations of satellites to provide space advertising. With the significant drop in the cost of getting satellites into space, and the growth of multiple satellite networks, or 'constellations', this is already feasible. Think, for example, of the SpaceX Starlink constellation, which at the time of writing has over 5,000 satellites and has a target of around 12,000, with a potential extension to 42,000. This isn't used for sky advertising, but it shows the possible scale.

There are broadly two ways that satellite advertising could be achieved. The relatively cheap approach is to use solar reflectors. This way, the light energy to generate the image comes from the Sun. The downsides of this approach are that the image would only be visible at dusk or dawn, and that it would be limited to showing relatively simple, static imagery such as a brand logo. The alternative would be to use lasers, which can operate all night and could produce more sophisticated imagery.

The study only covers the reflecting version and concludes that it is borderline economically viable in terms of the cost versus the exposure. Although the timing of visibility is limited, the reflector approach is likely to cause less international complaint than lasers, in that it wouldn't operate when the sky is

* 'Satellite Formation Flying for Space Advertising: From Technically Feasible to Economically Viable' – Shamil Biktimirov et al.

truly dark, a major concern for astronomers and one that most consumers would be unhappy with, after the initial novelty wore off. The laser approach is both less practical and would cause considerably more complaint.

Far more practical and cost effective, if more localised in viewing area, is the use of drone formations carrying LED lighting. Computer-controlled, these can be used to produce complex imagery, and are increasingly deployed to provide effects at major concerts and events. Drone swarms have now been used in the US (where there are significantly fewer planning hurdles to overcome than in Europe) to fly large-scale ads over cities. The specialist company Pixis has advertised Raid insect spray, the NBA, Nike, Volkswagen and more this way.

Even in the advertising environment of the US, this has proved controversial. For example, a campaign for the *Candy Crush* game in November 2022 caused outrage, with New York State senator Brad Hoylman quoted as saying: 'It's offensive to New Yorkers, to our local laws, to public safety, and to wildlife', in the way that it 'spoiled the city's skyline'. As it was illegal to fly drones over New York, the swarm was located over the less-regulated sky of New Jersey, but was visible from New York.

In anything involving regulation, the US is a special case (as is also true of China, where such displays are already relatively frequently used), but in Europe it is highly unlikely that such advertising would be allowed on a regular basis. There has been a small amount of drone advertising in London (for example, for the insurance company Beazley accompanying a company event on 26 April 2023), but were it to become more commonplace it would certainly be subject to greater controls.

The tendency is always to tighten up regulation on this kind of technology after the initial surge. It is also worth saying that while such advertising can create a buzz and get the advertiser news coverage, it has not been demonstrated to offer any significant benefit to the brands using it, and with the increasing concern over spoiling the night sky it may even be counter-productive, generating a negative impact for the advertiser.

Less dramatically, drones have also been used for banner advertising, much like a cheaper and safer modern version of the old banners behind light aircraft – but they face the same restrictions and issues with advertising effectiveness outside of jurisdictions with few controls.

Although much future gazing on the subject of advertising is about extreme and coercive approaches, the people in the real advertising business focus more on ways of tweaking existing modes of getting to their audience. Vast animated electronic billboards that float in the sky or plaster the sides of skyscrapers are not the vision that advertisers have of the future, which tends to be about putting across a message more subtly and effectively.

As far back as 2006, David Droga, then chief creative officer of the Publicis agency, commented:* 'In our industry's race to innovate and clients' rush to convert, we need to safeguard our one true asset. Consumer understanding. Otherwise, we risk bombarding them into rejection ... We need to ensure that as an industry we are not seduced by our own cleverness. In fact, at what point do we cross that line, that blurred line between ingenious communication and intrusive marketing?'

This viewpoint is still just as relevant today as it was then. At the 'Future of Advertising' conference held in London in 2024, the biggest focus was on AI, using it to produce advertising copy more cheaply, to better target digital advertising and to modify content on the fly. The other key area for development was new spaces opening up for advertising, notably via women's sport and the increasing availability of advertising on streaming platforms such as Netflix, Amazon Prime and Disney+. The future

---

* In *A History of Advertising* – see Further Discovery.

of effective advertising brainjacking is likely to be far more about winning over the audience with relevance and being present in the digital environments they access than it is about in-your-face attacks on their senses.

Following this view of possible futures, it's time to take a step back for an overview of the reality of brainjacking, and to get a final feel for how much power story has to inform, influence or manipulate.

IT'S THE STORY, STUPID 14

What has surprised me in researching and writing *Brainjacking* is how many parallels there were with a topic that I have written about before: parapsychology – alleged unexplained mental abilities such as telepathy, telekinesis, precognition and remote viewing, which I covered in *Extra Sensory*. There has already been some overlap here, both in the relevance of Derren Brown's work and in the scientific study of Yuri Geller we met in the deception chapter. Much of what can be represented as special mental abilities has turned out to be an attempt to play with our brains, deceiving others into accepting an unreal interpretation of what is happening: either consciously or unconsciously resorting to deception.

There is one other major lesson and parallel that emerges from the research I covered in *Extra Sensory*: when you make remarkable claims, you need to back it up with equally remarkable evidence. Many of the examples of scientific testing of psi phenomena either dated back to times when experimental controls were far laxer, or produced reports where professional illusionists fooled naïve scientists. But even in modern times, the issues leading to the replication crisis in the social sciences have appeared in the studies.

A researcher I included in *Extra Sensory* was American psychologist Daryl Bem of Cornell University in Ithica, New York, who shocked the world of psychological research in 2011 by publishing evidence for precognition,* or 'anomalous retroactive influences', as Bem described them – the alleged ability to be aware of an outcome before it occurs. After undertaking a series of experiments, Bem claimed that the chances of the null hypothesis being true and still getting his results was one in 134 billion. This is more than a little better than the typical test for significance used in psychology, which we have already seen is one in twenty.†

The best known of the experiments Bem undertook involved a group of university students who were presented with a computer screen showing two images of curtains. If one curtain was clicked, an image would be shown – if the other was clicked, there would be nothing. But there was no pattern to where the image would appear: which curtain revealed an image was purely random, and the decision of where to locate the image was made after the student had clicked – so there was no possibility that the student could have had some kind of foreknowledge of the outcome.

Whether or not the participants picked correctly should have been 50:50 over time – the result you would expect if they had guessed with no influences. And this was the case when ordinary images were used. But the truly bizarre result that Bem obtained was that if the image used was pornographic, the students did better than a random choice made possible. They picked the curtain that would reveal an image in 53.1 per cent of their guesses.

---

* Bem's 2011 paper was 'Feeling the Future: Experimental Evidence for the Anomalous Retroactive Influences on Cognition and Affect'.

† One in twenty is a far lower test level than, for example, in physics, which often goes for around one in 2 million: Bem was claiming far better than this, even.

Such a small shift from 50:50 doesn't sound much, and how significant it is depends on the number of trials undertaken. As an illustration, I just tossed a coin ten times and it came up with four heads and six tails. There was a 50:50 chance of a head or tail occurring, but in this example, because the sample size was small the outcome was actually 60:40 – a stronger ratio than Bem obtained in his experiment. However, I'm not getting excited: with just ten tosses, any apparent bias in the result had no significance. There was nothing odd about my coin.

The chances of Bem's result on this specific experiment happening if the null hypothesis was true was one in 100. The very low probability of one in 134 billion was obtained by combining the results of all the different experiments he undertook. These included tests where students chose between mirror images of pictures, or where they produced outcomes that suggested priming (see page 220), where the priming took place after they made the choice.

Randomness messes with minds

When I wrote *Extra Sensory*, I asked Bem about the approach taken to make the random selection, as the quality of random number generation could affect the outcome – and we weren't seeing huge variation from what might be expected from chance. Random numbers might seem to be a very straightforward concept, but they are anything but straightforward in reality, and human beings, with our excellent pattern-recognition abilities, can often be influenced by an apparent pattern in genuinely random outcomes.

We are very bad at understanding what a random string of events looks like. I mentioned above tossing a coin ten times and getting six tails. What might seem more remarkable about that little experiment is that, indicating heads as H and tails T, the sequence that I produced was H-T-T-T-T-T-H-T-H-H. That run of five tails in a row out of just ten tosses might seem remarkable, some kind of indication that the coin tossing wasn't producing random results. But bear in mind that the coin has no memory. This sequence is just as likely to come up as any other.

When people try to make a series of choices at random, they almost always fail to put in enough repeats and so are more predictable than a true random choice. This is known to have occurred, producing false results, in another series of parapsychology experiments featuring what was hoped to be a telepathy training device, devised by American psychologist Charles Tart at the University of California, Davis.*

The device worked by switching on a light against a randomly selected playing card (out of ten possible choices) in front of a 'sender'. He or she would then focus on the card and attempt to convey the value to another participant in a different room. After 'transmitting' a value, the sender pressed a button to switch on the light against the next card to be sent. When mathematicians analysed which cards were selected, they found a bias in the values. There weren't enough repeats.

It turned out that the random number generator was working fine – but the human part of the system was failing. Say the selection that has just been sent was the two of hearts. The sender then pushed the button to get the next card. If the light remained on against two of hearts, because the random selection happened to be the two of hearts again, the student assumed that their push of the button had not registered and would push again to get a different card.

Because the receivers also had the perception that a repeat was unlikely, if they were guessing which to choose, they were

* An analysis of the problems with Charles Tart's ESP training device is found in Martin Gardner's 1989 book *Science: Good, Bad, and Bogus*.

less likely to select the same card twice in a row. The combination of the two errors meant that their guesses had a better than one in ten chance of being correct. The experiment appeared to show evidence of telepathy. The error was enough to provide the small-scale statistical variation from true random guessing that is typical in this kind of experiment.

If, in Bem's case, there had been some problem with the random number selection that led to fewer repeats than should be the case, it could also have coincided with human guessing. I asked Bem about this and he said that they had run the trial with the random number generator doing the guessing and not got any significant result. When I suggested that there could be better tests using likely human biases – and this wouldn't guard against an inadequate random number generator producing a pattern such as too few repeats – Bem said that there was a 'near-infinite set of guessing strategies, and there was no reason to suspect a particular bias from the students' – but this seemed to miss the point that a similar problem to the Tart experiment could occur.

This all happened before the replication crisis in psychology. Since then, Bem's studies have often been highlighted among those that have fallen by the wayside, both for lack of reproducibility and doubts about the way he used statistics. There were also what have been described as 'serious methodological flaws', including changing the experimental protocol partway through experiments and the way that the different experimental results were combined. Because of the particularly dramatic topic of Bem's studies, the problems discovered here soon after publication were part of the trigger for the revelation of the wider replication crisis in psychology.

There is no suggestion that Bem was setting out to deliberately mislead. But the appearance of apparently impressive results for a phenomenon that stretches credibility required heavy-duty checking. And the same has been the case for the more unlikely feeling aspects of brainjacking.

Reality vs the big claims

As we have seen, the dramatic findings for both priming and nudges seem to have been exaggerated, again not through any deliberate attempt to mislead. It is not entirely surprising that this has happened in areas where leading researchers have written popular-science bestsellers. If it is possible to describe an outcome backed up by science that sounds incredible, it makes a much more exciting read than discovering that things are much as we expected them to be.

Similarly, as we have seen, the influencing attempts of the likes of Cambridge Analytica seem to have been exaggerated, presumably for commercial reasons. And that most mysterious of brainjacking phenomena, hypnosis, on closer examination, while sometimes definitely dramatic, seems to involve far less control over someone else's mind and actions than is often suggested to be the case.

In countries with good legal frameworks to protect the citizenry, what seems more likely to be the threat of deceitful brainjacking is in the way that artificial intelligence, social media and other influencers, and the manipulation of big data, can result in our getting an incorrect picture of the world. Things can, of course, be very different (and always have been) in authoritarian states.

The limit of information

Perhaps the most fascinating thing I have discovered in exploring brainjacking is the extent to which many of those who are professional brainjackers try to play down the influencing and manipulating aspects, insisting that their role is purely one of informing.

Each of my *University Challenge* teammates did to some degree. While each accepted that there can be an element of influence, the suggestion was that they mostly try to be neutral purveyors of information. But the feeling I have from looking at the many different ways that we modify others' brains is that it is often impossible to inform without also influencing. If information is neutral, having no effect on the way that we act or feel, then yes, we can be imparting pure information. But this is rarely the reality.

The University of Cambridge's Winton Centre for Risk and Evidence Communication, along with Sense about Science and the Science Media Centre, awards the Harding Prizes for Trustworthy Communication, which has the tagline 'for communication that helps'. According to the prize website:* 'When we have a decision to make, or we want to understand someone else's decision, we often look for a source of trustworthy evidence on the subject. Yet balanced, useful evidence can be hard to find ... The Harding Prizes are specifically for those who try to gather together the information that helps someone make a decision, or make their mind up about a subject, **without trying to tell them what to do**.' (Emphasis in original.)

I have a lot of respect for the Winton Centre (though at the time of writing their website suggests they are now closed), and its regular spokesperson Professor Sir David Spiegelhalter. And I understand that science aims to be objective and impersonal in its findings. Yet as soon as we start telling people about those findings (or anything else), we are telling a story. And however much we may aim to simply inform, I don't think there is a way to tell a story without a degree at least of influence – and quite often manipulation creeping in. Nor am I sure that this is as a bad a thing as seems to be suggested here.

I asked David Spiegelhalter about this and he told me: 'Any form of communication involves numerous personal judgements,

* https://hardingprize.online.

and so can never "objectively" present information. In particular, good storytelling should generate an emotional as well as intellectual interest in the developing narrative, and this may lead audiences to revise their opinions and even change their behaviour.

'However, just because it's impossible to be completely objective, this does not mean that communicators should not try to avoid pushing people into a specific response. By reflecting on one's own agenda, and testing stories out on different audiences, communicators can attempt to tell gripping stories that engage people in an issue, and perhaps make them question their assumptions, but without aiming for a particular response.

'With certain exceptions, trustworthy communication involves informing rather than persuading. Of course, skilful storytelling may persuade people to take an interest in the issue, and this seems reasonable – there is little point in being trustworthy if you are dull.'

I take the point – and communication of science is a very particular type of storytelling. Yet this still feels defensive: in exploring brainjacking we need to tell a more balanced story. We are without doubt regularly influenced and manipulated by the power of storytelling, just as we have been for thousands of years. It's a power that certainly needs control. As Spider-Man puts it so succinctly, with great power comes great responsibility – and storytelling truly does provide great power. But without the brainjacking that comes with storytelling we would not be human at all.

Evolutionary brainjacking

Very late in writing *Brainjacking*, I learned an extra insight into human development and brainjacking from Philip Ball's book *How Life Works*. The central message of the book is that the processes of life are far more complex than we typically envisage, and that the gene-centred viewpoint popularised by Richard Dawkins misses the wider picture of the nature of life. It's easy to think that evolution is just about changes in genes (or more accurately alleles: gene variants) – but it's far more.

This made me think of something covered in my book *The Universe Inside You*. I had noted:

> Scientists at the University of Michigan in Ann Arbor compared 14,000 matching genes in the human and chimpanzee genomes.* Of these, 233 of the chimp genes have changed as a result of positive selection – where natural selection appears to have kept a change that gives benefit to the species – as opposed to just 154 of the human genes. The lead researcher commented: 'The result overturns the view that, to promote humans to our current position as the dominant animal on the planet, we must have encountered considerable positive selection,' while a primatologist, Victoria Horner, commented 'We assume chimpanzees have changed less than us when that's actually not the case.'

This is a huge mistake, assigning total centrality to our genes. As Philip Ball points out, there is far more to the way organisms can change, and the implications for evolution than the genes alone. Apart from the genome (collection of genetic information) he quotes cardiologist Eric Topol in pointing out that an organism's development is affected by – and its evolution can involve – the transcriptome, proteome, epigenome, microbiome, immunome,

* The study in *Proceedings of the National Academy of Sciences* from 2007 on chimpanzee versus human genetic change was 'More genes underwent positive selection in chimpanzee evolution than in human evolution' by Margaret Bakewell et al.

physiome, anatome and exposome.* The total focus on genes in the comparison of humans with chimpanzees misses out on this – and brainjacking is a significant element in our evolution, resulting in far more change over the 6 million years since our and chimpanzees' paths from our common ancestor diverged than the genetic changes mentioned.

This demonstrates the power of brainjacking: it has played a major part in human evolution. To return to the quote from *How Life Works* I used in Chapter 2: 'One of our attributes that most distinguishes us from other animals is our construction of complex cultures, which rely critically on systems and technologies for passing on information and learning' – I would say brainjacking is *the* crucial attribute. Whether we are dealing with advertising or influencers, education or news, deepfakes or conspiracy theories, what is involved is that ancient, very human need to tell and to hear stories, as a result of which recipients change the way that they think. We can't avoid the concept of story, because it's at the heart of being human. We should embrace it – but with appropriate caution, trying to be more aware of just what that storytelling is doing to us.

As you finish this book, it is worth pausing a moment and asking yourself just what form the experience has taken for you. I hope that *Brainjacking* has informed and entertained. It would be great if it did influence you too. As for manipulation – you will have to decide what you have undergone.

If there is one takeaway, I would like to stress that it is to be more aware of brainjacking as it happens all around – both *to* you and *by* you. Embrace it where it's good; reject it where it is negative. But most of all, enjoy this particularly human activity.

---

* The various 'omes' refer to a whole range of layers of action and complexity that can be part of living organisms. So, for instance, the transcriptome is the way that DNA is transcribed into messenger RNA with various subsequent functions, through to the 'exposome', which is the environment.

FURTHER DISCOVERY 15

Artificial intelligence basics – for an overview of AI see *Artificial Intelligence* by Yorick Wilks (Icon Books, 2019).

Artificial intelligence disinformation – in *The Coming Wave* (Bodley Head, 2023), Mustafa Suleyman and Michael Bhaskar paint a dark picture of the future capabilities of AI, despite Suleyman being broadly in favour. Too much material here on other topics such as synthetic biology, but it is still useful.

Attention span – *The Studies Show* podcast episode 17: 'Your shrinking attention span' by Tom Chivers and Stuart Ritchie covers this topic, particularly concerning Johann Hari's claims.

Big data – for more on the ways that big data is used and abused see *Big Data* by Brian Clegg (Icon Books, 2017) and *Big Data* by Timandra Harkness (Bloomsbury, 2016).

Brain Gym – Ben Goldacre uncovers the problems with the Brain Gym approach in his book *I Think You'll Find It's a Bit More Complicated than That* (Fourth Estate, 2014).

Brainwashing – Kathleen Taylor's book *Brainwashing* (OUP, 2016) is the definitive introduction to brainwashing from a scientific perspective.

Cambridge Analytica – the chapter 'Cambridge Hyperbolytica' of David Sumpter's book *Outnumbered* (Bloomsbury Sigma, 2018) gives an excellent description of the difficulties of developing personality-based influencing from Facebook data.

Confidence tricks – in *The Confidence Game* (Canongate Books, 2016), Maria Konnikova explores the psychological mechanisms behind confidence tricks.

Consciousness – John Parrington's book *Consciousness* (Icon Books, 2023) gives a good overview of his theory of consciousness and the scientific evidence.

Disinformation and misinformation – *The Tiger that Isn't* (Profile Books, 2008) by Michael Blastland and Andrew Dilnot provides an excellent guide to getting a feel for the value of numbers we are presented with, and whether they should be trusted. *Beyond the Hype* (Elliott & Thompson, 2022) by Fiona Fox gives a good picture of the way that science can be presented in the media in a way that misleads. The BBC's radio show *More or Less,* hosted by Tim Harford, uncovers the misuse of statistics and other numbers and is available on the BBC Sounds app.

Environmentally dangerous advertising – *Badvertising* by Andrew Simms and Leo Murray (Pluto Press, 2023) is a polemic on the way advertising encourages us to over-consume and damage the planet. It can wildly overstate the case, but makes some interesting points.

Feynman's anecdotes – There is far more to enjoy from the early life of the famous physicist than his 'map of a cat' story, mentioned in the introductory chapter, in Richard Feynman's famous collection of anecdotes, *Surely You're Joking Mr Feynman!* (Vintage, 1992).

Fictional advertising – *The Space Merchants* by Frederik Pohl and Cyril Kornbluth from 1953 (Gateway, 2003) is still in print, while *The Merchants' War* by Frederik Pohl from 1984 can be sought out second-hand. Both are excellent sources for thoughts on the extremes to which advertising and marketing could go to if unchecked by the state and public opinion.

Flow – for more on the concept of flow in creativity, see *Flow: The Psychology of Happiness* by Mihaly Csikszentmihalyi (Rider, 2002).

Future advertising – although *A History of Advertising* by Stéphane Pincas and Marc Loiseau (2006) does anything but what it says on the tin (it only covers the era of the advertising agency and focuses almost entirely on one agency group, primarily in the US and France), it has some interesting thoughts on the future of advertising.

Growth mindset – *The Studies Show* podcast episode 8: 'Growth Mindset' by Tom Chivers and Stuart Ritchie covers this topic.

Hypnotism and stage magic – Derren Brown's *Tricks of the Mind* (Channel 4 Books, 2007) is a masterclass in the brainjacking aspects of these fields. Parts of it are written in an irritatingly mannered, 'quirky' fashion, but it is well worth persevering with.

Life – making us what we are – Philip Ball's *How Life Works* (Picador, 2024) gives a remarkable picture of the complexity of what shapes us (and all living things in different ways), far beyond just our genes.

Lydia Pinkham – *Female Complaints* (W.W. Norton, 1979) by Sarah Stage is a detailed account of Lydia Pinkham, her vegetable compound and how it became popular through advertising.

Marketing and brands – *On Brand* (Thames and Hudson, 2003) by Wally Olins gives a definitive picture of the nature of brands and the significance of marketing.

Marketing history – A useful overview is provided by *The Routledge Companion to Marketing History*, ed. Brian Jones and Mark Tadajewski (Routledge, 2016).

Mental powers – The parallel area of the science (or lack of it) of telepathy and other mental powers is covered in *Extra Sensory: The Science and Pseudoscience of Telepathy and other Powers of the Mind* (St Martin's Press, 2013) by Brian Clegg.

Patterns and probability – *Dice World* (Icon Books, 2014) by Brian Clegg includes the way we interface with the world through patterns and how probability can influence our brains and our understanding.

Propaganda – *Munitions of the Mind* (Manchester University Press, 2003) by Philip Taylor provides a scholarly but readable history of the concept.

Science of story – *Wonderworks* (Swift Press, 2021) by Angus Fletcher provides a fascinating, if over-long exploration of this topic.

Storytelling animals – In his book *The Storytelling Animal* (Mariner Books, 2013), Jonathan Gottschall argues convincingly that it is storytelling that makes us human.

Why we tell stories – *The Seven Basic Plots* (Bloomsbury, 2004) by Christopher Brooker covers the structure of stories and tries to explore why we tell them, but is limited on the latter topic.

INDEX